T0277263

Reading
Between
the Lines

Reading
Between
the Lines

The Biography of
'Cockney'
Cliff Lines

70 YEARS
in horseracing

RACING POST

First published by Pitch Publishing,
for and on behalf of the Racing Post, 2022

RACING POST

Racing Post
9 Donnington Park,
85 Birdham Road,
Chichester,
West Sussex,
PO20 7AJ
www.pitchpublishing.co.uk
info@pitchpublishing.co.uk

ISBN 978 1 83950 108 1

Typesetting and origination by Racing Post
Printed and bound in Great Britain by TJ Books, Padstow

CONTENTS

Dedication

To families and friends

ACKNOWLEDGEMENTS

THIS BOOK is dedicated to our families and friends without whose support and encouragement it would never have made it to press!

However, we would particularly like to thank the following for their time, memories and photographs: Sir Michael Stoute, Sue, Muriel and Malc, Barry and Eileen, Adrienne, Richard, Zoe, Becky, Debs, Julia, Jean-Luc and Robin, Claire, Kate, Carrie and Sean.

Thanks are also due to Shell Grainger at Pitch Publishing/Racing Post for picking up the idea at such an early stage and allowing us to run with it. Her patience and encouragement were heartening!

A percentage of the price of this book is being donated to Newmarket Pony Academy in recognition of the work they do providing opportunities for children who would otherwise not experience the joys of associating with ponies and horses.

THE EARLY YEARS

CLIFFORD VICTOR Lines was born on 14 February 1935, an improbable date for someone with not one romantic bone in their body! However, the location was more auspicious: the barracks of the Scots Greys in Edinburgh with whom his father was serving at the time. Cliff's first memory is aged about three, being sat astride one of the stunning grey horses by his father and screaming when he was taken off! It seems his life path was set early on. Unfortunately, Cliff's early equine education came to an abrupt end when, shortly after Cliff's first experience on horseback, his father, Bill, transferred to the RAF. The family had moved through several army placements including at Wilmslow and Aldershot before settling in Feltham, south-west London, where his father was squadron leader and it was here that Cliff grew up. It was not an unusual childhood and included, as childhood often did at that time, a stint with the Boys Brigade, some scrumping and a collection of birds' eggs.

There were six children. Cliff's eldest brother, Billy, a butcher by trade and a good dancer by choice, sadly was diagnosed with Multiple Sclerosis in his early thirties. Billy lived until he was 60, when his wife temporarily put him into a care home so she could have a week's respite. Regrettably, Billy picked up an infection while there. Cliff and his brothers went to visit him and Cliff remembers looking back as they were leaving and seeing tears in Billy's eyes. They knew they wouldn't see each other again.

Dave was the second eldest and now lives in Newmarket with his wife Rene. Dave was a child actor. One afternoon, Cliff and Dave went to the cinema in Hounslow to see one of the films Dave was in called *Trouble In The Air*. The boy Dave was playing went into a shop with a mate; as they were leaving, Dave's character asked the shopkeeper whether he had any broken biscuits to which he replied in the affirmative. Dave's character then replied, 'Well, mend them then!' Cliff and Dave burst out laughing and were told to shut up by the man in the row in front of them. Unfortunately, neither of them has improved their sense of humour since! As an adult, Dave initially went into the Navy before becoming a rep for Castrol and eventually he moved to Newmarket, where he went to work for Jeremy Hindley, a Newmarket trainer, as his maintenance man and driver.

The third child, another boy, was Eric, who became a welder. Eric had a canary who would sit on his shoulder and they would exchange kisses. Sadly, this caused Eric to get psittacosis and both his kidneys collapsed. He was on dialysis for ten years until his death.

Cliff was the fourth and, thankfully, the last boy! The next two children were both girls, Muriel who eventually followed Cliff to Newmarket with her husband Malcolm, and finally Irene who lives in Crawley.

All four boys were in the Boys Brigade and Cliff remembers following along at the back of the parade, pretending to blow his bugle but not having any idea how to actually play it! What he really enjoyed, however, was the annual camping trip. In fact, he loved camping so much that after the Boys Brigade camp he switched to the Scouts so he could go on their camping trip. Then the next one up was the Life Buoys (Sea Cadets) camping holiday. Then back to the Boys Brigade in time for their next trip!

Cliff's love of nature was apparent early. A neighbour taught him how to blow eggs and Cliff gradually built up one of the best collections among his mates; he was happy to scramble up trees, carefully inserting his hand into a nest and removing a single egg to take home, blowing the contents and adding the empty shell, fully labelled with species, date and place of gathering, to his collection. The same neighbour also took Cliff to St James' Park, London, where they found two featherless pigeon squabs. The neighbour was going to raise both, but, that night, one was killed by the cat, so the survivor was given to Cliff to raise, which he did successfully. The pigeon would sit on his shoulder, parrot-fashion, and would accompany Cliff to wherever he might be going. One day, Cliff and a friend were bird nesting on a railway bank and saw something blue covered in leaves and branches. They found a stick and poked it to ensure it wasn't a butterfly bomb (German SD 2 anti-personnel bombs dropped by the Luftwaffe during World War Two). Once they had confirmed it wasn't going to explode, they pulled it out and found it was a bag full of new shirts. They climbed back on to the bicycle, Cliff sitting across the handlebars with the bag on his lap and, as they were crossing the bridge over the railway, they saw a police car coming towards them. They showed the police what they had found and the police scrambled down the bank, rather less adeptly than the boys, and found two more bags, both containing leather jackets. The boys were disappointed that they never heard anything more about their discovery.

Cliff's next avian venture was pigeon racing: he built his own loft and got himself ten or so pigeons to race. The first pigeon successfully completed initial race and Cliff was hooked. Unfortunately, when the next race came around, Cliff's father was home on leave and they went to visit Cliff's uncle, so he was unable to race the pigeon. The next start was, therefore, a significant increase in distance for the bird; it was loaded on to a lorry and off they went. The next day at school, he was caught staring out of the window by a teacher. 'Lines! What are you looking at?' he was sharply reprimanded. 'Please sir, I am waiting for my racing pigeon to come home – he was released yesterday and it's his longest flight yet!' Cliff had discovered he could see his pigeon loft from the classroom window! Sadly, the further distance was too much and the pigeon never returned home. That was the end of the pigeon racing!

His love of lessons was less apparent than his love of nature. This was in the days where small, cheeky boys were still caned at school. Cliff occasionally had the cane across his hand from his class teacher; however, he soon discovered that if he got sent to the headmaster, rather than knock on the door and take the beating, he could rub his hand against the corner of the wall and the door coving and it would come up with a couple of red weal marks. On returning to the classroom, he would be asked to show his hand to the master and there were the 'cane' marks so he got off scot-free! Cliff remembers two school trips: a history outing to Hampton Court Palace was not his cup of tea; he hid behind curtains during the tour, but his toes stuck out, so he was spotted by the teacher and got into trouble. The second trip was when he was about 12 and they had a school outing to the abattoir. The reason this trip has stuck in his mind is that they were all given ice-creams after the tour! He particularly remembers one of his last teachers, Charlie Hawkes, who was the sports master. He was always kind to Cliff although Cliff was no good at sports: when they ran around the football pitch, Cliff always lagged behind; he was so small that his little legs just couldn't keep up with the others! However, his gymnastic skills were better thanks to his natural balance which was to stand him in good stead when he started riding later on. Yet, strangely, Cliff struggled on a family outing to Richmond ice-rink, spending most of the time on his backside while his older brother, Dave, literally skated rings around him. However, his exceptional balance, along with his core strength from riding, came into its own many years later when, in his fifties and visiting his children in Australia, he had an opportunity to try water-skiing for the first time. He proudly recalls standing up on his very first run, having stayed in the crouch slightly longer than a professional would, before completing the full circuit of the lake without falling. He can also do a yoga position called 'crow' which he is very pleased about, although it is the only yoga he knows! And don't challenge him to a push-up match – he still retains that natural core strength.

Cliff's father, Bill, had a yellow Labrador, but the dog lived away with Bill at the RAF barracks and Cliff only saw it when his dad came home on leave. It is a moot point whether Cliff was more excited to see the dog or the sweets his father always brought home with him. His father definitely came a poor third! Aged nine, while living in Feltham, Middlesex, Cliff persuaded his mother to allow him to have a puppy which he bought himself for £1. The collie-cross pup was the offspring of one of his school friend's dogs: he named the pup Laddie and trained him himself. Cliff claims Laddie was very well trained, but there is little evidence as to whether or not this might be true. The family certainly differ in their memories of his behaviour!

When he was about ten, Cliff swam across the River Thames at Runnymede for a dare. He made it across, but then realised he had no way back to the other bank where his friends were waiting for him. The only option was to swim for it! Cliff was exhausted from the first swim; he wasn't a strong swimmer and could only do doggy paddle. He was halfway back when a large paddle steamer full of tourists appeared. Cliff was terrified – there was no way they would see him in the murky water. Luckily, he had just made it safely to the far bank when the steamer drew level. Water, in all its states, seems to have had a beguilement for Cliff: a couple of years later, he was out with his brother, Eric, and some mates and they noticed the gravel pits had frozen over, so they decided to take a short cut across them. All eight walked together in a group rather than spreading out. Cliff can still hear the snaps and groans of the ice barely taking their weight to this day. Water was not the only element to catch Cliff's attention. Fire was fascinating, and so was what would burn. One day he decided to check whether one of Irene's dolls would melt or catch fire, so he tossed the doll into the open fire: she vanished in a puff of smoke! Cliff rushed outside in the hope of seeing the doll appear from the top of the chimney and the commotion brought Irene into the room at the critical moment, but there was nothing left to rescue. No one can remember what she was made of to vanish so completely, but, thankfully, Irene has now just about forgiven Cliff and his incendiary activities are now limited to the wood burner and the occasional bonfire under strict supervision!

Cliff always liked to use his initiative. He made his pocket money by collecting discarded lemonade bottles and returning them to the local shop. He got paid 2d per bottle. He told the neighbours from whom he collected them that the money was for the Scouts, although they never saw any of it. Eventually, he was returning so many bottles that the shopkeeper became suspicious and accused him of taking bottles from the back of the shop, bringing them round to the front and claiming the tuppence again!

There was no family connection with racing until one of his schoolmates (Tony Trevor, still a good friend despite moving to America to pursue a career in pharmacology) remarked, 'You're small: you should be a jockey.' At the time, Tony's mother was working in the local Job's Dairy where one of her colleagues was a warned-off jockey (known to Cliff as Mr Garnett). He kindly wrote off to various trainers to find a job for the young Lines. Cliff's only racing experience was a visit to Ascot with his father when he was ten years old. He was dumped at the top of the stands and told to stay there, which he did, until his father collected him at the end of the day. Cliff had only ridden once, a gypsy cob belonging to a friend. Cliff turned up for the promised ride after school one day and they set off, only to be stopped by a little girl on the leading rein without a saddle. Cliff was made to hand the saddle over and finish his ride bareback. They were out for nearly two hours. Unfortunately, the leading rein pony was in season and Cliff was on a colt: it was a very uncomfortable and painful experience! At the end of the two-hour ride, both ponies were turned back out into the field together and Cliff had his first sex education lesson!

Meanwhile, Cliff's elder brother David had already joined Ealing Studios and become a successful young actor, his more memorable roles including the son of Googie Withers and John McCallum in *It Always Rains on Sunday* and the telegraph boy in *Scott of the Antarctic*. However, Cliff had no interest in bright lights and greasepaint and was duly packed off by his parents to join Noel Murless who had replied to Mr Garnett offering the young Lines an apprenticeship. Cliff started the day after leaving school, the first Lines child to fly the nest.

SIR NOEL MURLESS

CHARLES FRANCIS Noel Murless set his heart on a career as a racehorse trainer at an early age. He was brought up during the First World War: his parents were busy, his father with the Army, his mother as a nurse with the VAD (Voluntary Air Detachment) and his younger brother Stuart was yet to be born. Noel's constant companion was his Welsh pony, Mary Jane, and he credits her for his amazing understanding of horses. His first trip to the races was as a nine-year-old, to the 1919 Grand National, which had returned to Aintree after being run at Gatwick for three years. Family neighbours, the Peels, had Poethlyn running in the race. He had won the Gatwick race the previous year and, ridden by Ernie Piggott (grandfather of Lester who was later to have such success as Murless's first jockey), he was backed down to 11-4 and won confidently. Murless's first visit to the races certainly lit a spark! Like so many children, he spent many happy hours reliving the race with himself as Ernie Piggott and Mary Jane as Poethlyn, all the while expounding on the credits and failings of the famous trainers of the time – Atty Perse, Alec Taylor and Dick Dawson – to those hairy pony ears.

After a few years riding out and schooling for various trainers, it was the Peels who pushed Murless into taking the next step. They got him a job with Frank Hartigan, an ex-army veterinary surgeon, who had ridden successfully and was a dual-purpose trainer based at Weyhill, a village on the Hampshire/Wiltshire border. Hartigan had already trained two 1,000 Guineas winners Vaucluse (1915) and Roseway (1919) when Noel started as a stable lad, doing his two, schooling over fences, getting occasional rides as an amateur but all the while learning the art

17

of training. After a short time at Weyhill, Noel was approached (after a fall over the Aintree fences) by Frank's brother, Hubert, to be assistant trainer at his yard on the Curragh in Ireland. Murless recalled that although Frank was the better trainer, Hubert was the nicer person and he quickly accepted the new position and became part of the family.

Murless began his own training career at Hambleton Lodge, Thirsk, in Yorkshire before moving to Hambleton House which he shared briefly with Ryan Price. In 1947, he was approached by Dewar to succeed Fred Darling as trainer at Beckhampton Stables in Wiltshire. The Beckhampton team were keen not to change things to any great extent when Fred Darling retired through ill health and they drew up a short list of three possible trainers to watch. Noel Murless was chosen as the new trainer because he was seen to carry the jockey's saddle from the weighing room to saddle up, rather than expecting the head lad to do so.

THE APPRENTICESHIP

When joined by a 14-year-old Cliff in 1949, Murless had already been champion trainer in his first season at Beckhampton, with Queenpot winning the 1,000 Guineas, The Cobbler finishing second, beaten a head, in the 2,000, and the great sprinter Abernant among a promising two-year-old crop. Sir Gordon Richards was the retained jockey.

Cliff left school as normal on the Friday afternoon but on Saturday 19 November, Cliff's father packed him a suitcase and took Cliff by train to Swindon, then a taxi to the yard. The taxi waited for Bill Lines, while Cliff was ushered into the canteen where the lads had just finished lunch. Cliff was one of 22 apprentices and was signed on for an initial five years, although this was later extended to seven years. The next day Cliff had to muck out in his suit trousers! His parents hadn't realised what was required to work in a stable yard and had only packed two new suits for Cliff to wear! It was also on his first day that Cliff became known as 'Cockney'. At evening stables, he was sent to the mash house to get the pony's feed and the head feed lad asked where he was from. The answer 'near London' simply provoked the reply, 'Right then, Cockney, here's your feed!' And that is how he was known from then on although he has never heard the Bow Bells.

One day, Mrs Murless and her daughter, Julie, went to visit Cliff in Savernake Hospital when he had pneumonia; the nurse asked whom they were there to see and Mrs Murless had to admit she didn't know 'Cockney's' real name! Thankfully, they were allowed in and told just to look around until they found him. All the lads were given nicknames when they started, usually connected with where they were from. A lad from Norwich, George Douglas, was called Norwich; Clive Brittain was Calne. There was already a Middlesex, so it was lucky that when Cliff was asked, he said London rather than Feltham; knowing stable lads' sense of humour that could have caused some embarrassment! Although, according to Mrs Murless, Cliff's father wasn't very pleased with the name 'Cockney', it was a long time before he generally became known as Cliff again.

Life as an apprentice in those days was tough. Wages were 10/- (50p) a week and, when you signed on, your trainer provided you with your first pair of britches, and a pair of boots and leather gaiters, but after that you had to buy all your own clothing and equipment. The dormitory was an old structure designed for the storage of equipment and machinery. It was a single-storey building with a bitumen floor. There was one large room which housed about 15 of the apprentices. Off the main room, there were four smaller rooms with lockers where the lads could store their clothes; it was not sensible to keep any valuables there as some of the older lads could pick locks, so nothing was safe. There was just a single bath in the washhouse along with some basins for washing yourself and your clothes, so Cliff used to send his clothes home for his mother to wash – not that she had a washing machine either! There was no central heating: condensation would run down the gloss-painted walls and the insides of the windows were covered in a thick layer of ice on winter mornings. The boys just had a sheet and a single blanket on the bed. It could have been worse: the lads in hostels in the north complained they often awoke to snow on the beds which had blown in through missing windows. Holiday allowance was two weeks a year. Amazingly, Cliff managed to save roughly 5/- (25p) a week (half his wages) which was kept for him in the office. Cliff took the money out when he went on his holiday, a trip back home to his parents.

Initially, the new apprentices didn't ride out at Beckhampton. They were never taught how to ride. They were told to tack up either the pony or the hack and, once they proved they could manage them and ride without falling off, Sir Noel drove them up to the gallops in the yard van; they were unceremoniously tipped out and, after the senior jockeys had ridden in the gallops, the apprentices were allowed to ride the horses home. Sir Noel smoked the oval 'Passing Cloud' cigarettes which were popular at the time and would always have one on the go in the van. He never finished them and chucked the remains out of the car window as they approached the gallops. One of the apprentices would rush back to find the stub and they would share it later. Otherwise, they had to spend their hard-earned 10/- (50p) on cigarettes when they went into town; they couldn't afford many, so would buy five and share them between them. Luckily, Cliff was a non-smoker, hence he was able to save more than the other lads.

The only person who helped Cliff with his riding was one of the paid lads, Billy Ray. Billy was an exceptional horseman and would ride all the particularly difficult horses: he could sit any number of bucks, plunges, spins and twists without coming off. He was also a kind person; on the coldest nights, he would sneak a small flask of brandy into the apprentice dormitory, hopeful that a quick swig for each of them would help keep them warm and raise their spirits a little.

A normal day as an apprentice at Beckhampton started with a wake-up call at 7am from the head lad (who had already given the horses their breakfast), mucking out, tacking up and riding out first lot, returning for a half a rasher of bacon and a fried egg breakfast in the canteen, then straight out again for a second lot. There were only two lots, so the rest of the morning was spent sweeping the yard and 'twisting in' to make a straw plait to lay across the front of the stable door. As Cliff is quick to point out, it's not something you can do now with the vast majority of horses bedded on shavings! Then it was back into the canteen for lunch; Cliff doesn't remember the food fondly! The afternoon was free to do as you wanted (which in the winter was just go back to bed to keep warm), then evening stables to do your two, or occasionally three if there was a spare because the paid lads were away racing. Murless looked round all the horses every evening and would check not just the animals themselves and their legs for heat or swelling, but also the tidiness of the stable, the cleanliness of the grooming kits which were laid out on a straw bale by the door, and that the horse had been groomed properly. To enable him to assess the latter, the lads had to empty their curry combs out into a small pile by the stable door to ensure there had been enough loose hair, dirt and dander removed each evening. Cliff would sneak the pile (once approved) into a matchbox to ensure he had enough for the following day! Two horses would be allocated to each lad to look after every spring. You could put your name down for one and Murless would allocate you a second horse. You'd normally get a horse that you had been riding and grooming during the winter, so the relationship was already established.

Sadly, historically, apprentices were callously bullied by the older lads. As well as being 'greased and polished', they could find themselves strung up in a hay-net and left there overnight unless they were wise enough to carry a pocket-knife to cut themselves free. Another of the senior lads' favourite tricks was to throw a naked apprentice into a frozen water trough in the middle of the night, often resulting in pneumonia and a stay at the nearest hospital. Not even promising the bullies some of your own food rations or tuck from home (if you were lucky enough to have parents who could afford to send you tuck) would stop them. Cliff always carries a penknife in his pocket to this day, but not everybody was prepared to tolerate the bullying and some apprentices returned home quite quickly. Despite all this, many of the lads said it was much harder before Murless came to Beckhampton. In Fred Darling's time at the yard, it was a harsh life for both horses and lads. Gordon Richards described him as ruthless with both. The lads had a 10pm curfew and if they came in any later than that, he would take a bullwhip to them. The bullying from older lads was much more sadistic, with humiliating initiations for the new apprentices. The horses would be 'strapped' at evening stables, which meant beating them with a wisp of knotted hay over their muscles before brushing them, sometimes so hard that they would sweat up. Murless immediately stopped this practice, finding it really stressed the horses, particularly the thin-skinned fillies. He preferred to use kinder methods for both horses and staff, often wandering around the yard at evening stables, just offering the horse a carrot or a handful of grass, to check on their wellbeing and levels of contentment. Murless took on two of Darling's top work riders, Tommy Seed, whom he promoted to head lad, and Tishy Morton. Any lad caught bullying the new apprentices would be punished. But they had to be caught. However, Murless's change of approach generally led to happier horses and a better working atmosphere among the staff.

There were also better days, however. Collecting plovers' eggs (often with another apprentice, Mick Leaman) from the heath (before it became illegal in 1964) and selling them to Sir Gordon Richards for his breakfast gave Cliff enough pocket money for an occasional day out in Marlborough, a quick trip to the pub or the pictures. Mick was also in charge of looking after the two cows that were kept at the yard and Cliff occasionally helped with the milking, but his technique was obviously lacking! When Cliff was helping, one of the cows always seemed to manage to stand in the bucket; the boys just skimmed the dirt out of that bucket before they took the milk to the canteen, but they made sure they knew which bucket their own milk came from! Another way the apprentices tried to supplement their meagre diet was by catching some of the wild rabbits that lived in a warren in the main paddock. One of the lads had a ferret, so the apprentices headed off to net all the escape tunnels and then popped the ferret down a hole. The lads then tapped their feet on the ground, which the ferret owner took to be the rabbits stampeding away from the ferret. One rabbit appeared and ran out of an unnetted tunnel, but there was no sign of the ferret; it had caught a rabbit in the tunnels early on during its exploration and was enjoying some fresh meat. The lads went hungry.

On the rare occasion the apprentices had an afternoon off, there was little public transport available between Beckhampton and either of the nearest towns, Marlborough or Devizes. Luckily, among the apprentices was a young Clive Brittain: he was the local boy from Calne, so knew his way around. It was from Clive that Cliff learnt the trick of hitching a ride home from Marlborough. The boys would grab hold of the back of a passing lorry, jumping off as it passed through Beckhampton, hopefully without being spotted by the driver! Cliff remembers the Tate and Lyle drivers were particularly kind and would stop to pick the lads up and let them ride in the cab; one even took him to London airport so he only had to walk two miles home when he had a week's holiday. However, the technique didn't always work. Unsurprisingly, some of the lorry drivers took a dislike to the lads clambering all over their lorries. One day, Cliff and a mate called Alan Ferguson thumbed a lift and jumped on to the back of a lorry as it slowed down on the hill coming out of Devizes towards Beckhampton; they climbed up the ropes hanging down the back of the lorry and settled themselves on the tarpaulin over the top. However, they must have been spotted because the driver pulled over and got out of the cab; he walked slowly all around the lorry while the boys crouched down quiet as mice. Anyway, they thought he was satisfied when he got back into the cab and drove off; however, on approaching the T-Junction into Beckhampton, instead of slowing down he put his foot on the accelerator. Cliff was halfway down the rope and managed to jump off but landed flat on his face on the tarmac. Alan, however, was carried on the top of the lorry all the way into Marlborough before he managed to get off. Luckily, the first passing car picked him up and drove him back to Beckhampton and he arrived at the yard not long after Cliff.

Clive Brittain already had a better knowledge of riding and horses than young Cliff when they started at Beckhampton. Like Cliff, Clive's family had little racing background; his father worked in the local bacon factory and his mother was busy looking after 13 children! However, at about seven years old, Clive became obsessed with the ponies living in the field opposite the house and had started to try and befriend them by offering them bread and cakes. Then he started to jump on their backs, grab a handful of mane and gallop across the field. One day, one of the ponies was spooked and the whole group galloped back across the field into their barn, dumping Clive into the old stone manger there. The owner was there and Clive was caught red-handed! Having received a cuff round the ear from both the ponies' owner and his mother, who was told of the incident, the owner, who was a dealer, then offered Clive a job helping him with the ponies. Clive learned to break them for riding and pulling a cart. Eventually, when Clive was about 13, he got a job riding 'flapping' ponies for a trainer near Bristol. He didn't stay there long and returned to Calne to see if he could get a job with Herbert Blagrave. Blagrave told him he already had an apprentice and to try Noel Murless down the road. Clive was initially seen by Murless's secretary, Humphrey Cotterill, who turned him down, saying he would be too big. But young Brittain wasn't easily put off and hung around the yard until Murless appeared. He told Murless that Blagrave had sent him and asked for a job as an apprentice. Murless agreed to give him a month's trial. Clive stayed with Murless for 23 years and his experience with recalcitrant ponies stood him in good stead as he was often given the more awkward horses to ride. In 1972, Clive set up as a trainer in his own right at Carlburg Stables in Newmarket, eventually becoming famous as the first British-based trainer to send out the winner of both the Japan Cup (Jupiter Island) and the Breeders' Cup (Pebbles) – quite an achievement in the 1980s when international travel for racehorses was still in its fledgling stage.

Cliff was trusted enough by Mrs Murless, his employer's wife, to be allowed to accompany their seven-year-old daughter Julie (later Lady Cecil, wife of Sir Henry) on a pony ride into the forest on a Sunday morning. The children would head off, Julie on her pony and Cliff on the hack on whom the apprentices learned their trade, for a ride around the forest, sometimes with a bit of tree climbing thrown in. They often got lost in the forest but would find their way back on to the road near Bishops Cannings (six miles as the crow flies but a lot further as children on ponies ride!) because they knew they could find an ice-cream van there. Julie would make Cliff buy her an ice-cream before they could head off home. One Sunday, three hours after they had set off, the search parties were out! Although they had lost their way in the forest as usual, Cliff and Julie had also lost track of time while climbing trees and were completely unperturbed! Luckily, the boss and his wife were very understanding. A sense of direction has never been one of Cliff's strong points. At eight years old, he got lost in Hampton Court maze and had to squeeze his way out, forcing himself through the bottom of the hedge! He has also been known to drive twice around the M25. His alternative route back to Newmarket from the westerly racecourses involved driving the horsebox through central London, going the wrong way down a one-way street and passing Buckingham Palace en route!

On his 15th birthday, Cliff was chosen to represent the yard in the Stable Lads Boxing. At 5st, there was only one other boxer in his 'novice' category. Clive Brittain was in the next weight up at 5st 7lbs and Mick Leaman, taking on the likes of Joe Mercer, was in the 6st category. The lads didn't have much actual boxing training, but their fitness was taken seriously with their coach, one of the paid lads Tishy Morton, taking them out for regular runs around Beckhampton, Avebury and Silbury while he rode his bicycle! The contest was held in Marlborough town hall and was well attended – when Cliff glanced up from a clinch, he spotted Noel Murless and Sir Gordon Richards sitting side by side in the audience. Cliff says his bout was like two school kids having a scrap – neither had the strength to hurt the other, but he won his bout on points and claimed the Fred Darling Trophy. There is a film of Cliff's fight on a Pathe News reel on YouTube and Cliff did actually manage to knock his opponent down, although he thinks he is more likely to have slipped! Clive made it through to the final, but was pulled out with a split lip. The following year Cliff moved up to the 5st 7lb category but was beaten early on by the eventual runner-up. In 1952 Cliff missed the boxing due to an injury; he had been on a camping holiday in Devon with Tony Trevor's family and the boys were skimming stones along the pebble beach. Cliff was ready to head home when Tony threw one last stone, which bounced awkwardly and caught Cliff just below the eye. X-rays revealed a fractured cheekbone and it didn't heal in time for the tournament. Over the years, Mick Leaman was often in the team, but because there were more lads at his weight, they had four or five bouts over two days. Cliff still has his Fred Darling Trophy, though. When Darling retired from training, he moved into a house opposite the yard. He had always been a great supporter of the stable lads boxing and if any of his staff were beaten through lack of fitness, woe betide the entire yard for days afterwards! One evening, he came round to the stables shortly after Cliff's victory and Murless introduced them. Gordon Richards loved the boxing and always made sure he was home from his annual holiday in St Moritz in time to support the lads.

Being so small and light, one of Cliff's earliest jobs was to help break in the yearlings by laying across their withers. They were broken in using a deep sand circle: there were no lunge pits. The yearlings were always lunged rather than driven; Cliff remembers Murless didn't believe in driving them because their mouths were still very soft and he didn't like the heavy weight of the driving reins pulling down on them. Cliff particularly remembers Dewar's yearlings as being wild: they used to come into the yard never having been handled and were therefore among the most difficult to break in.

In those days, many of the horses were broken in using cruppers which went under their tails. It was thought that putting the crupper on would get the steam out of the horse. Once the crupper was in place and you let the horse's tail down, it would plunge explosively and you had to keep a tight hold of the rein. It was a pretty risky job for the person putting the crupper on and buckling it up. They were never used on the horse once it was broken and thankfully are no longer used in the breaking-in process for Thoroughbred racehorses. Another piece of equipment that has thankfully gone out of fashion is the leather tongue-strap. There is no give in a piece of leather and the strap didn't move. Furthermore, they were often put on too tightly, causing the horse's tongue and mouth to swell, making the strap almost impossible to unbuckle and sometimes they needed to be cut off. The poor horses must have been in so much pain. Luckily, trainers seem to have returned to the more forgiving methods of a long piece of crepe bandage or using a pair of the wife's old tights to tie down a horse's tongue if it has a tendency to get it over the bit.

When a horse had its first start as a two-year-old, Murless would tack the horse up in the saddling boxes at the racecourse. The apprentice, who was leading the horse up for the race, would then be given a leg-up and would ride the saddled horse around the stable yard for a couple of minutes to ensure the horse was relaxed and comfortable before leading it down to the parade ring. It was much safer for Gordon Richards if when the horse was going to plunge, it plunged with an apprentice in the stable yard rather than with him in the parade ring!

Charlie Homer had initially worked for Fred Darling where he looked after Tudor Minstrel (1947 2,000 Guineas and St James' Palace winner) and he became part of the Murless team when Murless moved to Beckhampton. He was one of the boxing squad and had quite a punch on him! Cliff remembers him taking a blow to the mouth, spitting out a couple of teeth, then flooring his opponent with one hit! He called Cliff over one evening stables and sat him up on the horse he was mucking out. That was Cliff's first time sitting on a racehorse. It just happened to be a horse called Point d'Orgue. Cliff was obviously more adept at teaching himself how to ride than he was at listening to lessons in school. Luckily, he has wonderful natural balance which helped.

Amazingly, less than two years after joining the Murless yard and having never ridden before, on 6 August 1951 Cliff's riding was good enough for Sir Noel to put him up in a race at Chepstow on the large, strong, dark bay colt called Point d'Orgue which he had begun to ride regularly at home. Sir Noel approached Cliff three or four days before the race and asked Cliff whether he had managed to hold the horse in his work; he was known to take a hold and Cliff was only about 6st! Cliff confirmed he had been OK, although in all honesty he had been struggling to hold him off the heels of the horses in front: he knew he wouldn't get the ride otherwise! Murless had his own wooden, two-horse box and Cliff travelled to Chepstow on the box with the horse. His father and Mr Garnett made the trip from London to watch him. At the course, he had to borrow britches and boots: luckily the valet had spares and managed to find him some which fitted. Point D'Orgue had swerved badly at the tape start in his previous race and had only beaten one horse home. Down at the start at Chepstow, the instruction from the other apprentices was to make sure he kept out of their way, particularly when the tapes went up! Cliff and Point D'Orgue eventually finished second, beaten three lengths by Golden Lad. *Ruffs Guide to the Turf* credits Bill Rees with the victory, but Cliff is adamant that the winning jockey was Brian Swift, having tracked him on the rails from the start of the race. Whoever was riding, Golden Lad made the running and wasn't to be pegged back. Point D'Orgue won his next start at Bath, ridden by Sir Gordon Richards.

Cliff's next outing to the races, only a week later, was his first 'lead up' at Bath Racecourse. The filly, Crayke, had been bred by, and was owned by, Mrs Murless. She was one of Cliff's 'two', but was a bad-tempered mare and not easy to handle. However, she won a race at Nottingham at the end of her two-year-old season and the following year Cliff rode her at Newmarket. She was later sold to America where she became a decent broodmare.

While at Beckhampton, Murless had two fillies arrive as yearlings from the same stud. They were inseparable! One wouldn't go anywhere without the other and if they were forced to do so, chaos ensued. Coming home from exercise one day, one of the fillies whipped round and dropped her lad. Luckily, she stayed with the string and Murless was able to catch her. However, as soon as he grabbed the reins, the filly set off! Murless was running alongside her with his long, loping stride until he stumbled: he turned a complete somersault. It was quite some spectacle and the whole string were laughing. Luckily, Murless was unhurt.

The form of the Murless horses began to tail off. Mr Dewar who owned the yard removed his horses and sent them to Noel Cannon at Druid's Lodge to be trained. The four talented horses included Agitator, who won the Sussex Stakes and had been placed in the 2,000 Guineas.

The Lines family suspected Noel Cannon might actually have been one of the brothers of Mr Garnett who had got Cliff the job with Murless. Noel Cannon trained at Druid's Lodge on Salisbury Plain, not far from Beckhampton. At the turn of the century, it had been the location of the infamous 'Druid's Lodge Conspiracy' betting scandal. It is possible the Lines family were putting two and two together and making five, but we shall never know the truth. Mr Garnett never told the Lines family that he had been a jockey or about his racing career; nor did he ever speak about the Cannon family. At the investigation which got him warned off, he refused to disclose the other people who had been involved in the 'plot' and rumour has it that they paid him for his silence for many years thereafter. If it is true, Mr Garnett had a very sad life: not only was he estranged from his Cannon brothers, but his wife was in a mental home. He had a long-term partner and they adopted two boys. One died at 21; the other got married and had a daughter. However, he suffered badly from headaches and eventually committed suicide on Runnymede Hill: he sat down under an oak tree and took an overdose. It later became apparent that Mr Garnett's granddaughter had been diagnosed with a neurological condition and was not expected to live to adulthood.

Many critics had been prepared to backstab Murless when he first moved to Beckhampton, believing that he would not be anywhere near as good a trainer as Fred Darling. He soon silenced them with his 1,000 Guineas victory and by becoming champion trainer in his first season there. However, when Dewar's horses started to win for Cannon a few days after the move, the knives were out again. The fact that Murless had prepared them well and they were ready to run didn't enter into calculations, but the fact that all Murless's owners, barring Dewar, sent him their horses to train when he moved to Newmarket speaks volumes for their belief in him. He also had the promise of horses from H H Aga Khan once he moved.

Eventually, Murless told Dewar he would not be renewing the lease on Beckhampton and Dewar then sold the yards and house to Herbert Blagrave who was training at Beckhampton Grange, a few hundred yards down the road. Sir Gordon Richard's brother, Colin, was employed by Blagrave as a work-rider and could often be seen leading the stable pig around Beckhampton. Many stables historically kept pigs which ate all the leftover mash and generally kept the yard clean. Some yards in Newmarket even retain the pig-sties, although not with the intended residents, to this day. Sausages are particularly associated with Newmarket which is not surprising given the large number of stables there. At the turn of the century, there were over a dozen different butchers in Newmarket, each with their own secret sausage recipe. Newmarket sausages have been a standard offering at every breakfast in the town since the mid-1800s and, in 2012, the Newmarket sausage was granted PGI (protected geographical indicator of origin) status by the EU.

Colin Richards lived in Avebury, only a mile from Beckhampton. He had two daughters, Nina and Dulcie. One evening, Murless's head lad, Jack Blake, was cycling home from the pub: as he passed the straw barn, he pulled up and called out, 'Come out of there, Cockney!' A young Lines sheepishly emerged, shortly followed by Nina! Cliff swears there was nothing untoward going on – it was, after all, only their second date. Their first date had also been in the same location: an early indication perhaps of Cliff's reliance on his Scottish heritage providing the excuse for his reluctance to produce his wallet! However, when talking about Nina, his voice drops and his eyes soften. Unfortunately, with the move to Newmarket imminent, there was no chance of the relationship blossoming.

THE MOVE TO NEWMARKET

IN 1952, Murless took over the management of Sir Victor Sassoon's Eve Stud near Newmarket. When Sassoon died, Murless bought the stud from his widow, renaming it Woodditton Stud. He continued to stand stallions there, including Connaught and Welsh Pageant. In 1981, the stud was sold to Singapore-based Yong Nam-Seng, but it is now part of Sheikh Mohammed Al Maktoum's vast Darley/Godolphin empire and no longer stands stallions.

Murless was not disappointed to leave Beckhampton; he always complained he found Wiltshire winters cold and damp. Sir Alfred Butt had asked him to move to Newmarket and train for him at Clarehaven (now John Gosden's yard), but the accommodation on offer was unsatisfactory as Sir Alfred himself lived in the main house. Instead, Murless purchased Warren Place in Newmarket from the Maharajah of Baroda and, in the autumn of 1952 he moved his family and racing operation from Beckhampton to Warren Place. Cliff and many of the other members of staff moved with him. The horses and equipment were moved over several days on a variety of horseboxes and lorries. Cliff jumped on to the first horsebox in a bid to get the best bed!

Newmarket was a revelation to the young apprentices. They had been dubious about the move because the hostel in town had a poor reputation: it was reputedly like living through the times of Oliver Twist, being run by an ex-army sergeant-major who liked to maintain the strict discipline he had learned in the army and he had pretty archaic methods of doing so. However, a few of the Newmarket trainers' yards had their own hostels, such as Geoffrey Barling's and Sam Armstrong's. Luckily, Warren Place was one of these. The lads each had their own room with heating (although you had to put money in the meter, the lads soon learned how to fiddle the meter and remove the coins), a dining room, a communal TV room and a payphone which they could use whenever they wanted. Furthermore, the standard of food improved slightly, although Cliff was not impressed with the margarine being melted down and pasted on the toast with a pastry brush at breakfast time! He even remembers one lad, George 'Ginger' Link, picking up his plate in disgust and throwing it back at the cook before making a very hasty exit from the canteen! The standard and quantity of food improved significantly when Mrs Hall took over running the canteen a couple of years later; she lived in the main house and was a wonderful, caring mother figure to the boys. Breakfast improved to two eggs and two rashers of bacon as well as tomatoes. The tomatoes were fresh, grilled tomatoes and, although for Cliff tinned tomatoes are the epitome of the perfect cooked breakfast, he claims she cooked the best food he has ever eaten! It may be that post-war rationing had finished and good ingredients were easier to come by, but Cliff gives Mrs Hall all the credit for the improvement!

Entertainment during non-working hours was also significantly improved: as well as the TV room in the hostel, in town there were two cinemas (the Doric and the Kingsway) and the opportunity to go racing at the two Newmarket courses if you weren't working. The lads could either grab a lift on the horsebox if they had runners or they would squeeze into a taxi and split the fare. Some of the paid, married lads who had houses in town would even invite the apprentices for an evening meal or Christmas lunch.

Gordon Richards gave up his retainer with Dewar: it would have meant riding for Cannon who only had a small string and he wanted to continue riding as many winners as possible, so he knew he had to be associated with a large stable (with around 60 horses!). He was loath to leave his house on the Marlborough Downs: early in his career, he had started with Captain Hogg who had become private trainer to Lord Glanely in the early 1930s, an association which had also involved a transfer of the string to Newmarket. Richards retained his job as stable first jockey but didn't want to move to the house in Exning that Lord

Glanely had for him and it was agreed he could remain in his home on the Marlborough Downs and travel up to Newmarket twice a week to ride work and stay in digs overnight. He may have known there would have been a lack of plovers' eggs in Newmarket! Also, although he thought Newmarket racecourses were among the fairest in the world, he wasn't a fan of the gallops, considering they dried up too quickly with the sun and wind and that the Marlborough Downs contained more moss, and so were springier and better for training racehorses, particularly those with poor conformation or leg injuries. Already in the 1930s, he thought there were too many other strings and horses in Newmarket. At that time, racehorses in the town were counted in their hundreds, but current estimates gauge the number to be around 3,000 horses! Despite knowing how much additional travel it would necessitate to continue riding work in Newmarket when Murless moved, Richards stayed put in his house on the Marlborough Downs.

Many of the apprentices never got a ride in public; Cliff recalls they were just cheap labour. They were initially taken on for a five-year apprenticeship, but this would be extended to seven years if the apprentice was getting rides in races. Two of Cliff's friends, Clive Brittain and Mick Leaman (the latter had started with Murless at Hambleton, York, and moved with him to Beckhampton), never had a ride despite remaining with Murless when he moved to Newmarket and staying with him until he retired. In those days, if either party didn't like the situation, it wasn't possible to just swap an apprenticeship from one yard to another, which possibly offered better pay or more chances of rides. If an apprentice hadn't blotted their copybook after five years, they could become a paid lad. If they did anything amiss, the result would be a sacking and the possibility of becoming blacklisted, preventing the culprit from being able to get a job in another racing yard, particularly a decent one.

The move to Newmarket also reignited Cliff's interest in the fairer sex! All the staff at Murless's were lads; although one girl joined the yard shortly after the string arrived at Warren Place; she was twice Cliff's age. When Mr Cotterill retired as Murless's secretary, he was replaced by Mrs Hall's daughter, Maureen, but she went out with, and eventually married, Clive Brittain. Cliff soon realised that Captain Boyd-Rochfort, who was training at Freemason Lodge on the Bury Road, had quite a few girls riding out. As the strings passed each other on the heath, Cliff plucked up the courage to start chatting to a few of them.

One evening, after a night on the town, Cliff was cycling back up the Moulton Road to his digs when he spotted a couple, silhouetted in the moonlight, walking across the road. Then he realised their feet weren't touching the ground and they disappeared into the locked, red heathmen's hut on the side of Warren Hill. He quickly swung his bicycle around and pedalled as fast as he could back down the hill to the pub at the bottom. There he jumped into a taxi. No way was he cycling up there again that night! Although Newmarket has a few ghost stories – for example, Fred Archer can often be seen riding his grey Scotch Pearl across Newmarket Heath or the beat of shod hooves can be heard in Park Lane, but there is nothing to be seen – no one else has reported sighting Cliff's ghosts.

The Murless's looked after Cliff extremely well. When he was about 17 or 18, he was having problems with breathing through his nose and a visit to his doctor in Newmarket resulted in a stay in hospital, having the nasal cartilage removed along with some polyps. Cliff hasn't been able to smell anything since that day, which is not ideal when preparing for a date night and he can't tell the difference between the bottles for the hair gel and the garlic oil! Unfortunately, the surgery didn't help Cliff's breathing, so Mrs Murless had Cliff referred to a specialist on Harley Street. The specialist discovered an infection affecting the antrum and the bone was being eaten away. There was no need to have had cartilage and polyps removed. The specialist peeled away the skin and associated tissue from Cliff's lower face and chipped away the infected pieces of bone at the back of his nose with a hammer and chisel. However, when Cliff came round after the operation, his whole face was black and he was in excruciating pain. He remained in hospital for ten days with ice-packs over his face until he got fed up and put his hot water bottle on his face. That helped, so he alternated the hot water bottle and ice-packs. When he was discharged, the hospital charged him over £100 and wouldn't let him leave until it was paid. Luckily, he had just enough money to cover it. He mentioned it to Mrs Murless when he arrived back in Newmarket and she reimbursed him the next day.

In 1953, Cliff was called up for National Service. He and a lad from Major Holliday's called Alan Wellburn took the train from Newmarket to Cambridge. Wellburn passed his medical and went off to do his two years' National Service but Cliff had an asthma attack during the examination and so was exempted. When he returned to Newmarket, Murless accused him of shaking up the hay in the hayloft before he went to the interview to ensure he got off! Holliday kept Wellburn's job open for him and he and Cliff met up again later at Major Holliday's yard, La Grange, with Hethersett.

The hacks at Warren Place weren't always the safest conveyances. One morning, as the string was crossing the road outside the yard, Murless's hack whipped round and dropped him. Unfortunately, he broke his shoulder and was unable to ride out for a few weeks. Mrs Murless also rode out with the string on a racehorse called Buckhound who had won a few races; although no superstar himself, he was very consistent and often used as the lead horse for important gallops. One morning, Murless told the lads to put boots on the hack. They duly did so and brought him out for Murless. Murless enquired why on earth the hack was wearing boots. The lad explained that Murless had told him to put boots on the hack which was what he had done. Murless roared, 'I said put Boots on the hack this morning! Boots "the lad" to ride him! Not boots on his feet!' Boots had just started as an apprentice, but in due course proved himself to be a genuine lad and good worker.

One of the fillies Cliff used to ride was called Regicide. She was a pretty tricky ride as she used to fly-jump going on to the gallops. One morning, she was misbehaving in her normal way before a piece of work in which Gordon Richards was riding. Cliff refused to be beaten by her and managed to get her on to the gallop and jump off with the others. She won the gallop easily. A few days later, Sir Gordon was called on to ride her work on Side Hill. Cliff warned him not to smack her if she fly-jumped because she would do six more. Regicide fly-jumped. Gordon automatically smacked her. Off she went, fly-jumping across the heath! She caught Gordon unawares, he lost his balance and went forward on to her neck; her head came back and caught him in the face, giving him a terrible black eye and forcing him to miss three days' racing. He quickly got off the bouncing filly and gave her back to Cliff to ride. When Cliff came back to the yard, Gordon was being driven out in his Rolls-Royce by his chauffeur. He wound down the window and asked Cliff, 'What did you put under her saddle, drawing pins?' A week or so later, towards the end of the season, Cliff was due to ride her as second string in a two-year-old maiden, but she didn't run. He still believes Gordon was worried Cliff and Regicide would beat him and he didn't want the two horses to run against each other. As it turned out, Regicide didn't train on as a three-year-old and never made it to a racecourse.

In 1955, Murless's old mentor Hubert Hartigan died. Murless was sent one of his horses, Hugh Lupus, to train. Hugh Lupus had won the Irish 2,000 Guineas but missed the Derby through injury. Despite his tendency to try to savage his poor lead horse, Riseborough, Hugh Lupus won five races for Murless as a four-year-old, including the Hardwicke Stakes, Royal Ascot and the Champion Stakes, Newmarket. He became a successful sire, one of his best progeny being a horse Cliff would eventually look after, Hethersett. Riseborough, meanwhile, was still racing and Cliff finished third on him at Newbury. The horse was rather set in his ways and you had to just sit on him in a race; Cliff wasn't allowed to pick his whip up or give him a smack in any way. Riseborough earned his oats as a very good lead horse rather than by winning much prize-money.

Murless didn't stand for any abuse of the horses. One evening stables, a lad called Ginger Williams was dismissed. He had been with Murless a few years, having started with him as an apprentice at Beckhampton. Williams was one of the lucky ones who got his apprentice licence out; he had been due to ride one of the horses he looked after in an apprentice race at Newmarket, but once he was down at the start, the horse whipped round and deposited him on the turf before galloping off across the heath. That night at evening stables, Ginger hadn't realised Murless had entered the barn and his horse was messing about, so he kicked it in the belly. Murless went mad. It was instant dismissal. The head lad, Jim White, was sent to clear all Ginger's possessions from the dormitory and escort him from the premises. Ginger Williams then joined the navy and was with them for seven years. He had been a good boxer and had achieved three knock-outs in the Stable Lads Boxing tournament over the years. However, the standard of boxing in the navy was at a different level and he soon gave up!

Lester Piggott was very aware that Murless didn't like too much use of the whip, particularly during a horse's first race. But not all jockeys had the same level of appreciation of this instruction and for Lester it definitely only applied to a horse's first race! Cliff looked after a big black horse called Carnoustie. He wasn't fit for his first race and blew up. His next start was at Ascot and his odds were 25-1, but he had had a very hard race to win by a neck. He didn't forget it! Next time out at Newmarket, he was 2-1 on, the horse he had beaten at Ascot being his main danger: Carnoustie's jockey on this occasion was Scobie Breasley and when he pulled his whip through, running down into the dip, the horse veered right across the track, away from the whip, and finished last. The horse that Carnoustie had beaten at Ascot won the race. The jockeys couldn't use their whips on him after that second race. In Britain nowadays, the whips are foam-padded and air-cushioned. There is only one accredited supplier in this country and the jockey's whips are checked by the Clerk of the Scales to ensure they meet strict criteria. The rules about when and where a whip can be used on a horse have also been significantly revised over the years; among other changes, a whip can now only be used seven times during the entire race on the flat and they may only be used on the horse's hindquarters, never in the forehand position. The welfare of the horse is paramount.

PLANES, TRAINS AND HORSEBOXES

WHEN, AGED 16, Noel Murless first started in racing with Frank Hartigan, having a runner meant a long day. The lads would have to be up early, candles were lit in the lamps and the pony and trap prepared to take the tack, equipment and forage from Weyhill to Andover Station. The railway companies were still privately owned and were used to travelling horses; they would provide water for them and the vans were always well prepared, clean, safe, warm and comfortable. Meanwhile the lad had to get up, get the horse ready, lead it from the yard to the station at Andover, box it on to the train, disembark at, for instance, Esher if the races were at Hurst Park or Kempton, then lead the horse another five miles, past Hampton Court, to the racecourse. Once at the racecourse, the horse's shoes had to be changed for racing plates and his mane plaited. After the race, the horse would be groomed again, the racing plates replaced with his usual shoes, the lad would lead him back to Esher for the train journey back to Andover, the racing equipment needed to be unloaded from the train and into the pony and trap, then the runner walked back (uphill all the way) from Andover Station to the stable yard at Weyhill. Once that was done, the horse had to be 'strapped' for half an hour before the lad could start on his own two, which he still had to muck out, groom and feed as normal before bed. For a day taking a horse to the races the wages were 5/- (25p).

Luckily for Cliff, transportation of racehorses had progressed a little by the time he was an apprentice. Although horses were still transported by train, particularly from large training centres such as Newmarket, Murless had invested in his own wooden, two-horse box. They would leave the day before the race and return the day after, whereas now many of these journeys are done in one day. For important meetings, such as the Derby and Ascot, Murless would also have an empty horsebox following his own in case it should break down. That way there would be minimal disruption to the horses' journey. This meant Cliff only travelled a horse by train once, from Newmarket to Newcastle, stopping at Doncaster to jump out and grab a sandwich and coffee from the platform. He felt the horses travelled better on the train than on a horsebox; they enjoyed it as it was a smoother journey, without all the stops and starts, roundabouts and junctions, not to mention potholes in the road!

In the late 1960s, Cliff decided to supplement his income by working occasionally as a flying groom for BKS Air Transport on his days off from Warren Place. He flew mainly between the UK and Europe. One nasty incident occurred at Castle Donnington while he was loading a horse on to a plane: there was a lot of screaming and shouting and people running across the tarmac, away from the plane. Cliff stood in the doorway watching them, then turned back to the horse, ignoring all the hullabaloo outside, and carried on with his job. Someone saw him still standing in the plane and starting screaming, 'Get out, get out, the plane's going to blow up!' It turned out that there was a fire by one of the fuel tanks and the crew were worried that the flames could spread and the whole plane would explode. Luckily, by the time Cliff paid attention and jumped out of the plane, the fire brigade had been and managed to put the fire out! On the return flight, there was a bad head wind and the pilot was very short on fuel and only just managed to land.

The final straw for Cliff was the crash in 1968 at Heathrow Airport. The BKS Airspeed Ambassador plane had been converted to carry horses and was flying from Deauville to Heathrow, but metal fatigue in one of the flap-opening rods caused the landing flaps not to open correctly. Six of the eight people (five flying grooms and three flight crew) and all eight horses on board (belonging to William Hill the bookmaker) were killed when the plane cartwheeled across Terminal One which was still under construction. Two flying grooms survived but were badly injured. Over 20 other people at the airport had minor injuries and two other planes were damaged beyond repair. Luckily, Cliff wasn't on that flight, but he didn't really enjoy the work and those two near-misses were enough to keep his feet firmly on the ground for a while.

In 1983, Cliff took the Michael Stoute-trained Royal Heroine to America for the Yellow Ribbon Stakes on a passenger flight, meaning the filly had to travel in the belly of the plane. Cliff remembers the hold area being like a dancehall it was so huge, but it was bitterly cold and the horse needed to be well rugged up; indeed, she had three rugs on. The air hostesses were excited to discover they had a horse on the flight and took it in turns to pop down to the hold to meet her, but they must have been freezing in their skimpy outfits. Luckily, Cliff and the lad, Angus 'Silky' Brown, were able to travel upstairs with the other passengers, although they had free access to the hold to check on Royal Heroine's wellbeing throughout the flight.

However, Cliff's first overseas adventures were largely thanks to a horse owned by the Queen, which he was lucky enough to look after early in his career with Noel Murless.

LANDAU
1951 bay colt by Dante out of Sun Chariot

Before 1954, Cliff had only been abroad once when his elder brother, Billy, and a mate had taken him for a two-week holiday on the Isle of Wight. Despite winning the 'knobbly knees' competition, his brother decided Cliff was cramping their style with the ladies and he was sent home after a week.

Then along came the Queen's colt Landau, one of the horses Cliff had been allocated to look after during his time with Murless. Cliff had broken him in and ridden him through the winter, as well as doing him at evening stables. In 1953, Sir Gordon Richards had won the Derby for the first time on Pinza despite the buckle on his reins coming undone; it was his 28th attempt in the race and he beat the Queen's horse Aureole. Up in the Royal box afterwards, Prince Philip asked whether Richards planned to retire now he had the Derby under his belt. Before he had a chance to reply, the Queen butted in, insisting he would not be retiring as he would be riding her own colt, Landau, in the following year's Derby. It was not to be.

Sir Gordon Richards never really liked Landau and when he went to Buckingham Palace to receive his knighthood, which had been announced shortly before Pinza's Derby victory, the Queen asked how Landau was because he was due to run on the Friday. Apparently, Sir Gordon pulled a face because the Queen later sent her racing manager, Captain Charles Moore, to ask what the face meant and he quickly had to reply he wasn't sure what to make of the horse! He had thought him rather a cocky horse early on, but was now worried he was soft and wouldn't go through with a run when coming under pressure. Cliff disputes Sir Gordon's assessment of his horse and wonders how he came by such an opinion because he never even rode him at home! Despite Sir Gordon's misgivings, Landau won nicely that Friday: in fact, he won three races as a two-year-old. On the back of those successes, he was fancied for the 1954 2,000 Guineas. He jumped well, but Richards took him back into the middle of the pack, which Landau resented. It was a strange tactic because Richards's advice on how to ride Newmarket is to jump out and sit handy. Landau was the last horse still on the bridle at the bushes, but he put his head in the air and refused to go on when asked. Sir Gordon later reflected, 'There is no doubt he lacked resolution and ran very moderately.' Cliff knew it was wrong to have disappointed the horse and feels that if Sir Gordon hadn't taken him back having jumped so well, Landau would have run a much better race. The race was won by Darius. The Queen believed in Landau and called in a neurologist from London, Charles Brook, to treat him. He put one hand on the horse's withers and one on his girth, supposedly treating the electrical impulses in the nervous system. Brook claimed the treatment had a soporific effect on the horse, but Cliff, who was stood in the box holding Landau, felt it was himself becoming sleepy: Landau just became colty!

One evening, the Queen Mother came to look round evening stables, bringing with her Queen Elizabeth and Princess Margaret. When they came to Landau's box, Princess Margaret sat down on the edge of the half-bale of hay on which Cliff's tools were neatly laid out for inspection. The half-bale collapsed, depositing the princess on the floor! Luckily, it was all taken in good humour, but all this rather distracted attention from the horse. Later, the Queen remembered and sent the head lad back to ask Cliff which brand of boot polish he used because Landau looked so shiny!

After the 2,000 Guineas, Landau finished second in the Lingfield Derby Trial and was fancied by some for the Derby. Sir Gordon again claimed he was soft, having headed the winner while travelling the better. However, for the Derby itself, Sir Gordon was unavailable having been bought down in a pile-up at Salisbury a couple of weeks previously and suffering a head injury, which left him with recurring headaches. He suggested Willie Snaith, the stable's second jockey and known for riding as a lightweight, should deputise. Willie was thrilled to be given the ride despite more senior jockeys being available.

Willie Snaith was born in Gateshead in 1928, the son of a cobbler who died when Willie was just five years old. Willie left school at 14 and briefly worked in a woollen mill before becoming apprenticed to trainer Sam Armstrong in Middleham. He was only 4ft 11in tall, so weight was never going to be an issue! He moved to Newmarket when Sam Armstrong moved to Warren Place to train for the Maharajah of Baroda and became champion apprentice in 1949. Once out of his apprenticeship, he was attached to the Murless and Captain Boyd-Rochfort yards while still getting rides for Sam Armstrong. During his career, Willie rode five winners for the Queen, including Landau in the Sussex Stakes. He rode in the Epsom Derby seven times and was placed twice. He also spent the winters riding in India. In 1961, he had a bad fall at Lingfield, puncturing a lung and rupturing his spleen, but continued to race ride until 1973 when a bad asthma attack forced him to relinquish his licence. However, he continued in the industry as work rider with Henry Cecil. Eventually quitting the saddle, he became a tour guide, initially for Hoofbeats and latterly at the National Horseracing Museum in Newmarket where his tales made him immensely popular with the visitors. In 2004, he received an MBE from the Queen. On meeting her to collect his honour, Willie recalls that he bowed low and said, 'Good afternoon, Your Majesty' and she replied, 'Good afternoon to you too. It has been a very long time since I last saw you,' remembering him from his days with Noel Murless when he was riding for her. She wanted to talk about Landau and his Sussex Stakes victory in 1954. Willie sadly died in 2019, aged 91. Always a popular figure around town, there is a road named after him in Newmarket and he re-opened the local Tesco superstore after a major revamp.

Cliff, Landau and his lead horse arrived at Epsom two days ahead of the Derby. The morning before the race, the horses had a gentle canter around the track to accustom Landau to the gradients. It was Cliff's only ever ride on the course, but at least he can claim to have ridden a Group 1 winner around Epsom! In the race itself, Snaith thought he and Landau had every chance rounding Tattenham Corner, but, unfortunately, Landau did not stay the distance and eventually reverted to a mile. The race was won by Never Say Die, ridden by Lester Piggott, winning his first Derby!

Sir Gordon had recovered from the Salisbury fall in time to ride at Royal Ascot, winning the Rous Stakes over a mile on Landau. He was also able to ride Landau in his next engagement: the Eclipse Stakes at Sandown where he gained a more positive, although still rather begrudging, assessment from the jockey after having battled back in the final furlong to clinch third place, just beaten a short head for second by 2,000 Guineas winner, Darius. Landau was the last horse Sir Gordon Richards ever rode in a race. Cliff was leading him back to the stables after the Eclipse Stakes but keeping an eye on the stable's next runner, a two-year-old filly, also owned by the Queen, named Abergeldie, who was already in the parade ring ready for the next race. Cliff regularly rode her at exercise because she was a difficult ride due to her tendency to rear. She could not be led because of the rearing and used to be chased from behind at home. As was her way, Abergeldie was misbehaving in the paddock and the travelling head lad rushed over and grabbed her from the lad leading her, rather than chasing her along from behind. The lad leading her was an experienced lad who had looked after Abernant, so the incident about to occur was possibly the fault of the travelling lad interfering, but whoever was to blame it shouldn't have happened. The filly reared and went right over, throwing Sir Gordon and then falling on top of him. She struggled to get up but slipped and landed on Sir Gordon a second time crushing his pelvis. The Queen was in the paddock and witnessed the accident. It was horrific and Sir Gordon was lucky to survive: he admits he should have made the lad let go the first time she went up. In his autobiography, *My Story*, he says he had already made plans to retire at the end of that season as he 'knew he was already past his peak and wanted to go out at the top rather than struggle on when his abilities were failing'. Sadly, Abergeldie certainly saw to it that he kept his word. His pelvis was operated on at the hospital in Newbury and it wasn't until a week later, when doctors made him stand for the first time since the surgery, that he realised his ribs were also very painful and X-rays showed that he had broken four of them. Sir Gordon announced his retirement from the saddle and was able to set up as a trainer at his beloved Beckhampton for the next season, Colonel Warden having said he would not be training there the following season. Sir Gordon Richards ended his riding career having ridden more than 4,870 winners from 21,834 rides; he was champion jockey 26 times and his record number of wins in a season was 269. All quite an achievement considering there was no evening racing nor any Sunday racing in those days.

Over a mile, Landau had already won the Rous Memorial Stakes at Royal Ascot, ridden by Sir Gordon Richards, and he finished his English campaign with a win in the Sussex Stakes at Goodwood, with Willie Snaith, retaining the ride after Sir Gordon's retirement, made all the running. An audacious plan was hatched to run Landau in the Washington International at Laurel Park, USA, making him the first horse to carry the Queen's colours in a race outside the British Isles. As his lad, Cliff accompanied him. It was Cliff's first plane trip. About a week before the race, Landau was loaded into the airplane stalls along with King of The Tudors who had beaten Landau in the Eclipse. The stalls were then loaded on to the plane and Cliff sat with the horses during the flight. A few days before the race, Landau got bad 'run downs' on his hind legs which became infected. Leading him across the track to the parade ring before the race, Cliff knew his horse wasn't right; he was wearing a large sheet with a Union Jack on which was blowing in the wind, but the horse was behaving like an old sheep. However, Landau belonged to the Queen and it had been a long journey, so run he did, ridden by Willie Snaith. He made the running, but when they hit the home straight, he dropped out. Landau returned home to Newmarket, but he didn't run again. Before Cliff had left for America, Murless had instructed him to bring home one of the concrete, jockey-shaped hitching posts which were used at Laurel Park to tie the horses to. As they were packing up, Cliff remembered he was supposed to take a 'jockey' home and asked which one he could take: he got short shrift from the officials! Yet one did appear soon afterwards and stood outside Warren Place for many years; it was still there when Henry Cecil was training at the yard, painted in his racing colours.

In 1954, the Queen became champion owner. While a large proportion of the prize-money would have been thanks to Aureole, Landau certainly played his part with his victories at Royal Ascot and Goodwood along with his third place in the Eclipse Stakes. Aureole was trained by Captain Boyd-Rochford and as a four-year-old in 1954 he won the Coronation Cup, the Hardwicke Stakes at Royal Ascot and the King George VI and Queen Elizabeth Stakes.

Landau was subsequently sold to E.A. Underwood for a record 21,000 guineas to stand at stud in Australia. The purchaser requested Cliff accompany the horse to Australia to which Murless kindly agreed. Cliff was 19 years old. On 1 January 1955, Cliff and Landau boarded the *Port Freemantle* and departed from King George V dock in London. Cliff's mother Isabella and his sister Irene were there to see him off.

It was a six-week sea voyage to Adelaide. Landau was in a wooden stall on the top deck which was open to the air, along with one other horse and a large selection of goats and pigs which Landau wasn't too keen on! There was also a sheepdog which took a liking to Cliff and, in typical Cliff fashion, vice versa, so Cliff allowed the dog to sleep with him in his cabin. The crew thought Cliff might be prepared to look after both horses, but the other horse was quite nasty, so Cliff turned that offer down very quickly and the bosun was left in charge of it. Cliff was being paid by Mr Underwood just to look after the one horse: he was treated as a guest on the trip, eating with the captain at his table, rather than eating with the crew. He only had to look after Landau and was not expected to help sweep the decks or perform similar duties, much to the annoyance of the crew! However, on the first day Cliff was unused to the routine on board and he had to ask what to do with the droppings when he mucked out. He was told just to chuck them overboard. The first time he attempted this, he let go of the fork which fell into the sea and sank as the straw blew back into his face! He quickly learned to check the wind direction before throwing anything else overboard and luckily there were plenty of spare forks for mucking out the other animals.

During the voyage, a bad storm blew up one night. The boat was rolling, pitching and yawing. Cliff decided to put a tarpaulin up over the stable to protect Landau as the waves were coming in and splashing over the top of the stable, soaking the horse and his bed. Cliff had to stand on the top railing round the deck to get the tarpaulin up, so he tied a length of rope around his waist and then tied the other end on to the railings. Luckily, he managed to get the tarpaulin in place and to stay on his feet because no one would have seen him if he had gone overboard.

Cliff still has the certificate from the captain confirming that he had completed the voyage and crossed the Equator. The boat arrived in Adelaide early on the Sunday morning and Cliff and Landau travelled by box to Mr Underwood's Warlaby Stud just outside Melbourne, arriving at lunchtime. Mr Underwood was thrilled with how well Landau looked when he arrived. He was well enough to start doing swinging canters after three weeks, in preparation for the stud season. The other horse, which the bosun had been looking after, certainly looked as though he had been at sea for six weeks. Sir Noel had told Cliff to return home as soon as the horse was delivered, but Mr Underwood asked Cliff what he wanted to do and managed not to find a return flight for three weeks, so Cliff had his first experience of Australia. It was not to be his last! The Underwoods kindly had Cliff to stay with them in their bungalow on the stud and Mr Underwood showed him around and took him to a couple of local race meetings before he flew back to the

UK (which took four days thanks to a brief stopover in Singapore) and normal work was resumed.

Today, the stallions fly down to Australia and are there in roughly 36 hours! They undertake two weeks' quarantine either side of the flight and many of them shuttle, doing five months covering Northern Hemisphere time, then quarantine and fly to Australia or New Zealand, two weeks' post-arrival quarantine, then five months covering Southern Hemisphere time before returning to the Northern Hemisphere around Christmas time and getting a couple of weeks' break before starting all over again.

RACECOURSE SUCCESS

CLIFF'S FIRST winner as an apprentice was on Prairies, owned by Sir Victor Sassoon, in a three-year-old maiden at Pontefract on 3 August 1955.

On her first start, Prairies had been ridden by Lester Piggott at Newmarket and finished unplaced. Cliff then rode her at Alexandra Park and his father was there with Tony Trevor's next-door neighbour. Tony's neighbour leaned over the rails to the paddock and asked Cliff how he thought she would go. 'Close' was Cliff's reply. It was his first tip! Prairies

```
724.

4.30—Frank Pease Plate. £207 ; 3y ;
                   5f.
4952PRAIRIES 8-2*          C Lines 1
 660 Beethoven 8-12        E Britt 2
(552)Bluebottle 9-7       S Clayton 3
 495 Minerva 8-9          E Mercer 4
  64 Ship's Recall 8-4*
                         J Seagrave 5
 480 Conductress 8-4*
                          G W Green 6
S.P.: 11/8 Beethoven, 3 Minerva,
7/2 PRAIRIES, 5 Bluebottle, 33
others.
   Tote: 10/1.   Places: 4/-, 2/10.
Straight Forecast: 24/5.
   2l, ½l, hd, 6l, 3l.   1/4½.   N
MURLESS. (SIR VICTOR SASSOON.)
```

finished second at 20-1 and had been beaten a short head by Piggott on Murless's other runner, Lady Supreme, who was odds-on favourite. Cliff's instructions from Murless had been '... Don't cut Lester's throat!' Suffice to say Piggott was not amused by Cliff finishing only a short head behind him. Despite this close call, on the morning of the Pontefract race Lester Piggott came up to Cliff in the yard and said, 'You won't win on her today, she'll finish last.' Lester fancied Elsey's horse, Beethoven, ridden by Edgar Britt, an Australian jockey who was plying his trade in the UK having been brought over as retained jockey for the Maharajah of Baroda. Apparently, the betting public agreed with

Lester. In the morning papers, Prairies was quoted at 7-2, but by the off she had drifted to 10-1. However, Cliff thought she won quite easily and had significantly improved from her previous race – he couldn't pull her up! Unfortunately for Cliff, she was retired to stud soon after her win, despite her evident improvement between races.

Cliff's next ride was at Bath on Peruke. She was second-favourite and Cliff fancied his chances. Unfortunately, he was unused to the tight turns at Bath and he allowed Peruke to drift off the rail, allowing Joe Mercer through on his inside on Clyde Light. Peruke eventually finished third. Sadly, the tight course is the only thing Cliff remembers about Bath: over 2,000 years of Roman history and the beautiful Georgian architecture passed him by completely!

His only other win as an apprentice was on Anthracite, a bay filly by Abernant, owned by the Queen, in a two-year-old maiden at Thirsk on 27 July 1956. Cliff remembers Anthracite being another easy winner: she had shortened to evens favourite at the start of the race. Her next race was at York and Cliff was replaced by Doug Smith, but she didn't figure at the finish.

Obviously, with the ups came the downs: for instance, the occasion when Cliff was due to ride a horse called Chiperone at Lewes. The 11-

10 favourite was Game Rights, ridden by Ken Gethin. The white flag was up and Cliff and Ken set off, but the gate never went up and both jockeys found themselves on their backsides. Cliff had been caught across the face by the tape and his upper lip was bleeding badly. The two riderless horses were cantering loose across the open Downs. The starter took one look at Cliff, blood everywhere, and told him he wouldn't be fit to ride and would have to

684. THIRSK
Friday, July 27.
(FIRM GOING.)
2.15—Coxwold (M.) Stakes. £486
3s ; 2y (maidens at starting) ; 5f.
475³ANTHRACITE 8-2*	C Lines	1
327³Tournedo 8-12	E Hide	2
646 Tate's Pearl 8-9	D Buckle	3
457 Constantius 8-12	R Parnell	4
390 Dentrilla 8-9	A Roberts	5
540 Pitaport 8-9	E Britt	6
330 Mistinguette 8-9	J Mercer	7
621 Grey Rose 8-9	F Barlow	8
312 Dollar Loan 8-9	R Fawdon	9
172 Gilded Pen 8-9	D Gunn	0
405²Footstool 8-9	V Mitchell	0
Pendlemist 8-9	S Nesbitt	0
515 Saucy Dream 8-9		
	G Littlewood	13

S.P.: Evens ANTHRACITE, 6/4 Constantius, 10 Mistinguette, 100/7 Pitaport, 20 Footstool, 25 others.
Tote: 4/1. Places: 2/6, 5/7, 17/9.
3l, 3l, 4l, 1½l, nk.   1/0½. N
MURLESS. (THE QUEEN.)

withdraw. Cliff argued his case. Meanwhile, Gethin had got to his feet and set off in pursuit of the horses. Chiperone had stopped to graze after about a furlong, so Gethin swung himself up and set off down to the mile start where Game Rights had come to a halt. A hiker suddenly emerged from the gorse bushes and helped round up Game Rights; however, the favourite had put his foot through his reins and broken them. Gethin thought quickly and asked the hiker for his boot laces to mend the reins and was duly given them. 'That will teach him to go wandering across Lewes Downs when there is a race meeting in progress,' said Gethin, remounting Game Rights and handing Chiperone back to Cliff, who had arrived late on the scene! They rode back to the start together and the race got under way. However, their efforts were in vain: the exertions had taken their toll on the horses and both were beaten by Boisterous; Cliff was two lengths second on Chiperone, but Game Rights was unplaced. Boisterous was trained by Arthur Budgett at Whatcombe. Having been recently turned out in the paddock, it was a last-minute decision to run, yet the horse cruised past Cliff! Chiperone won next time out.

Despite over 100 rides during his time with Murless, the competition to be given these opportunities was extremely tough. Sir Noel usually retained two top-class jockeys and owners are unlikely to want to put an apprentice up when the likes of Sir Gordon Richards, Lester Piggott, Willie Snaith or Sandy Barclay are available. With all the other stable apprentices waiting in the wings, rides were hard to come by and Cliff was usually only given chances either on the difficult horses which no one else would ride, or the no hopers. For example, he never got back on either of the horses he won on; they were both ridden by the senior stable jockeys once they had proved their ability. Worse still, he once rode a horse called Ten Bells for the Queen at Nottingham, finishing fourth in a competitive maiden. His next run was in an apprentice race at York and Cliff didn't get the ride! Josh Gifford, who wasn't even connected with the yard, was called up. That sort of treatment really knocks the confidence, particularly for the young. It wasn't just hard for the apprentices: in fact, competition was so tough that one year, when Cliff had had 12 rides, Murless's retained second jockey, Geoff

Lewis, turned to Cliff and said, 'Cockney, it's too hard to get rides here, I'm going back to Epsom.' When Cliff asked why, Geoff pointed out, 'Well, you've had more rides than I have this year!' Geoff eventually returned to Murless as first jockey towards the end of 1970. Murless had lost patience with Sandy Barclay, who was becoming less reliable and more wayward every day, and sacked him. Geoff Lewis agreed on the understanding that he would be free to ride Mill Reef when required. He immediately won the Champion Stakes at Newmarket on Lorenzaccio. The following year saw him winning the Derby on Mill Reef for Paul Mellon and Ian Balding as well as the Coronation Cup for his new connections. He went on to ride Mysterious, the half-sister to J O Tobin, to her Oaks and Guineas victories in 1973.

THE ONES THAT GOT AWAY!

IN 1955, Murless tried to get hold of the Queen's racing manager, Sir Charles Moore, but he was on holiday in the Caribbean. Murless had two runners in the same race, the Rosemary Stakes at Hurst Park, the Queen's filly Carrozza and his own filly, Shaken Bridge. Carrozza was a tiny, delicate bay filly, leased to the Queen from the National Stud and Murless thought Shaken Bridge was the more forward of the two, so wanted Lester Piggott to ride her and to put Cliff on Carrozza to give her a nice introduction. Unfortunately, he was unable to contact Moore, so felt he ought to put Piggott on the Queen's filly. Carrozza beat Shaken Bridge by half a length. Shortly afterwards, Carrozza reared over backwards, badly damaging her withers and needing to be put away for two months. When she reappeared later that year, she was unplaced in two starts. However, it was as a three-year-old that Carrozza blossomed, although she didn't grow much over the winter and barely stood 15 hands high, she really came to herself during a mild spring. She started her campaign at Epsom, winning the Princess Elizabeth Stakes; she recovered well, so Murless ran her in the 1,000 Guineas where she finished fourth, ridden by Bill Rickaby because Piggott had chosen to ride the yard's favoured runner Sijui, who was unplaced.

Her next start was to be the Oaks at Epsom. Although she was only carrying the second colours of the Queen, Carrozza squeezed through on the rails and clung on grimly to win in a photo finish. It was the first Royal victory in the Oaks at Epsom and the Queen proudly led her little filly into the winner's enclosure. Murless described it as 'the most brilliant race of Lester's career', while Sir Gordon Richards, summing up his successor, commented, 'The secret of Lester's success is his confidence in his own genius.'

On the other hand, Shaken Bridge never won a race despite giving Cliff the feel of a good filly. Although he doesn't remember doing so, he apparently reported to Mrs Murless that the filly was a cow, for which he got a telling off from Billy Ray! Perhaps unsurprisingly, he didn't get the ride on her the next time she ran and was replaced by the stable second jockey, Wally Swinburn Snr.

Wally Swinburn Snr had started as an apprentice with Sam Armstrong when he was based in Newmarket, riding his first winner at Warwick in 1953 before becoming second jockey to Noel Murless at Warren Place. Cliff was still getting rides and Lester Piggott was first jockey. Wally then moved to Ireland where he completed two seasons with Paddy Prendergast before becoming jockey to Dermot Weld. He became Irish Flat champion jockey in 1976 and 1977 and was the first Irish jockey to ride 100 winners in season, his final tally of 101 beating Johnny Roe's record of 87 by some way. Epsom 1981 should have been a special weekend for the family when Walter won the Derby on Shergar: Wally Snr was due to ride Blue Wind in the Oaks, only to find himself jocked off by Lester Piggott. He was based at various times in Britain, India, France and Ireland.

However, Shaken Bridge was not an enthusiastic racehorse: as soon as she came under pressure and was asked to extend, whether on the gallops at home or at the races, her head would go up in the air and she would stop trying. Cliff did later have the temerity to point out to Mrs Murless that the best race she ever ran was when he rode her against Carrozza!

* * *

Cliff was first person to lay across Crepello when he was being broken in. However, unused to having any weight on his back, the horse plunged then came back up, catching Cliff, who was lying across his withers, between the pommel of the saddle and the back of the horse's neck, crushing Cliff between the two. Cliff recalls it as being very painful and thought he had broken his ribs. Cliff looked after Crepello at evening stables all through the winter but didn't put his name down to do him, assuming he would be given him anyway, and nor did any of the other lads put their names down. However, at allocation time a new lad started, a tall Irishman called Jim LeGunner, and the horse was given to him to do.

Instead, Cliff was given a horse called Troika owned by the Queen, which sadly had a suspected brain tumour and ran into a tree in the woods, killing himself. The other horse Cliff was allocated that year was Shearwater (by My Babu ex Sea Parrott) who was a real handful! Cliff recalls, 'He wasn't vicious but he was a bit naughty.' One evening stables, Murless told Cliff he would give Calne (Clive Brittain) a ride on Shearwater the following day. Clive and Shearwater went into the paddock with the rest of the string, but Shearwater started acting up, so Clive took him away into a corner of the paddock. Shearwater refused to come out of the corner! Cliff got the ride back very quickly. However, Shearwater would buck and jump and kick to try and get the rider off which would upset the rest of the string. Eventually, he was banned from walking round the paddock with the string and he had to go out on his own with just a lead horse; throughout the winter, he was only allowed on the Waterhall Gallops. He was bred and owned by Colonel Giles Loder, who, when Murless told him Shearwater was so difficult, replied, 'I love to see my horses with a bit of go in them!' Shearwater was unraced at two but won the Craven Stakes, Newmarket, (Lester Piggott) at three on his first start at odds of about 10-1. His next race was the Brighton Derby Trial and he was three lengths clear coming out of the dip. The other lads said to Cliff, 'Go and collect your winnings; he's trotted up,' but Shearwater had other ideas and finished third. He never won again, always pulling himself up when he hit the front and allowing other horses to pass him.

Meanwhile, as a two-year-old in 1956, Crepello was beaten first time out in the Windsor Castle Stakes, Piggott claiming he could have won but Murless had told him not to give him a hard race because of his delicate tendons. Crepello was a good-looking horse but had straight forelegs and was heavy-shouldered: he always wore protective bandages which were sewn on around his front legs. He went on to win the Dewhurst and the following year he won the 2,000 Guineas and the Derby ridden by Lester Piggott, beating Ballymoss. Lester did his best to protect those tendons from the infamous Epsom camber, keeping him on a tight rein, biding his time and letting Ballymoss get first run; he didn't allow Crepello to quicken until they met the rising ground. However, the undulations had unsurprisingly taken their toll and he returned home jarred up. Murless was keen to put him away until the St Leger to give him plenty of time to recover, but his owner, Sir Victor Sassoon, wanted him to run in the King George VI and Queen Elizabeth Stakes at Ascot. Murless reluctantly agreed, but it rained and rained, and on the morning of the race there was a terrific thunderstorm which led to false patches on the course. Murless withdrew him. Crepello was to be rerouted to the St Voltigeur at York as a prep race for the St Leger. However, his fragile tendons had begun to cause significant problems and he was retired to stud. He had only had five starts but had won the last three of them, all Group 1 races, and Lester Piggott rated him as being one of the top five horses he had ridden. Standing at his owner Victor Sassoon's Eve Stud in Woodditton, Newmarket, he was leading sire in Great Britain and Ireland in 1969 and Champion Broodmare Sire in 1974.

* * *

Jockey's skull caps became compulsory on the Flat from 10 September 1956. They were very different from the skull caps worn today and were little more than a leather cap with no chin strap, so could easily come off in a fall. A few days after they became compulsory, Cliff had a ride on Lady Murless's nice, two-year-old filly Sijui in The Hastings Maiden Stakes at Yarmouth but he had no skull cap. Lady Murless drove Cliff to the races and he hoped to borrow one from one of the other jockeys at the course, but only one jockey had the same-sized head and he refused to lend his cap to Cliff, although he didn't himself have a ride in the race. Cliff had to stand down and watch the horse canter to victory under another jockey, Paul Tulk (not, thankfully, the one who refused to lend him the skull cap!).

Cliff thinks that during his apprenticeship he had six seconds and readily admits that he should have won on a couple of them when he was beaten a short head. He recalls one race at Windsor where he was in a photo-finish with Michael Beary, but the photo-finish equipment had broken down. Cliff swears he won, but the stewards awarded the race to Beary because he was the senior jockey.

In 1954, the Aga Khan had transferred his racing interests from England to France, where the horses were to be trained by Alec Head, owing to the lower costs and higher prize-money: a move which was to be replicated in the early 2000s by the current Aga Khan for the same reasons. However, his son Prince Aly Khan kept the horses in which he had a share in training with Murless. In 1957, H.H. The Aga Khan sadly died, but in the draft of yearlings which arrived from Ireland that autumn was what Murless described as 'an awful monkey', hence she was given to Cliff to ride! In 1958, Cliff's apprenticeship came to an end: he wasn't going to get rides for Murless and he was encouraged by a colleague, Derek Mayes, to become a professional jockey which he still had an ambition to do. Derek was older than Cliff and had been with Murless since the Beckhampton days, having been a successful pony racer as a boy. This 'mate' encouraged him to take a job with Joe Hartigan in Cheshire where he had the promise of occasional rides. Cliff's one regret was leaving the unraced two-year-old filly of the Aga Khan's at Murless's. He had been riding her on a regular basis and he thought she was rather special. He had, foolishly perhaps, told Derek how much he thought of her. Once Derek had manoeuvred Cliff safely out of the way, Derek asked to do her and became her regular rider. 'The awful monkey' turned out to be none other than the grey flying machine, Petite Etoile. Murless recalls her being 'a peculiar animal'. For some reason, she liked to have another grey in front of her in the string. Murless gave her plenty of time to mature and her first outing was in May 1958 in a two-runner race at Manchester. She got loose twice on the way from the stables to the course and then again in the paddock. She was eventually beaten eight lengths. She then won at Sandown and her next start was the Molecomb Stakes at Goodwood, but Piggott missed the start and she was beaten again, Piggott claiming it was because the grass had been left too long! Her final race as a two-year-old was at Sandown in August, which she duly won. She progressed over the winter and trotted up in the Free Handicap at Newmarket in her first start as a three-year-old. Cliff can't understand how Lester Piggott chose Collyria over Petite Etoile in the 1,000 Guineas; she had only run once as a two-year-old, finishing runner-up at Sandown to a French colt, Saint Crispin, and had reportedly not done well over the winter, so hadn't had a prep race before the 1,000 Guineas. Doug Smith didn't have a ride in the race, so came to ride Petite Etoile in her final piece of work at home. Piggott didn't ride in that gallop, so possibly didn't realise what he was missing. Petite Etoile had quicker acceleration than a Ferrari and streaked clear when Smith asked her coming into the dip. She held on to win by a length and Collyria finished fourth. Her time was two seconds faster than the colts in the 2,000 Guineas. Petite Etoile was eventually the winner of 14 races and finished second in her other five starts. Her wins included 1,000 Guineas, Epsom Oaks, Sussex Stakes, Yorkshire Oaks, Champion Stakes and the Coronation Cup (twice). Her pedigree is still current in the Aga Khan's broodmare band, being the ancestress of Zarkava who was unbeaten in seven races in France including the Prix de l'Arc de Triomphe. Petite Etoile retired from racing in 1961 and was the last horse of note that the family had trained in Great Britain until the current Aga Khan decided to send horses to two English-based trainers, Michael Stoute and Fulke Johnson-Houghton, in 1978.

1958 AND BEYOND

1958 WAS a pivotal year for Cliff. Not only did his apprenticeship come to an end and he left Newmarket for Cheshire, but before the move he got married! His chat-up lines out on the heath to the girls in the Boyd-Rochfort string had evidently worked. He had been dating June (known as Danny) Davie, who was one of the first girls to ride out there. She looked after a couple of good horses herself. Danny had a sister, Jill, and their mother Sybil was an accomplished professional pianist. Obviously, once married, Cliff was no longer able to live in the lads' hostel; Sir Noel very kindly offered to let the newlyweds live in a flat in the main house, but Cliff had already sorted out a flat in the beautiful Warren Towers. Situated next door to Warren Place, at the top of Warren Hill overlooking the training grounds, Warren Towers was a large, red-brick, neo-Tudor-style house with wooden panelling in the main rooms. It had been owned by the dukes of Rutland, but, during the war, Warren Towers became a Barnardo's evacuation centre for boys. The house had been converted into nine flats; there were large gardens with an orangery, squash courts and a sauna and it was run by a lady dressed in appropriate costume for the age of the house: a long dark skirt with a silver chatelaine around her waist.

Sadly, the property was later sold to Sheikh Mohammed, the original house demolished and replaced by an ugly, modern, concrete and red-brick house, surrounded by a high breeze-block wall, said to house around 80 people. It was nicknamed 'Pentonville' by Greville Starkey and is still known as that by many locals.

Joe Hartigan

Joe Hartigan was the son of Frank, with whom Murless had spent his early years. Frank was a good trainer and had trained the horse Elsinore, on which Gordon Richards broke the record for the number of winners (246) ridden in a season, set in 1885 by Fred Archer, as well as winning the Grand National with Foin Goylan. Joe was the yard's amateur rider before becoming assistant to his father. He then spent a couple of years at Beckhampton as assistant to Murless before setting up in Cheshire on his own. Cliff remembers him as being a 'very nice guy', probably more like his uncle Hubert than his father. He trained a couple of jumpers and the rest of the string consisted of Flat horses, but there were only about a dozen to 15 horses in training altogether. Joe Hartigan went on to become an author. One of his books published in 1977 was entitled *'To Become a Racehorse Trainer'* and suggested ways of achieving success for those wanting to enter the profession.

Cliff had a few rides for Joe but without success. To make matters worse, during his spell in Cheshire, Cliff also had to continue to do his two as well as riding work. One day, one of his horses, Stem Christie (Michael Scudamore), was running in the Topham Trophy at Aintree and Cliff was leading up. Unfortunately, the horse and jockey parted company over on the far side of the course. Cliff had to run across the course to catch Stem Christie, but the grass was wet and he was wearing a new pair of suede shoes of which he was inordinately proud. The horse was fine, but the shoes were ruined! Cliff also rode at Liverpool while he was with Hartigan, but it was the second string in a two-year-old Flat race; he has never faced the famous Aintree fences!

Not only had Cliff given up Petite Etoile to move to Chester, but another of his favourite horses, Boccaccio. He was riding at Chester one day and found his old mate was also running; Piggott was riding. Boccaccio duly won the Great Cheshire Handicap. However, Cliff has few regrets about the move. He feels the experience of seeing how different yards were run was pivotal to his achievements in later years. To be successful, it is necessary to experience working at the top and bottom levels in an industry and to see different methods, giving you the option of choosing which methods work best under different circumstances.

On 17 October 1958, Cliff and Danny had their first child: a daughter, Adrienne, was born in Nantwich Hospital. Shortly before this, Cliff had taken his driving test. One of the other lads in the yard, Terry Devlin, had given Cliff a few driving lessons, so Cliff was used to driving his own car, which he had already bought in anticipation. However, for the test he had to use an instructor's car, so he booked himself a driving lesson. His first attempt in the instructor's car, with the instructor sat alongside, saw the car kangaroo-hopping through the village as Cliff fiddled with the unfamiliar choke! At the end of the lesson, Cliff pulled up and the instructor turned and asked when his test was booked for. 'Tomorrow,' replied Cliff. The instructor just wished him luck. Fortunately, Cliff passed his test soon afterwards on the second attempt. Cliff then gave Terry Devlin some handy hints, such as needing to stop at a stop sign rather than keeping driving just because there was no other traffic on the road, so Terry could pass his test which he hadn't yet taken when teaching Cliff!

Joe Hartigan then moved from Cheshire to Middleham in Yorkshire. Hartigan asked Cliff whether he would be joining him in Middleham, so Cliff went to have a look around. It was a small village with cobbled streets, although there were five pubs! But he was not a lover of what he saw, feeling it would be like living in a goldfish bowl with everyone knowing your business. He had also heard how cold the winters there were! He told Hartigan that he did not fancy the move, so Joe Hartigan kindly sorted Cliff out with a job with Toby Balding in Hampshire.

Toby Balding

Gerald Barnard Balding Jr (known as Toby) was born in 1935; his brother Ian followed in 1938. Their father (also Gerald) was one of the best polo players in the world at that time. Gerald returned to England from New Jersey, USA, in 1946 and began training jumpers in Gloucestershire. Ian started riding for Herbert Blagrave in 1962 and initially pursued a career as an amateur jockey, riding against the likes of John Oaksey, Bob McCreery and the Biddlecombes, while Toby, after a few rides in point-to-points, including for the Queen Mother, was forced straight into training after his father's untimely death at the age of 54.

Toby Balding was based in Weyhill, Hampshire, and, although a dual-purpose trainer, he was more famous for his achievements in National Hunt, being one of the few trainers to have won the 'big three' jumps races: the Grand National (Highland Wedding and Little Polveir), the Cheltenham Gold Cup (Cool Ground) and the Champion Hurdle (Beech Road and Morley Street). However, he did also have a small string of Flat horses that made their mark, such as New World in the 1959 Portland Handicap and Green Ruby, winner of the 1986 Ayr Gold Cup and the Goodwood Stewards Cup. Other big flat wins came courtesy of Decent Fellow in the 1977 John Porter Stakes and Sea Freedom in the 1997 Ascot Stakes.

Toby was elected an honorary member of the Jockey Club in 2006 and was, for a time, director of the British Horseracing Authority. He was given an OBE for services to racing in 2011, but sadly died in 2014. However, the Balding name lives on in racing with his nephew, Andrew, a leading trainer and his niece, Claire, a presenter and author.

While with the Balding team, Cliff would also occasionally ride out for one of the neighbours, Richard Sturdy. One of the colts he rode, Barbary Pirate, was particularly difficult and aggressive. He would dive down on to the ground and throw himself around in an attempt to rid himself of the jockey. Sometimes the staff from the nearby army barracks at Weyhill would come and ride out there. One of them rode Barbary Pirate a couple of times, but when he dismounted to lead the colt back to the yard, Barbary Pirate would swing his head round and make a grab for the major's testicles. He only just missed, and after the second occurrence the major refused to ride him again. When Lester Piggott rode Barbary Pirate at the races, the horse ducked out just after the winning post and Lester was dropped. Luckily, the horse cantered away or Piggott could have been gelded!

In 1961, while Cliff was at Toby Balding's, the Murless yard became embroiled in a doping scandal that rocked the racing world. Doping had become widespread in England. Indeed, even the Queen's horses were not immune. Her favoured runner for the 1957 Oaks, Mulberry

Harbour, trained by Captain Boyd-Rochfort, was suspected of having been doped when running in the race won by Carrozza in the Queen's second colours. Mulberry Harbour had been sat in second rounding Tattenham Corner, but when asked to quicken and make her challenge, she lost her action in a stride and quickly went backwards. She was distressed on her return to the racecourse stables; however, in the excitement of having had a royal winner of a Classic race, the stewards forgot to order a dope test on the disappointing Mulberry Harbour.

Pinturischio, owned by Sir Victor Sassoon and trained by Murless, was a big, backward colt but had showed plenty of promise in his homework, so was the intended Derby horse for the yard that year. The lads struggled to get their tongues around the name, so he was known as 'Pint of Sherry' in the yard. He had his debut delayed by a bout of coughing, but he eventually started in the Wood Ditton Stakes at Newmarket, ridden by Lester Piggott and won easily at 2-5. His next race was the 2,000 Guineas where he went off as 7-4 favourite but could only finish fourth. The first- and second-placed horses were both 66-1 outsiders. Murless felt that maybe the trip and going hadn't suited him, but he was still on course for the Derby. Murless had received a tip-off that Pinturischio was likely to be 'nobbled', but he assumed it would be before the Derby, rather than before his prep race in the Dante at York. However, a week before the York race, when Pinturischio was already trading at 6-1 favourite for the Derby, the dopers got to him and he was very sick. Unsurprisingly, he drifted in the Derby betting. Amazingly, Murless managed to get him well enough to resume exercise and Piggott came to ride him, but that piece of work was enough to cause the trainer to scratch him from the Derby. The dopers had found out that he had resumed work and revisited the yard. He had been doped, not just once but twice, with a substance that was normally used as elephant laxative. He was never the same horse again and his racing career was over.

Although no one was ever prosecuted in connection with the Pinturischio case itself, there was a well-known gang of dopers around at the time, run by a bookie called Bill Roper. Trainers were being blamed for doping horses, which they hadn't, and the authorities were not investigating horses which had been doped. It all came to a head later when there was an attempt to dope horses at the yard of the Queen Mother's trainer, Major Peter Cazalet. At around the same time, the Duke of Norfolk, who had been senior steward of the Jockey Club, announced that two of his horses had been doped and he had had them tested privately to prove it. Bill Roper had a Swiss mistress called Micheline Lugeon. The way they worked it was that she would turn up at a selected yard in a chauffeur-driven car (Roper playing the role of chauffeur) posing as a French owner looking to place her racehorses with the trainer. She would be shown around, with Roper following and taking notes about the yard layout and security (if there was any). He would chat to the lads and either bribe one of them or get his own gang to break in at night. They targeted fancied runners in small fields and, once the target had been hit, they would back the other horses in the race.

When the Pinturischio story broke, the trainers started to talk among themselves. Fred Rimell recalled that Lugeon had appeared at his yard shortly before the 1961 Grand National and had shown particular interest in a grey horse called Nicolaus Silver. He saw her at the races a few days later with people he knew to be dubious, so switched his National runner, putting another grey in Nicolaus Silver's box. The ringer was duly doped and Nicolaus Silver went on to win the Grand National.

Eventually, the gang became cocky and foolish. In August 1962, in a three-runner race at Lewes, there were joint odds-on favourites Countess and Lucky Seven, and 20-1 outsider Dear Joe. Countess looked half asleep and duly finished last. The man placing bets on both the other two horses was recognised as Bill Roper. Still the Jockey Club did nothing. Eventually, in October 1963, Roper, Lugeon and some of their accomplices were brought to trial at Lewes Assizes. The Pinturischio affair was not brought up as part of a deal with one of Murless's lads, Snuffy Lawler, who had turned Queen's Evidence to tell of his refusal to dope St Paddy (a horse he looked after) for the gang prior to the 1960 Derby. With the gang unable to get at St Paddy through Lawlor, he had, as expected, won the Derby. At the end of the trial, the gang were found guilty, but Roper only got three years and Lugeon one year. No one at Warren Place could understand Snuffy's actions in working for the gang. He was a single lad with a room in the hostel; he was lucky with his horses, having done Carrozza and Arctic Explorer (an Eclipse winner) as well as St Paddy. He lost his job and was shunned throughout town. Although Snuffy had turned Queen's Evidence, saving himself from a prison sentence, he was, unsurprisingly, not able to get another job in racing, ending his days in a Stable Lads Welfare accommodation flat, a bottle of whisky his only friend.

For Cliff, meanwhile, no winners were forthcoming from either Hartigan or from Toby Balding in Hampshire. The calibre of horses at both yards was not the same as at Murless's and, as everybody in racing knows, it is difficult to get outside rides if your face in not regularly seen aboard winners. Cliff approached Sir Gordon Richards for a job at Beckhampton, but there was no house, just a caravan, and Scobie Breasley and Nelson Guest were already in situ as first and second retained jockey. Piggott had been offered the job as first jockey to Sir Gordon Richards, but eventually turned it down in favour of riding as first jockey for Murless.

RETURN TO NEWMARKET, 1961

MAJOR HOLLIDAY – LA GRANGE

It wasn't long before Cliff was offered a job, with a house, back in Newmarket at La Grange Stables. La Grange is based in a triangle between the Fordham and Snailwell Roads. It was built in the late-1870s by Tom Jennings and is typical of the high Victorian period, made with distinctive local red brick, the main yard angled to face the sun all day but kept cool with built-in air vents flowing up from each individual box to housings on the ridge roof. The pig sties remain to this day.

His employer would be Major Lionel Holliday, who was an extremely wealthy, northern, aniline dye manufacturer and one of the leading owner/breeders in the UK at the time. The dye manufacturing business had been started by Major Holliday's grandfather, Read, in 1860, but was taken over by the government in 1915. Major Holliday used his share to set up the business again in his own name. His main stud was Copgrove Hall Stud near Harrogate, which he bought in 1936, and this was where he kept the majority of his mares and foals, but in 1946, he also bought Sandwich Stud in Cheveley, Newmarket, where his stallions, including Hethersett, were housed. Sandwich Stud also served as a base for his mares when they were visiting Newmarket-based stallions. That same year, he also bought La Grange Stables as well as his house, Sunnyside on Park Lane, where he lived until 1964 when he returned to Copgrove Hall. The house at Sunnyside was subsequently demolished for the development of a new housing estate.

Major Holliday had a reputation for being a difficult and tough character, the archetypal Yorkshireman! He had employed a succession of 13 private trainers in as many years at La Grange; however, when questioned about the rapid turnover in his trainers, Major Holliday's retort was, 'They came to me on a bicycle and left in a Rolls-Royce!' When Major Dick Hern arrived in 1958, Ryan Jarvis in the next-door Phantom House Stables hailed him with, 'I hope you've packed your toothbrush – it's all you're going to need!' It was Major Hern's first training licence, but he proved Ryan Jarvis wrong, bringing quite some success to the yard and remaining there until the end of the 1962 season when he was head-hunted to train for the Astor family at their private stables at West Ilsley, Berkshire.

Major Hern had been associated with horses throughout his life, growing up hunting with various Somerset packs before following his father into the Army in 1939 and seeing active service in north Africa and later Italy. On leaving the Army, Major Hern became a qualified riding instructor and was appointed coach to the British three-day-event team who returned from the 1952 Olympics in Helsinki with gold medals around their necks. He was late into racing, becoming an assistant trainer at the age of 31. It was six years later in 1957, aged 37, that he successfully applied for the position of private trainer to Major Lionel Holliday. Major Hern was the incumbent trainer when Cliff first arrived at La Grange.

HETHERSETT
1959 bay colt by Hugh Lupus out of Bride Elect

Hethersett was a really kind, placid horse; he didn't know what it was to be naughty and Cliff became very fond of him. However, he wasn't the luckiest horse on the racecourse. Despite not being Hethersett's lad initially, Cliff was his regular pilot at home. He was a lazy horse and very green in his work. Once Cliff felt Hethersett was going a bit better and thought he might be a nice horse, he contacted Harry Carr and suggested he should come and ride him work. At the time, Holliday didn't have a stable jockey as such. Carr came and rode Hethersett a piece of work: there were five horses in the work and Cliff led. Hethersett duly went by him and, on pulling up, Carr told Cliff he thought Hethersett was a nice horse but would need a race or two to get him fit, so Cliff didn't back him first time out and, of course, Hethersett bolted up in the Duke of Edinburgh Stakes at Ascot first time out as a two-year-old, winning by five lengths at 20-1. His next start was the Doncaster Timeform Gold Cup (Group 1) (now the *Racing Post* Trophy), but he was struck into from behind, losing the skin off his hind leg from the hock to the fetlock joint, and finished a disappointing fifth as a result.

As a three-year-old in 1962, Hethersett won the Derby Trial at Brighton impressively, again ridden by Harry Carr. Brighton was often used as a Derby trial due to the course being downhill and left-handed, similar to Epsom. Cliff felt it was a better course to use than Lingfield, where the bend was so sharp that, if you were on the wrong leg, the horse would fail to corner and would run straight across the track. Hethersett's Brighton victory was enough for him to be installed as 9-2 favourite for the Derby. However, at Tattenham Corner, Wally Swinburn (senior), riding Romulus, clipped the heels of the horse in front of him, his own mount fell and brought down five others, including Hethersett. Harry Carr broke his shoulder, but when he woke up in hospital, he asked how far he and Hethersett had won the Derby by! He was already 45 years old and his riding days were numbered. Carr eventually retired on the advice of his doctors in the middle of the 1964 season and took over the management of Genesis Green Stud in Wickhambrook, near Newmarket, the same stud now owned by the Swinburn family. Hethersett was badly bruised and shaken and only walked for the next five weeks, so was not particularly fit for his next race, the Gordon Stakes at Goodwood, where he finished only seventh on the firm ground. Cliff's brother-in-law, Malcolm, had had a bet on Hethersett in the Derby, but Cliff told him not to worry, he'd get it back in the St Leger. By the time of the York Ebor meeting, Major Hern had managed to get some more work into the horse and the rain came, easing the ground a little. Hethersett won his Leger prep race, the Great Voltigeur, by a short head.

Cliff was, in fact, the third lad to look after Hethersett. His first lad was Alan Wellburn, who had returned from National Service but he left at the end of the horse's two-year-old career. The next lad to look after Hethersett was Don Alcock, but he left soon after the Derby to move to West Ilsley with Major Hern. Don wasn't the nicest lad and would accuse Cliff of not picking the horse's feet out after morning exercise by chucking stones out into the yard from Hethersett's box. Cliff wasn't sorry to see him go. Cliff knew Hethersett's ability, so wasn't letting another lad have a chance at the pool money Cliff knew he was capable of earning! He already had two horses, so he gave up a horse to Titch King (which went on to win for Titch) to do Hethersett.

Hethersett had very sensitive soles and they would bruise easily; even standing on a hard divot would cause him to knuckle over. He was shod behind with three-quarter shoes. In the run-up to the St Leger, Cliff decided that, in order to protect his feet, it would be safer to lead him across the heath to the gallops, so he wasn't carrying any weight in case he did stand on a stone or hard divot, then Cliff would jump on at the bottom of the canter. Cliff reckons he walked about 50 miles a day!

The night before the St Leger it rained all night. Major Hern joked with Cliff that he had overdone his rain dance, but Cliff was confident that Hethersett would handle the ground and he was proved right. Hethersett took the lead over a furlong out and won by a comfortable four lengths, with the Derby winner, Larkspur, back in sixth. Meanwhile, Cliff's brother-in-law, Malc, was chasing his Derby losses and put on, what was for him, a large bet of £7 at 12-1: that was equivalent to a week's housekeeping and had caused Malc a lot of worries. However, all was well and their winnings paid for his and Muriel's first holiday abroad. They went to London then and there to book it and paid £120 for a fortnight in Spain. Cliff had also given the tip to his father, but parents always know better than their children and Bill eventually admitted to Cliff that he didn't think the horse could win, so hadn't backed him.

Meanwhile, away from the yard, Cliff had bought his second-hand car back with him when he left Chester. Unfortunately, it was beginning to show its age and, after evening stables one day, Cliff tried to drive home from the yard on the Fordham Road but the brakes failed crossing the clocktower roundabout. He tried to pull on the handbrake, but it came off in his hand! He steered past the back of the Rutland and continued to the flat where he lived at the time, continually bumping into the edge of the pavement to try and slow the car down. Eventually it came to a halt. Luckily, it was only a few days later that Hethersett won the St Leger: Cliff had backed him and also received a nice £300 present from Major Holliday, which, together with Cliff's share of the pool money, paid for a new car.

Hethersett's final race was the Champion Stakes at Newmarket; the distance was on the short side for him, but he finished a brave second. Hethersett's exploits enabled Holliday to claim the champion owner and champion breeder crowns and Major Hern to win his first champion trainer title.

Hethersett had little chance to prove himself at stud, dying in 1966 at only seven years old from a brain tumour, which Major Hern speculated might have arisen from his fall in the Derby. However, he showed considerable promise, siring 1969 Derby winner Blakeney and the filly Highest Hope, winner of the Prix Vermeille. He is also the broodmare antecedent of Harzand, winner of both the Epsom and Irish Derbies in 2016 and now standing as a sire himself at HH The Aga Khan's Gilltown Stud.

Prior to Hethersett's St Leger victory, Major Hern had been head-hunted by the Astors and he went to train at their private yard at West Ilsley, near Lambourn, taking the jockey Stan Clayton with him, which freed up a nice house on Duchess Drive that Cliff and Danny moved into with Major Holliday's blessing. Major Holliday wasn't enthusiastic about Hern's resignation, but the latter knew what Holliday could be like and he wasn't going to hang around! Major Hern was briefly succeeded by Captain Jimmy James, but he was not a talented trainer and only held the job for about ten months. One day, the Captain chose to send a group of horses to the beach for a canter, Cliff and Hethersett included, which was much enjoyed by those involved. The head lad, Jim Meany, held a temporary licence when Capt. James resigned (after much, not very subtle, prompting from Major Holliday!) and suddenly the horses started to win! Jim Meany was training when Pushful won the Futurity at Doncaster. He had finished second but was promoted to first on the disqualification of the Irish winner and Cliff, Pushful's regular work rider at home, received another present from Major Holliday in his wage packet.

Before Hethersett, Cliff had ridden his half-brother Proud Chieftain on the gallops. This Proud Chieftain won both the Rosebery Handicap at Kempton and the Magnet Cup at York in 1961 and was looked after, like Hethersett initially, by Alan Wellburn. Cliff was later to name his own horse Proud Chieftain and his house Hethersett.

After Captain James, Walter Wharton (senior) took over training at La Grange. He had originally trained a few horses for the Major in the north.

Cliff looked after Vaguely Noble's half-brother, Attractive (1962 chestnut colt by Acropolis out of Noble Lassie), who was a home-bred of Major Holliday's and arrived at the yard directly from the Major's Copgrove Stud in Yorkshire. The Major always named his horses starting with the initial letter of the sire's name, whereas the Aga Khan starts with the first letter of the dam's name. Attractive was a big horse and didn't run as a two-year-old. Cliff had liked the look of him and decided to do him. He could rear occasionally and was always hollering but he wasn't nasty. The more work he did, the more Cliff liked him. One day, Wally Wharton sent Cliff for a long trot down Cheveley Road, along Duchess Drive, turn right at the junction to come out on Woodditton Road, turn right again and trot up the hill. At the pub on Cheveley Road, Attractive jumped into the middle of the road and reared straight up in the air. Luckily, the roads were a lot quieter then and, once Attractive settled down, they continued on their way. One day, Taffy Williams (the father of current trainer, Stuart Williams) got the leg up on Attractive; he didn't get the same feel as Cliff and thought the colt was moderate. Cliff managed to get the ride back and Attractive continued to improve with each piece of work. He ran a nice first race while continuing to progress at home. His third run was at Alexandra Park, ridden by Bill Williamson; Cliff backed him and he won as expected. His next piece of work was with a horse who had finished fourth in the Guineas, which Joe Mercer had come to ride in the work. Cliff recalls hitting the rising ground and going past Mercer as though his horse was standing still. A few days later, Cliff looked at Attractive's front legs at evening stables; he noticed the tendon wasn't straight. Wally Wharton came and felt the legs when he was looking round. Neither said anything to the other. A couple of days later, the tendon was completely bowed. Attractive was sold overseas as a stallion. Cliff took another horse to the airport a few weeks later to go racing and heard a screaming and hollering that could only be one horse! It was Attractive; he had completed his quarantine and was about to head off to his new stud career overseas, but he had recognised Cliff!

A smart, staying filly whom Cliff looked after at this time was Never A Fear (1962 chesnut filly by Never Say Die out of Cherished). She ran in the Oaks Trial at Lingfield, but Major Holliday wasn't able to attend so he watched on television. Joe Mercer rode. Joe wasn't a hold-up jockey and was usually the first jockey to kick in a race: he never came with a late run; it just wasn't his style. At Lingfield, Never A Fear started as favourite, but Joe kicked her in the belly running down the hill towards the bend; consequently, she was going so fast that she couldn't corner and went straight across the track. Instead of staying where he was and running up that rail, Joe pulled the filly back across to the inside, giving away tens of lengths! She finished second and got a jaw-breaker for her efforts. The Major saw all this on television and swore Joe Mercer would never ride for him again. He never did. However, it didn't seem to harm Joe's career! He rode over 2,800 winners, including the likes of Brigadier Gerard, Bustino, Highclere, Kris and Time Charter. He was stable jockey to Major Hern from 1962 to 1976 and was often described as one of the most stylish jockeys in a finish. Although Major Holliday wasn't a betting man, Cliff was, so when Never A Fear was beaten a short head at Ascot at 25-1, ridden by Ron Hutchinson who never picked up his stick, there were a few choice words from her lad!

Sadly, Major Holliday died in 1965 and his son, Brook, took over. Cliff had found Major Holliday a very good employer and admits that he might have stayed there forever if the Major hadn't died. Sadly, Brook Holliday was nothing like his father and shortly afterwards Cliff decided to return to Sir Noel Murless at Warren Place as one of the trainer's key work riders. Wally Walton tried to persuade Cliff to stay on as he was looking after a good two-year-old filly who was a half-sister to Never A Fear, called Heath Rose (1964 bay filly by Hugh Lupus ex

Cherished) whom Cliff got on with better than many of the lads. He recalls she was a beautiful homebred filly who had won comfortably at Kempton first time out, her only start as a two-year-old, when ridden by Bill Williamson. She became more difficult after Cliff left – she used to throw head around a great deal, possibly because she never had her teeth done, so she had sharp points on many of her teeth and the inside of her mouth would get badly cut. When she was still a two-year-old, Bill Stubbs used to ride her. One day, Wharton decided she needed a change of hands because she was throwing her head around and told Cliff to start riding her. Cliff argued that her mouth needed to heal, so Wharton eventually agreed to let Cliff lunge her instead, providing he did it in his own time. Cliff tried lunging her for a week to give her mouth a chance to heal, but her teeth were so sharp that as soon as she had a bridle on again the cuts in her mouth would reoccur. In fact, the poor filly's teeth were so bad that there would be blood dripping from her mouth after a race. Routine dental visits for the horses were not the norm at that time, but, usually, if a horse did have recognised problems with its teeth, the vet would have been called.

Wharton told Cliff that he thought Heath Rose would win the Guineas and he would get Cliff a good drink from Brook Holliday if he stayed at La Grange. Cliff agreed about her potential but had already sussed Brook Holliday's reluctance to put his hand in his pocket to thank the lads. He retorted, 'I know she will win the Guineas but as to the drink – she's just won a £10,000 race and all I got was four pounds, two shillings and tuppence!' The Major wasn't someone to cut corners and would have had her teeth rasped had he still been alive but Brook was very tight with money. Sadly, this resulted in connections trying different methods to stop her throwing her head around. At the start of her three-year-old career, they tried putting a drop cross noseband on her at home, but it was too tight and Heath Rose panicked and became extremely het up. Despite the poor filly having a constantly painful mouth, she was rated as one of the best three-year-old fillies in Europe, although she only won one of her five races. She finished third in the Prix Vermeille. Her next race was the Prix de l'Arc de Triomphe at Longchamp, but there she bolted to the start. In the race itself, she jumped out and made the running; she was still in front 100 yards out but had expended too much energy, eventually finishing fifth in a blanket finish, beaten heads and necks totalling less than a length. Cliff reflects that, had she not bolted to the start, she would probably have won. How good would she have been if her teeth had been looked after properly from the start?

Vaguely Noble (1965 bay colt by Vienna ex Noble Lassie) arrived at La Grange as a two-year-old the year after Cliff left. He needed to be broken in twice because he was a big, strong horse with a bad temperament, but they eventually got him right. He was beaten into second place in both of his first two races when trained by Wharton for Brook Holliday. However, with the advent of softer, autumn ground, he was able to show his true colours when he won first the Sandwich Stakes at Ascot by 12 lengths, ridden by Bill Williamson, then he inflicted a long-looking, seven-length defeat on his opposition with victory in the Observer Gold Cup (Group 1) at Doncaster. At the end of his two-year-old career, he was part of the dispersal at Tattersalls of Major Holliday's stock to settle death duties. The opening bid was 80,000 guineas and Vaguely Noble was finally sold for 136,000 guineas, then a record price for a racehorse. It was too much to expect to win in prize-money: he wasn't even entered in the Classics, and the cost would have to be recouped in stud fees. It certainly looked a reckless purchase at that stage with Vaguely Noble's sire, Vienna, not even being a top-class stallion himself.

The purchaser was a Californian, Dr Robert Franklyn, who initially transferred Vaguely Noble to Ireland to be trained by Paddy Prendergast. A few days later, Dr Franklyn sold a half share to Nelson Bunker Hunt and they subsequently moved Vaguely Noble to Sea Bird's trainer, Etienne Pollet, in France, with the aim of winning the Prix de l'Arc de Triomphe. Vaguely Noble won his first two starts as a three-year-old before disappointing in the Grand Prix de Saint Cloud when he bolted to the start. Pollet's favoured jockey, Deforge, was also given some criticism in the racing press at the time for lying too far out of his ground in what was a high-class race. Bill Williamson, who had got on so well with him as a two-year-old, was reunited with Vaguely

Noble for the Prix de Chantilly and the colt returned to winning ways. Williamson kept the ride for the Arc where Vaguely Noble trounced a high-quality field, including seven winners of 11 Classic races, only needing to be pushed out hands and heels to win by three lengths from Sir Ivor, winner of the Epsom Derby, who was a further four lengths clear of the third horse. At this point, Vaguely Noble was syndicated for two million pounds and retired to stud at Gainesway Farm in the United States. He became a great sire of turf horses, his progeny including Dahlia, Nobiliary, Empery, Gay Mecene and Jet Ski Lady as well as the broodmare sire of horses such as Golden Fleece, Indian Skimmer and Touching Wood.

Brook Holliday started selling bloodstock and winding down the yard almost straight after his father died. Poor Walter Wharton was sacked in 1967 and had to start to rebuild his business in the north, initially at Richmond before moving to Melton Mowbray. La Grange was sold.

RETURN TO WARREN PLACE, 1966

ON LEAVING La Grange, Cliff returned to Warren Place in 1966 and it appears that they were delighted to have him back. As a married lad with children, Cliff had preferential quarters on the yard and initially had the end house (one of only four lad's houses) on Warren Place until he moved into the bungalow by the paddock, which had recently been vacated by Clive and Maureen Brittain.

By this time, Murless had about 80 horses in training, which was a good-sized string in those days. He still used to go round all the horses every night checking their legs, as he had at Beckhampton. It would be impossible to do now with the size of some of the strings – imagine checking the legs of 200-plus horses! However, many are out at spelling or pre-training yards, but one wonders how trainers can keep track of what all the horses are doing.

In 1965, Eph Smith had joined Murless as a work rider, having had a very successful career as a jockey. Eph had moved to Newmarket in 1936 to become first jockey to Sir Jack Jarvis, winning two Classics on Lord Roseberry's Blue Peter. He also rode in the Queen's colours many times for Captain Boyd-Rochfort, including winning the King George VI and Queen Elizabeth Diamond Stakes at Ascot on Aureole. Eph wore a hearing aid, having suffered from deafness since childhood. He didn't wear it while racing, so however much another jockey shouted at him, they would get no response! One morning, riding work on Warren Hill, his hearing aid fell out. Luckily, he had a well-trained Labrador. He collected the dog from the car and took him to the area where he thought he had lost the device and the dog found it for him. Eph often used to visit Cliff's house at Warren Place for a drink. One day, he told Cliff that he had struggled mentally as a retained jockey for Ted Leader and he had often been prescribed anti-depressants by the doctor. Tragically, Eph Smith's body was found in a shallow brook at Snailwell near Newmarket in August 1972. His labrador was sat at the side of the road waiting for help, but it was too late. The verdict given was death by misadventure. Heartbreakingly, some years later, Eph's younger brother Doug, a successful jockey and trainer himself, committed suicide by throwing himself into the family swimming pool and drowning.

By 1966, Piggott was riding more and more horses for Vincent O'Brien and was often choosing to ride his horses over Murless's. Sir Noel decided that the following season he would need to revert to having a fully retained jockey again rather than using Piggott when available. It was announced that George Moore would come over from Australia to join the Murless team.

George Moore was born in Queensland in 1923 and moved to Brisbane to become an apprentice jockey in 1938. Despite teaming up with leading Sydney trainer, Tommy Smith, and becoming champion jockey in Sydney ten times between 1957 and 1969, it was a tempestuous relationship with neither man liking the other. It culminated with Moore, having had a rollocking from Smith after riding out one morning, retorting that when Smith had been a jockey, he couldn't keep his seat on a rocking horse! During a period of suspension from riding in Australia in the mid-fifties (for owning and backing a winner in a race in which he rode another horse), Moore was encouraged to try his hand in Europe, which led to him winning the 1959 2,000 Guineas on Taboun and the Prix de l'Arc de Triomphe on Saint Crispin. The following year, he won the Prix du Jockey Club on Charlottesville and the Ascot Gold Cup on Sheshoon. However, his brief spell with Murless was probably the most fruitful period of his career as a jockey. They won the 2,000 Guineas and Derby with Royal Palace, the 1,000 Guineas with Fleet and the King George and Queen Elizabeth Diamond Stakes with Busted. When he left Murless, Moore returned to Australia to train, later moving to Hong Kong where he was champion trainer on 11 occasions. George Moore rode 2,278 winners around the world and was given an OBE in 1972. He died in 2008, aged 84.

Sandy Barclay was barely out of his apprenticeship when he got the retainer as second jockey with Murless in November 1966. He came down from Scotland and was suddenly riding Classic winners, shooting him to stardom at a young age. Sadly, like so many who achieve fame too early, the more he shone on the racecourse, the less enthusiasm he had for the more mundane side of life. He modelled himself on Piggott and horses ran for him, but he became frustrated when he got beaten and started swinging his whip. He eventually lost the magic that he had had.

Murless had a set of starting stalls installed in the paddock when they became compulsory for some Flat race starts in 1966. Cliff took the first horse in with two others and the boss told him to give it plenty of rein to ensure he wasn't hanging on to its mouth when the stalls opened. Cliff did so, the stalls opened, the horse jumped and Cliff was sent somersaulting backwards! He wasn't holding on to the neck strap and hadn't realised how quickly the horse would jump! Murless was a great proponent of starting stalls and worked hard to get them introduced. There was some talk that it would result in a loss of jockey skills, since riders wouldn't have to get a horse to line up and get a good break, but they still need to get their mounts to break well from the stalls. Starting from stalls certainly prevents situations such as the one at Leicester involving Harry Wragg: a large field of inexperienced two-year-olds were lining up at the tapes; Gordon Richards was on the red-hot favourite but was struggling to get into the line. The starter told the jockeys to take a turn and come in again, not realising Harry Wragg had lined up directly under his rostrum and couldn't be seen. As they came in again, the starter let them go, allowing Wragg a four-length start, the same advantage he held over the rest of the field at the finishing post!

The following year, starting stalls were in more common usage at the major courses, which was just as well for Fleet (1964 bay filly by Immortality out of Review) who was winter favourite for the 1,000 Guineas. She started her Classic campaign by refusing to jump off at the start in the Classic Trial at Thirsk where they were still using the conventional tapes; she stood broadside to the tapes and was being held by the assistant starter when the starter let the field go! She took no part in her trial race. Her next start was the 1,000 Guineas; the stalls were used for the first time for that race and she duly jumped off and won, having been midfield throughout the race and making her challenge running into the dip. She was never asked to face the starting tapes again. George Moore rode her in the 1,000 Guineas and again in the Oaks where she finished fourth, a lack of stamina being her undoing. She then won the Coronation Stakes at Ascot over a mile impressively and was stepped back up to 1m2f for the Eclipse. Moore stuck with her in preference to Busted (the best son Crepello had), but she appeared not to stay the trip in that race either. She had one final start, the Sir Michael Sobell Stakes, back over a mile and although she won, she wasn't suited by the soft autumn ground and was retired to stud, a date with Crepello her reward.

Meanwhile, George Moore switched to Busted (1963 bay colt by Crepello out of Sans Le Sou) for the King George. Busted had been trained by R. N. Fetherstonhaugh in Ireland as a two- and three-year-old and was ridden by Peter Boothman. He had been fancied for the Irish Derby as a three-year-old, but he went about 20 lengths clear before failing to get home and being overtaken by the rest of the field. As a three-year-old, he was headstrong and would race too freely, so although he showed himself to be a useful colt in Ireland, he was not achieving his potential. He was transferred to Murless for his four-year-old career, primarily as a lead horse for Royal Palace who was being prepared for the Derby. Murless put his daughter, Julie, on Busted to settle him at home. When racing, George Moore would adopt the same tactics as Julie and ride him from behind to settle him. The result was that he went through the season unbeaten, starting with the Coronation Stakes at Sandown in April. Unfortunately, he returned home with a pulled muscle and, needing some time off to recover, he was unable to assist Royal Palace in his Derby preparation. His main aim was the King George VI and Queen Elizabeth Stakes, but having been off the track since April it was decided to give him a prep run in the Eclipse, taking on Fleet who would be ridden by George Moore. Bill Rickaby was given the ride on Busted who won impressively before following up with an easy victory in the King George VI itself. He was supposed to go for the Arc and was not pressed to win his prep race, the Prix Henri Foy, but he sustained a suspensory injury while training for it; Murless felt his leg one evening and that was it. He was retired to his owner Stanhope Joel's Snailwell Stud, just outside Newmarket. He proved successful as a stallion, with Bustino and Mtoto among his offspring. Busted died of a heart attack at home aged 25 in 1988.

ROYAL PALACE
1964 bay colt by Ballymoss out of Crystal Palace

Royal Palace was allocated to Murless's head lad, Spider Gibson (the grandfather of Dale Gibson, currently executive director of the Professional Jockeys Association). However, as head lad, Spider often had other duties, so Cliff was quite frequently called on to ride the colt. Although he was only a small horse, he was effective! Having finished his two-year-old season showing impressive acceleration to win the Royal Lodge Stakes at Ascot despite having missed the break, the racing world was looking forward to him being a possible triple crown contender. The main worry was whether he would have enough speed for the 2,000 Guineas. However, the co-favourite, Bold Lad, met trouble in running and was unable to mount a challenge, and Royal Palace was just able to hold on by a fast-diminishing short head from the French challenger Taj Dewan. Next stop the Derby. With 22 runners and starting the race from the stalls for the first time, it took a while to load all the horses. Royal Palace took all the shenanigans in his stride: he wasn't upset by the delay and was quickly away, settling into his rhythm in midfield. He took up the running in the straight and was unchallenged, winning emphatically by 2½ lengths. The triple crown looked a certainty! Unfortunately, as is the way of racing, it was not to be. Royal Palace knocked a joint before his St Leger prep race, the Great Voltigeur, and was forced to miss it. Although he resumed work, Murless deemed he was not ready for the St Leger and he was forced to miss his triple crown opportunity. He was re-routed to the Champion Stakes. Cliff rode Royal Palace in his last gallop before the Champion Stakes and in the race Royal Palace was beaten into third place. Despite having no chance of beating the first two, George Moore went to give him a smack around his flanks, but his whip flew out of his hand. After the race, Murless claimed he knew he was over the top; he probably did because in that last work he told Cliff not to draw upsides but to stay in behind. Cliff also thought the horse might be over the top because he wasn't giving him the same feel as he had done earlier in the season; in fact, he doubted whether he would have been able to draw alongside the other horses. Murless was obviously trying not to give him too much to do in that final piece of work.

Unusually for a Derby winner, Royal Palace remained in training as a four-year-old, kicking off with an easy win in the Coronation Stakes at Sandown and following that up by taking the Coronation Cup at Epsom and the Prince of Wales's Stakes at Royal Ascot. On to the Eclipse: Yves St-Martin, riding Taj Dewan, took up the running after the final turn and claimed he had won the race. It looked as though St-Martin was correct watching on television, with Sandy Barclay appearing to have given the Murless colt too much to do, but the photo-finish camera gave the race to Royal Palace. Sir Ivor, that year's Derby winner, was in third. Royal Palace was stepped back up in trip to 1m4f for the King George VI and Queen Elizabeth Stakes at Ascot. As they straightened for home, Barclay began to ask Royal Palace for an effort. He quickened, nicely initially, but failed to get away and started to hang left. This allowed the French challengers, Topyo and then Felicio, to come up on his inside. Topyo faltered and Felicio was hard ridden to maintain his challenge, with John Oaksey (the commentator) describing his jockey's style as 'an imitation of a demented windmill'. But Royal Palace struggled on bravely, without Barclay having to resort to his whip, and held on to win by a fast-diminishing half a length. Royal Palace pulled up lame on his near fore. He had torn the suspensory ligament badly, explaining why he had started to hang. He was retired to Egerton Stud in Newmarket before moving to the National Stud. His best Flat winner was the Queen's filly Dunfermline (winner of the 1977 Epsom Oaks and St Leger), but he also sired the triple Champion Hurdle winner See You Then. Royal Palace died in 1991 aged 27 and is buried at the National Stud in Newmarket.

Murless was not always happy with George Moore's riding. He had a tendency to make his run too soon, even during work. Cliff remembers being third of a group of four on the Limekilns, with George Moore on the fourth. With 3½ furlongs still to go, Moore came flying past! During races, Moore used to hit the horses around the flanks rather than the quarters and Murless thought he was waving his whip at the horses because of the lack of weals on the quarters. However, one morning, as the string were crossing the Bury Road to get to Limekilns, the horses were sweating: they knew they were doing some work when they crossed the road to go to the Limekilns. Murless noticed black marks down the flanks through the sweat on a particular horse and queried what they were. The horse had only run a couple of days previously and the whip marks stood out through the sweat.

On another occasion, Cliff was riding work on Long Hill with Willie Snaith on the lead horse. There were three of them upsides in behind the leader, Cliff on the left, Gary Moore (George's son, later an extremely successful trainer in Hong Kong) in the centre and Geoff Lewis on the right. Willie set off too fast, so the three let him go. Willie's horse stopped suddenly two furlongs from the end of the gallop as a result of having gone too fast and poor Gary's horse went straight into the back of him, slicing into the tendon. Gary was mortified and Geoff Lewis wanted to say they didn't know who had caused the injury. Cliff made Gary tell Murless what had happened, believing it was always better to tell the truth. Gary explained what had happened and that he had nowhere to go. Murless had a brief eruption, but then realised it was an accident and calmed down. The injured horse eventually recovered and continued racing.

A popular race for unraced horses at the Craven meeting, the Wood Ditton Stakes had a reputation for being a bad race. However, King's Favourite, whom Cliff looked after, won the Wood Ditton and followed up with wins at York and Doncaster. He stayed in training as a four-year-old. The plan was to start in the Rubbing House Stakes (now the Earl of Sefton Stakes), which is run the same day as the Wood Ditton. At evening stables, the day before the race, Murless suggested to Cliff that he felt he was short of a piece of work. Cliff felt he had been fit enough the year before when making his racecourse debut, so checked his diary which showed he had had as many gallops as the previous year. On consideration, Cliff decided that, even if he was one gallop short, he shouldn't get beaten: he wasn't a big horse who took much getting fit. Also, none of the other horses would be race-fit: there were no opportunities to run them before the Craven meeting in those days, unless you were Vincent O'Brien with access to horse flights to Cagnes-sur-Mer in France! King's Favourite won convincingly, ridden by Geoff Lewis with Cliff's money on!

Cliff seemed to be particularly lucky with 'black' (dark bay/brown) horses. As well as Hethersett and Sir Victor Sassoon's Boccaccio, who won the 1957 Autumn Foal Stakes at Newbury, he looked after Mrs Hue-Williams's Sun Rock (1964 bay colt by Ballymoss out of Blue Prelude), a half-brother to champion hurdler Magic Court. Sun Rock stood in the stable next to the office at Warren Place which had fitted rubber matting stuck to the floor. He was a peculiar horse who wouldn't go past on the left side of another horse: Cliff tried it one morning and failed, so switched to the right and Sun Rock took off! He only ran once as a two-year-old but started his three-year-old season well, winning at Sandown, and with possible Classic pretentions in mind he was sent to the Derby trials, finishing second in the Chester Vase, but then he disappointed at Lingfield. George Moore rode him and didn't listen to Cliff about only passing on the right, so the poor horse got a hiding. Next time Cliff told him again about passing on the right and this time Moore paid attention, took the correct route and the horse quickened impressively. Sun Rock came to himself in the latter half of the season, winning the Summer Cup Handicap at Newbury, the Gordon Stakes at Goodwood (this victory taking Murless's winnings for that year past £200,000, ten years after he had become the first trainer ever to pass £100,000) and finishing the season with a win in the Peter Hastings Stakes at Newbury. Sun Rock stayed in training as a four-year-old and started the season promisingly enough, finishing third in the Jockey Club Stakes at Newmarket, but otherwise was unable to reproduce his three-year-old form. He was sold as a stallion to Colombia.

Cliff's other 'lucky' superstition was number four. J O Tobin was number four when he won the Swaps Stakes.

CONNAUGHT
1965 bay colt by St Paddy out of Nagaika

Connaught only had one run as a two-year-old, having refused to enter the stalls on his intended debut, but certainly came into his own at three. His prowess was being talked about around the Newmarket pubs before he even set foot on a racecourse that year. However, things didn't go to plan initially: his debut was due to be in the Greenham Stakes at Newbury, but once again he refused to enter the stalls and he continued to have his ups and downs throughout the season. His next start was in the 2,000 Guineas at Newmarket, although the Derby was to be his main objective. Plenty of additional stalls schooling at home saw him enter them without a problem, but he didn't figure in the race itself, not being a natural miler. On to the Chester Vase, where his jockey, Sandy Barclay, took the lead four furlongs out but didn't ride him out to the line, allowing the ante-post second favourite for the Derby, Remand, to pass him. Barclay made amends with his ride in the Derby, but Connaught had no answer to Sir Ivor's turn of foot and finished a respectable second, beaten a length and a half, with Remand well back in fourth.

Connaught was brought out again quickly to run in the King Edward VII Stakes at Royal Ascot. It was a tough ask, but he was thriving on his racing and, taking the lead at halfway, he strode clear to win by an easy four lengths. His next start was due to be the Gordon Stakes at Goodwood, but he trod on a wasps' nest when being led over Trundle Hill to the course and got loose. Charlie Dyson, the travelling head lad and all of 12st, was sent racing down the course to collect him. (The press referred to Charlie as a top work rider, but he was a little on the heavy side for that role!) Unsurprisingly, Connaught was covered in stings and had to be withdrawn. Connaught was doing himself very well all this time and through missing this race he became positively plump! So Murless took matters into his own hands and decided to work Connaught on the Limekilns before his next race, ignoring Newmarket

Jockey Club instructions that the Limekilns were closed. Unfortunately, Humphrey Cottrill, another trainer, reported him and Murless incurred the wrath of the Newmarket Estates manager. Fortunately, it was just what Connaught needed and, stripping a lot fitter, off he went to York to run in the Great Voltigeur. Barclay was aware that the St Leger was just around the corner and unfortunately decided to hold on to the colt, rather than send him on as normal. This resulted in a barging match with Riboccare, which the latter won by a neck. However, the stewards on the day deemed the fault lay at Riboccare's door, despite him being half the size of Connaught, and the placings were reversed.

By the time the St Leger came around, the ground had turned soft: Connaught failed to act on it and could only finish fifth, despite starting favourite. He stayed in training as a four-year-old, winning the Coronation Stakes (now the Brigadier Gerard) at Sandown and the Prince of Wales's Stakes at Royal Ascot, breaking the track record by four seconds. Unfortunately, he then developed a respiratory infection and didn't run again for three months. His temperamental streak resurfaced before the Scarborough Stakes at Doncaster, where he was reluctant to leave the pre-parade ring before finishing third to Karabas and Hotfoot. As a five-year-old, he started well, winning the Westbury Stakes at Sandown, then breaking his own track record when winning the Prince of Wales's Stakes again. Once again, he was reluctant to enter the stalls before the Eclipse and then swerved coming out and almost unseated Barclay. However, it was a three-horse affair and he managed to win convincingly from Karabas, again setting a new course record in the process. He was retired to stud where he produced a steady stream of good class winners of both codes before being retired in the mid-1980s. He died in 1987 at the age of 22.

In 1969/70, one of the horses Cliff looked after, Queenborough II, was a tall, weak horse and didn't come into training until he was three. He stood roughly 16.2 hands high. Cliff got on well with him although he reputedly didn't have a great temperament. Cliff thought he felt like a nice horse and Queenborough II upheld Cliff's faith, winning his first race, the September Stakes at Doncaster, when ridden by Sandy Barclay. Despite being slowly away, he was able to beat more experienced runners without coming under pressure. His next race was in the Brodrick Stakes at Ayr and Murless sent him to Scotland a week before his race. When he was walking around the parade ring, the vet noticed he was lame and mentioned the fact to Lady Murless. She replied that he was a big, soft horse: he just had a slightly sore heel in front and was making a fuss about nothing. He was allowed to run and Sandy Barclay rode him: he needed a couple of backhanders but he won. Ten minutes after the race, his coronet split open and there was pus everywhere. Maybe he wasn't as soft as they believed, winning with a huge abscess in his foot. Unsurprisingly, after this incident, Queenborough II became a little reluctant to put his best foot forward, particularly when coming under pressure in a race, but he continued to work well with the good horses at home. Willie Snaith rode him while Cliff was away on holiday and when Cliff returned, Queenborough II was favourite for the Bunbury Cup on the Newmarket July Course: they both really fancied him. Unfortunately, Queenborough II was never sighted. Sandy Barclay then got the sack and Queenborough II's last race was in the Arden Stakes at Warwick, ridden by Geoff Lewis, who was taking over as retained jockey.

Cliff's instructions were 'This horse could win (despite there being a 2-1 on shot in the race, being ridden by Ron Hutchinson for John Dunlop). When you get to the start, don't stand still. If you stand still, he will start shaking like a jelly and you've had it. If you keep him walking around until they call you in, he'll be OK. In the race don't move on him, just sit. If you move, he'll curl up. Just let him do what he wants to do himself.' Geoff Lewis carried out his instructions to perfection! He jumped off in front and although the odds-on favourite came upsides in the final furlong, Geoff Lewis didn't move, sitting with his hands on the horse's withers. They flashed past the post together and a photo-finish was called. It was then discovered that the photo-finish camera had broken down, but the judge gave Queenborough II the verdict! His next engagement was to go through the sales ring at Tattersalls where he was bought by Dennis Rayson who asked Cliff to ride the horse back to the yard. Cliff was a little reluctant because it was dark and Dennis Rayson was based in part of Harraton Court Stables in Exning (now Gay Kelleway's Queen Alexandra Stables). However, he agreed to ride the horse across the heath to the yard at Exning. He was speaking to Rayson about the horse when the well-known entertainer and multi-millionaire Des O'Connor (who had a regular slot on ITV Saturday night television) appeared. 'Thank you for bringing my horse home,' he said and handed Cliff £3! Rayson then ran the horse at Aintree (there was still Flat racing there then), but, unfortunately, he started breaking blood vessels and was unable to win again.

In the early seventiess, Cliff was riding the Hue-Williams's Altesse Royale (1968 chesnut filly by Saint Crespin out of Bleu Azur). She won her two-year-old maiden at Lingfield first time out when ridden by Sandy Barclay who commented that that was about as good as she was. Cliff was a bit upset because he rather liked her, but he continued to ride her throughout the winter. She was left unclipped and sweated profusely in her heavy rug, trotting around the indoor ride, and it took a lot of brushing to keep her clean! One evening in the spring, Murless told Cliff to switch from Altesse Royale and ride a horse called Saintly Song. Saintly Song was looked after by Robert Street who had been riding him every day. Saintly Song wasn't the nicest ride as he would whip round and mess about and Rob just used to let him do it rather than try and correct the horse. Saintly Song had ability and had won the St James's Palace Stakes at Royal Ascot, but Cliff wasn't too pleased to be told to switch. Eph Smith was switched on to Altesse Royale. Having ridden her at home, Eph backed Altesse Royale at 33-1 for the Guineas but didn't tell anyone. She wasn't generally well fancied, having finished second in the Nell Gwyn, and Geoff Lewis chose to ride the stable's other runner, Cheveley Park winner, Magic Flute. Yves Saint-Martin came in for the ride on Altesse Royale and she turned around the Nell Gwyn form, winning by 1½ lengths from Super Honey. Magic Flute finished fourth. Murless found out about Eph's bet and didn't speak to him for weeks! Altesse Royale then went on to win the Oaks by three lengths, ridden by Geoff Lewis, who, only a few days earlier, had won the Derby on Mill Reef. She then went on to take the Irish Oaks before a training injury forced her retirement from racing and she returned home to stud.

STABLE LADS STRIKE, 1975

IN 1975, the Newmarket lads decided to go out on strike over their conditions of employment. They wanted more money and more time off (they were working seven days a week with one Sunday afternoon in three being the only time they had to themselves). At the time, the average lad was paid £28 a week, scarcely enough to buy more than basic food and the occasional pint of beer, and £5 for a winner which was taxed. Not all the yards had hostels and it was impossible to afford to rent a house as well as buy food and drink for a family. Stable lads had been represented by the Trade and General Workers Union since the early 1920s, but only about half the lads in Newmarket were members. Negotiations for better conditions had been going on for months with the National Trainers' Federation, but they had failed to secure a deal despite there being sympathy within the industry for the lads' grievances. Eventually, the union called for the lads to strike.

Cliff was very much against going out on strike: he knew how well Murless looked after them and didn't want to upset his employer. However, he was heavily pressurised by the other lads in the yard. Eventually, he agreed to join the strike provided more than half the other lads in the yard went out. At the last minute, many of the Murless lads changed their mind and eventually Cliff realised only about six of them had attended the strike.

When Newmarket Racecourse opened their gates for the Guineas Meeting on Thursday, 1 May 1975, pickets tried to stop anyone from entering, but this failed, so around 200 strikers headed for the course itself and staged a sit-in. This is where the atmosphere soured: the agreement had been that there would be no disruption to racing, but it appeared that some of the more vociferous lads had egged the others on and they managed to stop the runners going to post for the first race. Eventually, the police were able to move the lads on and the delayed first race went ahead. However, this was not enough to stop the strikers and they moved down the course and picketed the start before the second race. Initially, the jockeys were in support of the strikers, many of them having come through the apprenticeship system themselves, but this action angered them. Some jockeys charged the picketers in an attempt to break them up and managed to break through the demonstrators and make it down to the start. The crowd wanted racing to go ahead and, egged on by Willie Carson who had been pulled off his horse by the picketers, they joined in, clambering over the fences and ducking under the rails. Fights broke out between the racegoers and the strikers. Eventually, the police managed to break up the fights and the crowds returned to the grandstand. However, it turned out that the strikers had not finished.

On the Friday night, it would appear they 'borrowed' a bulldozer and managed to plough up the turf at the mile start. The 2,000 Guineas on the Saturday had to be started with tapes rather than starting stalls. The race was won by Bolkonski, ridden by Frankie Dettori's father, Gianfranco. The lad who did Bolkonski (Tommy Dickie) was one of the strikers and he refused to lead the horse into the winner's enclosure. He was employed by Henry Cecil (Murless's son-in-law) and, while he considered Cecil a good employer, he had a wife and two children. His weekly take-home pay of £28 did not go very far. The dispute rumbled on until an agreement was reached in July 1975. However, it was a hollow victory: the strike split families, some couples even getting divorced, and more than 70 of the strikers were sacked on their return to work. In the wake of this disruption, the Stable Lads Welfare Trust was set up and now deals with employment negotiations with the National Trainers Federation. The lads get more time off, expenses when they go away racing and a percentage of the winnings of any horses they look after. Still, Willie Carson reflects even now that, although conditions have changed for the better, the only lads who will get rich are those who become jockeys, or the few who look after champions. He says, 'It will always be an existence rather than a career.'

Cliff hated the way the more mutinous strikers were behaving, disrupting racing and causing trouble, so he returned to work before the strike ended; he approached Sir Noel one Saturday to ask for his job back and was told to turn up as normal on the Monday. The lads all thought the strikers would get the sack or at least be punished by only being allowed to ride the walkers in the covered school rather than riding work. But Murless was a more sympathetic employer and Cliff recalls that he never held their actions against them and it wasn't mentioned again.

FAMILY LIFE

CLIFF WAS always one to try and make an extra bob or two. He and his mate John McGarr bought a large flock of chickens to keep on an allotment at the back of Barry Lynham Drive and they sold the eggs. After his brother-in-law, Malcolm, had completed his National Service, he got a job working for Lincoln Cars in the parts department. During the week, he was the bookies runner, gathering all the bets from around the factory and ringing them through to the local bookmaker rather than learning the car parts from the thick volume sitting on his desk! Luckily, his co-workers were delighted to have someone acting as bookies runner, so they just showed him which part they needed in the huge manual! At the weekends, he would load up the car boot with goods that were supplied by a neighbour and come down to Newmarket to stay with Cliff for the weekend. Cliff and Malc would then sell this merchandise, starting with Jack and Joan Button who had a shop in Wickhambrook. After visiting the Buttons, Cliff and Malc would then drive around the stable yards, selling from the car boot and finishing on Sunday lunchtime at the Coronation Hotel where they would sell their wares to the jockeys who used to lunch there. The goods varied from bri-nylon shirts to sheets, toys at Christmas time and even condoms! It was rather like Trotters Independent Traders!

Occasionally they also had some rugs to sell, in which case they would knock on front doors, roll the rug out across the front room before the homeowners had a chance to speak, and point out how well the rug went with the décor. The chicken eggs from the allotment hens would fill the boot for the return journey to London. The egg enterprise was going well, so Cliff and John decided to expand into rabbits. However, they hadn't realised the significance of the phrase 'to breed like rabbits' and pretty soon they were overrun! There were 300 rabbits to skin and gut before they could be taken to the butcher to be sold: they were only paid by carcass weight, which was not a lot by the time they were ready for the butcher. The work involved for so little return brought a speedy end to that particular money-making scheme!

Eventually, Muriel and Malcolm moved to Newmarket: house prices were between two and three thousand pounds here as opposed to about six thousand or more around London. One weekend, Cliff decided Malc needed a riding lesson and legged Malc up on to a grey pony in the paddock. There was no tack. The pony set off, thanks to a smack on the backside from Cliff, and Malc slid off inelegantly! The spot where he hit the earth is the site where the house that he and Muriel bought now stands! This meant they needed someone else to bring the supplies for sales from London and occasionally Cliff's brother, Eric, would be roped into bringing the goods down. He wasn't too keen on doing the condom run, worried he would have some explaining to do if he was stopped by the police! Occasionally, one of the lads would come to the house for supplies. If Muriel opened the door, they would ask for a word with Malc, but, if he wasn't around, they would often leave empty-handed because they were too embarrassed to ask Muriel for the condoms they had come for.

Adrienne remembers that initially the family were living at Malvern Close in a bungalow with a garden backed by stunning, mature, walnut trees. It was while Danny and Cliff were living here, they had a young girl as a lodger briefly, but she had a downstairs bedroom and the curtains didn't quite close. This encouraged the local peeping tom. Cliff, always keen to catch a wrongdoer, and aided and abetted by John McGarr who lived a couple of houses down, set electric wires around and across the garden in an effort to deter him! The peeping tom was sneaking down a back alley from the nearby stud and coming in through the back gate. Cliff and John hid in the garage one evening, ready to switch the battery on when he appeared (they didn't want to electrocute the wrong person!). He was so busy peeping that they were able to creep out and catch him without the need for any electrical traps.

He was so surprised that he made no attempt to struggle and waited with them while the police were called and came to pick him up for a night in the cells.

In 1964, the Lines family moved to Duchess Drive and on 7 December 1964 Cliff and Danny welcomed their second child. Richard was born at Ely Hospital. When Danny went into labour with Richard, a kindly neighbour, Mrs Lanham, had to take her to the hospital because Cliff wasn't well and was suffering from flu. Adrienne had started school the previous year at the Catholic school by the Severals in Newmarket. The family wasn't Catholic, but the head lad's wife at Holliday's was; she was very friendly with the nuns at the school and managed to get Adrienne a place at the convent, although Cliff did have to pay her school fees. When he was old enough, Richard followed his sister into the convent school at Newmarket (although after his first year, Cliff no longer had to pay school fees).

Once the family moved back to Warren Place, Cliff decided to teach the children the art of horsemanship. He bought Welsh mountain ponies in batches of about six at a time at a price of £30 each, unbroken, from the Balaton Lodge Equine Research Station (later the Animal Health Trust) in Newmarket. The ponies were initially kept with Adrienne's best friend, Angela. Unfortunately, one of the ponies rolled and got under the fence. A passer-by kindly went to catch it and return it but left the paddock gate open! The six ponies all broke out and were running loose around the Cheveley Road area of Newmarket, up the road and through private gardens! Cliff was told he would have to move them, so he rented some paddocks from Mrs Lanham on the Fordham Road. Cliff and the children broke the ponies in and brought them on. Once they were ready, Richard and Adrienne would ride the ponies around the local competition circuit and, as soon as Cliff thought a horse had reached its peak, the pony would be sold on, often from under the children riding them on lead-rein at the gymkhanas. Otherwise, Adrienne and Richard would return from school to find their favourite ponies had been sold and there was a new batch in the paddock waiting to be broken in. Richard would run and hide behind the shed in tears! Cliff remembers one in particular – a big, strong, black pony with a long mane and forelock. He wasn't nasty but was always rather nervous and didn't like to be caught: he would stand with wild, black eyes scowling out from under his foretop and he would always contrive to be at the back of the group. However, he was good to break in and was sold to someone in Cheshire. Cliff warned the purchaser that the pony needed to be kept on a lead rein. The farmer put his son on the black beauty, who, one day, bolted and made straight for the stone wall round the field. Luckily, the little lad fell off long before the pony jumped the wall. The pony was then rebroken to harness and started buggy racing; he could trot as fast as most horses could canter and became one of the leading harness-racing ponies in the country.

Sometimes you have to be cruel to be kind and prove who is in charge for the horse's own good. One of the ponies would often rear. Richard was trying to ride the pony and it just wouldn't stop rearing wherever he went or whatever he did. Cliff spun the pony round until it fell on the ground. He put a sack over the pony's head and sat on it. The pony's ribs were heaving then suddenly stopped. Cliff thought he had suffocated it! He stood up, removed the sack and the pony rose to its feet. It never reared again but turned into one of the best gymkhana ponies Cliff had. Another common remedy for this, which Cliff used occasionally, is to break an egg over the pony's head as it comes up. This supposedly simulates blood trickling down the face as if the horse had cracked its head on something. The tricky part is having an egg in your pocket and getting it into your hand at precisely the right time to crack over the horse's head without breaking it en route!

Adrienne's favourite was a cream filly with blue eyes named Opal, which Cliff had bought for her as she was becoming more competitive. Opal was a serious little jumper: she was only about 13 hands, but together they beat all the larger ponies and older children. Richard also had a good pony at this time called Grey Shadow. The ponies were moved to a farmer's paddocks and barn in Kennett behind The Cock pub. At the time, Cliff was looking after some ponies for an Australian friend, so he had Opal covered by the friend's stallion. Cliff's knowledge of breeding fell well behind his knowledge of racing: Opal was also a novice, so when it came time for Opal to foal, she remained standing and Cliff caught the foal (as well as the afterbirth!) in his arms. The pretty palomino foal was weaned quickly and sold on.

As well as teaching Adrienne and Richard how to ride, Cliff also taught Dick Parry. Cliff knew Dick's mother, who lived in Kennett, and he would drop Richard off at the Parrys' house when he left for work and Dick's mother would ensure Richard caught the school bus. One day, Dick expressed an interest in learning to ride and Cliff found an ex-racehorse for him and started to teach him. Cliff recalls that he took to it very well and was soon riding around the village on his own. However, a close call with a muck lorry, which was speeding through the village and didn't slow down on approaching Dick, nearly put him off completely. Dick was a session saxophonist and a childhood friendship with David Gilmour led to him playing with Pink Floyd on the *Dark Side of the Moon* album, on songs such as 'Money' and 'Shine On You Crazy Diamond', as well as touring with him.

If Cliff couldn't be making money, then he would try to be saving it. If anything needed mending, he would have first attempt at it! Cars, lawn-mowers, etc., would all be taken apart then put back together again – although not always successfully! Even a bent nail would be straightened and reused. Sometimes he was successful: he did the wallpapering when the family moved house (with help from Adrienne as he and Danny would argue too much!) and he even made his own trailer to take the children's ponies to their shows! When Cliff bought Adrienne her first bike, she couldn't reach the pedals, so Cliff fixed blocks of wood to them until she grew into it and they could be removed! He would never have considered buying a bicycle the correct size if he could solve the problem without any expense! He also made her a netball hoop which was fixed up in the garden. Adrienne loved netball and soon became top goal shooter in the area, thanks to Cliff's home-made hoop.

Holidays could be hit and miss. Initially, the family would go to the Isle of Sheppey, which they loved, and visit Cliff's parents in Hounslow. Even though Cliff went there at least twice a year, they always seemed to take a different route! Later on, Danny's sister, Jill, and her husband, Barry, persuaded Cliff and Danny to take the children on camping holidays in France and Spain. On the first occasion, they decided to all squeeze into one car and drive to the ferry. With Cliff in charge and his sense of direction, it was always going to be pretty much pot luck where they would end up! Once they found somewhere suitable to camp, there came the drama of putting up the tent. The children soon learned the correct way from other campers, otherwise they could have been waiting all night! Another year, Cliff's brother, Dave, and his wife, Rene, came along. One morning, Cliff took the car to fill up with petrol and drove back to the family. The trailer with all the camping equipment was re-attached. Of course, Cliff and Dave both assumed the other had checked the trailer connections. It was a windy day and halfway down a mountain pass Cliff noticed in his wing mirror that there was a loose trailer picking up speed and over-taking the car. A second glance confirmed it was their trailer! Luckily, there was no other traffic and the trailer met up with a grassy bank at the side of the pass and survived undamaged, rather than plummeting headlong into the ravine.

On another occasion, they had got lost and decided to stop at the roadside and cook breakfast. The men went off for a wander and Danny, Rene, Adrienne and Richard were noticed by the local police, who pulled over and approached them. Neither of the policemen could speak any English and none of the English could speak any French, so luckily whatever law was being broken was forgotten and they were allowed to continue with their breakfast.

Back in England, Cliff didn't have much better luck with the horse trailer than he had with the camping trailer in Spain. He had gone to Kempton alone to collect a pony for one of the children. He loaded the pony and set off on the trip home, but when they were circling the first roundabout, the pony moved to the front of the trailer, tipping the weight forward which pulled the back of the car down, lifting the front wheels right off the road! Cliff sat and thought for a couple of minutes about what to do. He managed to slide out of the car, went round to the trailer and moved the pony back into the rear of the trailer. He filled the front of the trailer with bits and pieces from the car, along with buckets and hay-nets to stop the pony being able to move back into the front. The car's front wheels returned to earth and Cliff was able to drive home safely, albeit he didn't exceed 20 miles an hour down the motorway in case it should happen again!

Cliff and Laddie

Mr Garnett with Cliff's father, Bill Lines

Bill Lines and Prince Philip

Cliff and his mother at London Docks before heading to Australia with Landau

Fred Darling boxing cup

Landau at exercise, Cliff riding

Landau with G. Richards

Landau with Cliff

Leading up Landau prior to The Derby

Landau arrives in Washington

Landau and Cliff at the docks

Carrozza (Piggott) and Shaken Bridge (Lines)

Hethersett and Harry Carr

Hethersett wins the St Leger

Hethersett and Cliff on the beach

Cliff and Adrienne

Adrienne in her party dress

Family on equine research station ponies

Adrienne on Opal, Richard on Grey Shadow

Adrienne and Richard, Isle of Sheppey

Cliff on a donkey at Clacton

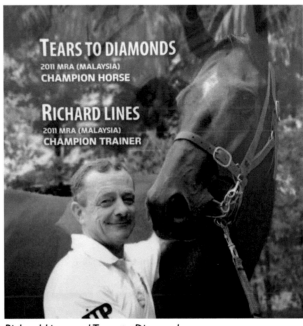

Richard Lines and Tears to Diamonds

Cliff and J O Tobin

Richard and George Best

J O Tobin wins, W. Shoemaker rides

RICHARD LINES

WITH ALL the early experience at home, Richard was allowed to help his father muck out and feed around Michael Stoute's yard at Beech Hurst after school and he also rode out first lot before school, and three lots at weekends and during school holidays. Richard remembers being the only person who wanted a third lot on Saturdays!

When Richard was 13, Cliff bought him an Arab cross called Bossy Boots. The plan was to teach Richard to race ride on him in pony races, so, one Saturday, Bossy Boots joined the Stoute string, which was cantering up Long Hill, for third lot. At the end of the canter, Richard was tailed off! Cliff was riding the hack and cantered over to Richard, criticising him all the way about not laying up with the string! Richard tried to explain that the pony simply wasn't good enough to lay up! Suffice to say, Bossy Boots never made it to a pony race and was promptly retired to the job of hack at Stoute's other yard, Freemason Lodge.

When Richard was 16, Cliff took him and Adrienne to Australia. By then, Adrienne had married Timmy Clark, so he went as well. Cliff's old friend, John McGarr, was emigrating to train at the Warwick Farm track near Sydney. John and Cliff had worked together at Murless's and for Major Hern at La Grange, although McGarr had initially been apprenticed to Willie Stephenson at Royston. The plan was for Richard to gain some riding experience in Australia for a year or so. McGarr had 15 horses and Richard spent most of his time riding work for McGarr and other local trainers. A typical day as an apprentice in 1980s Australia was very different from Cliff's experiences in 1950s England. The apprentice would start work at 4am in the morning with mucking out, but by 5am he would be working his first horse. They would warm up with a quick trot before working. The strapper (a non-riding lad) would bring out Richard's next mount and take the first one back to the yard to be washed down. The horse would be back in its box within 20 minutes. By 8am, Richard would have ridden six to eight different horses.

Richard's talent was spotted and it was suggested that he should get a licence. He was soon noted as a future champion apprentice by Bert Lillye in the Australian press who wrote, 'Today I want to introduce another champion of the future. He is Richard Lines, who rode for the first time at Kembla Grange, last Saturday. He had three mounts, but I saw enough to convince me that he has everything needed to make Sydney's top apprentice within three years. He has been well tutored and boasts more experience than most apprentices his age.' McGarr's horses were generally backward types, and, although Richard got plenty of experience riding them in races, he didn't have any winners. After Richard had had about 70 rides, McGarr retired, but he was impressed with what he saw in Richard and took him down to leading Sydney trainer Neville Begg, who really got him going as an apprentice. Between August and December that year, Richard rode 24 winners. Like Cliff when he went to America, Richard considers that the most useful thing he learned from his initial spell in Australia was judgement of pace. He also found the Australia tracks were very tight and always on the turn; the senior jockeys didn't give an inch, but if you came more than three wide off the rails you were sure to be in for a rollocking from the trainer!

Richard returned to England in 1982 following visa problems: he was quickly snapped up as apprentice by Michael Stoute, for whom he rode three winners that season. The following winter he spent in Maryland, riding at both Pimlico and Bowie to further his experience. Next season in the UK, he had another six winners, but with Walter Swinburn, Ernie Johnson and Tony Kimberley all attached to the Stoute yard as senior jockeys, rides were not easy to come by and Richard had to seriously consider his future. Luckily, an apprenticeship with William Hastings-Bass (later Lord Huntingdon) materialised and Richard was allowed to transfer his indentures.

John Virgo, a world championship-level snooker player, was the friend of a friend of Cliff's called Steve, who lived in London. John and Steve owned a horse called Jokist, who was in training with an ex-Stoute assistant, Richard Shaw. Richard Lines was called upon to ride Jokist for his first race, but the horse was awash with sweat going down to the start and Richard reported to the trainer that the horse felt completely wrong and needed treatment on his back. Unsurprisingly, the horse ran very badly and the jockey's words were misreported as saying that the horse wouldn't win a seller. Richard Shaw called in the equine chiropractor who agreed the horse was completely wrong. Once he was right again, Virgo demanded that Robert Street should ride the horse. Virgo was a gambler and wanted inside information on the Barry Hills horses where Robert worked. Jokist won easily. He was eventually retired to Willie Jarvis as a hack.

In 1984, Richard was in the line for Champion Apprentice, only needing to win The Mirror Final at York on 13 October to win the chance of a working holiday in Kenya. He rode Miss Bali Beach, who had finished third in the Cambridgeshire. Richard rated her the best horse he had ridden on the track at that time, although he had ridden Shareef Dancer at Stoute's a couple of pieces of work before he won the Irish Derby. He already had his regular trip to Australia lined up, so would have had the choice of winter sunshine in two countries! By then, he had ridden 43 winners, including the 24 in Australia. He had ridden his first treble for William Hastings-Bass on Derring Miss, Shuteye and First Pleasure at Windsor on 30 July 1984 in consecutive races. Unfortunately, Miss Bali Beach failed to shine on this occasion and Richard returned to Australia for the winter.

Richard's sister Adrienne and her husband Tim Clark had decided on their first visit that their future lay in Australia. On returning to the UK, they had sorted out the required visas and work permits and returned to work at Muskoka Farm in the Newcastle area of the Gold Coast, living in a caravan and working for John McGarr. It was not long before Tim's qualities were recognised and he took over the running of Muskoka Farm for Bob LaPointe, a Canadian who had moved to Australia at the age of 26. Tim was training a few horses, so Richard often went over in the winter to help them out and ride trackwork. He continued to ride in Australia during the winters and was attached to leading trainer Brian Mayfield-Smith, for whom he won the 1988 Journalist's Plate at Randwick in 1988. It was while riding trackwork for Mayfield-Smith that Richard met Liam Birchley, who was foreman at the time. Birchley was keen to train himself but wanted to experience training methods in other countries. Richard linked him up as assistant to Neil Drysdale, a leading trainer in the USA. Birchley returned to Australia and took out his licence, training at Muskoka Farms. In 1994, Birchley repaid the compliment by giving Richard his first winner back in Australia for his final stint as a jockey: Furacao in the Victoria Barracks Handicap at Rosehill. Richard kept the ride of Furacao for the Golden Slipper, but the horse wasn't good enough to win.

During his time as a jockey, Richard rode around the world, including seasons in Macau, Singapore, Malaysia and Dubai. During his stint in Dubai, Richard was primarily riding for Bill Mather, but he also rode a few winners for Paddy Rudkin, who had been head-lad to Henry Cecil before starting a successful training career in Dubai, and Richard Shaw who had been assistant to Michael Stoute. Cliff would often go out for a holiday and ended up riding out as well! Richard Shaw was training Arabians as well as Thoroughbreds in Dubai, so Richard Lines would ride both. One day, he was riding one of the Arabs at Longchamp when one of the spectators asked where he was from. Richard Lines replied he was from Australia, but his father overheard and quickly corrected him, 'No, you're not! You're British!' It was the very early days of racing in Dubai and Cliff remembers Richard weighing out for a race; they were using bathroom scales! Richard was also over in Dubai in 1997, the year the World Cup meeting was delayed due to rain. Cliff remembers trying to walk through the restaurant, but the water was up to his knees! Helicopters were brought in to dry up the track and the meeting was held a week late, with Michael Stoute's Singspiel coming home victorious. However, Cliff had to return home before the rescheduled meeting, so missed the great occasion.

By the mid-90s, Richard was giving serious thought to becoming a trainer when he gave up riding and decided that his future lay in Asia.

He started as a stable supervisor in Penang in 1997 before taking out his own training licence in 2002/03, training 16 winners in his first season. Although he enjoyed his time in Penang, some of his owners wanted to have runners in Kuala Lumpur where the Selangor Turf Club were making efforts to increase the attractiveness of their racing for owners and trainers alike. He has been Champion Trainer there every year for the past 11 years (2011–21). In 2011, his horse Tears to Diamonds won Horse of the Year after winning five races in a row, culminating in victory in the Group 1 Penang Gold Cup. He also trained Taichi Master to win both the Group 3 Sports TOTO Supreme Challenge Trophy and the Group 1 Coronation Cup in 2013.

Both Cliff and Richard feel they have benefitted enormously from riding in different countries and learning different techniques of both riding and training around the world. Richard still often phones Cliff to discuss a horse he may be having a problem with: they have a good chat to discuss different methods of doing something and Richard will, sometimes, put the advice into practice.

Adrienne continues to manage the financial side of Muskoka Farms, despite Bob LaPointe having sold the farm, along with his fast-food chains and car wash businesses. Cliff would often visit the family there during the winter. One year, John Warren, who later became the Queen's racing manager but was then a bloodstock agent, was also staying, presumably to look at yearlings. The family had known him for a while because he had been a stable lad with William Hastings-Bass when Richard was apprenticed there. Warren rather fancied himself at tennis and challenged Cliff to a game. Cliff won and has never been forgiven!

J O TOBIN

1974 bay/brown colt by Never Bend ex Hill Shade

TOWARDS THE end of 1976, the Newmarket rumour mill was in full swing and stories abounded that Noel Murless, having been champion trainer nine times, was planning to retire and hand over the reins to his son-in-law, Henry Cecil. Murless confirmed that Henry Cecil would take over as the trainer at Warren Place, but stated that he himself would carry on training half a dozen horses in order to train the brilliant J O Tobin for the following season's Classics, and he planned to find a small yard in order to become private trainer to George Pope. However, the colt's owner/breeder George Pope decided to bring the horse home to America, along with the other horses he had in training with Murless.

Sir Noel Murless had won 21 Classic races and was champion trainer eight times during his career, quite eclipsing his contemporaries. His owners included all the leading owners and breeders of the day, such as the Queen, Prince Aly Khan, Sir Victor Sassoon, Jim Joel and the Earl of Derby. In the preface to his biography, *The Guv'nor* by Tim Fitzgeorge-Parker, Murless claims he had four greats in his life: Abernant, Crepello, Petite Etoile and Sir Gordon Richards. Cliff had associations with all of them, but for him the greatest was still to come: Shergar.

J O Tobin had been broken in in America before coming to Warren Place. He was named after a friend of the owner called Joseph Oliver Tobin. Cliff was away one day and Willie Snaith had been given the leg up on J O in the indoor school; it would be fair to say the two hadn't gelled as J O Tobin was quite a bouncy horse and Willie was delighted to hand the reins back to Cliff to be his regular partner on the gallops. Cliff recalls that although he was a colt, he needed to be treated like a filly, with delicacy and care. He was quite highly strung and could get wound up if you didn't handle him correctly. He needed the jockey to sit still and make a fuss of him, otherwise he could whip round. However, like all the best horses, he had some spirit about him and, walking home, Cliff would always need to drop his irons early because J O liked to drop his head and put in three big bucks after a good exercise! Having done that, he was content to walk home quietly.

J O Tobin was champion two-year-old in the UK in 1976. When Piggott came to ride him work before his first race, Cliff said, 'Lester, this is a good horse, don't show him up!' Piggott won the gallop by 12 lengths! He asked his wife, Susan, to drive alongside and check what speed they were going at; she clocked them at 43 miles per hour. J O Tobin won his first three races, a maiden at Newmarket, followed by the Group 2 Richmond Stakes at Goodwood, where he started at 8-11 favourite, beating Priors Walk and Tachypous, who went on to win the Middle Park Stakes. His season culminated with victory in the 7f Champagne Stakes at Doncaster. He was 4-9 favourite and the performance was described by Timeform simply as 'breath taking'. Piggott sat motionless until the final furlong when J O swept four lengths clear of his rivals, beating the filly Durtal, who went on to win the Cheveley Park Stakes and was rated the best two-year-old filly in Britain. This performance earned him a weight of 133 lbs in the Free Handicap, five pounds ahead of the next horse. In his autobiography, Lester Piggott says, '… the great thing about this horse was his stride. I can only describe him as having an action like a panther, clawing at the ground and devouring it with a huge enthusiasm for his task. When you changed your hands on J O Tobin and asked him to pick up, he seemed to stretch and get lower to the ground, and his acceleration was amazing.' He rated J O Tobin as one of the best two-year-olds he has ever ridden, alongside My Swallow.

J O's final two-year-old start was to be in the Grand Criterium at Longchamp, but the ground was a swamp and he could only finish third to Blushing Groom, probably not staying out the mile in the bottomless ground, although Piggott felt he 'looked a little less robust than usual and felt ill at ease'.

Cliff, on hearing of Sir Noel's probable retirement, had been offered, and had accepted, a job as assistant head lad at Beech Hurst for Michael Stoute. George Pope wanted Cliff to accompany J O Tobin to America as his work rider. Lester Piggott recalled that J O Tobin didn't like to have anyone other than 'Cockney' around him. One work morning, J O Tobin had refused to cross the Norwich Road on to the Limekilns when Piggott was riding him work. Luckily, Cliff was close behind on foot and as soon as Cliff got a hand on his bridle, he was happy to follow Cliff across the road and on to the gallop. Cliff was very much the horse's security blanket. Sadly, Cliff's marriage to Danny had recently broken down, so he was keen to get away and Stoute kindly agreed to let him go.

In the USA, J O Tobin was to be trained by John H. (Johnny) Adams. Adams had been a successful jockey for over 24 years with 3,270 victories to his name, including the 1954 Preakness on Hasty Road as well as two wins in the Santa Anita Handicap (Kayak in 1939 and War Knight in 1946). On his retirement from race riding in 1958, Adams had gone to work for the Popes at El Peco in northern California. Murless would go over every autumn and choose which yearlings from El Peco he wanted to train. They would arrive at Warren Place in the winter already broken in. Adams was allowed to train the Murless rejects. Once Murless announced his retirement, all the El Peco horses were returned to California.

In America, the horses were stabled with just a webbing strap across the doorway, rather than the solid wooden door they have in the UK. They appeared to adapt very quickly; however, one day J O decided to have a roll and managed to get his back legs stuck under the webbing. Cliff had to get hold of his headcollar and drag him backwards to free him, so he could stand up. After that, the webbing was dispensed with and the bottom half of the stable door was kept closed!

In the stable next to J O Tobin was another of Pope's ex-Murless horses called Jumping Hill. He had won the Hunt Cup at Ascot the previous year and returned to America on the same flight as J O Tobin. One day, Jumping Hill developed a large haematoma on his belly towards the back. Cliff advised the lad (who was also the groom for J O Tobin) to get some warm water and a cloth to foment the haematoma to try and get it to burst. The next thing Cliff heard was a tremendous crashing – he rushed to the box to find the lazy lad had tried to tie a warm sponge over the lump with baling twine, knotting it across the top of Jumping Hill's quarters. As soon as the horse felt the twine tighten across his quarters, he thought he was being attacked by a predator and started kicking and bucking madly. He drew quite a crowd with his performance. Cliff ducked under the webbing into the box and managed to get hold of the poor, petrified horse; another lad passed him a pair of scissors and Cliff was able to cut the twine. As soon as he did that, the horse stopped plunging but he had cut his hind legs badly. Unsurprisingly, the idle groom was given the sack.

J O Tobin tended to work alone as he did enough that way and he could be too keen with another horse. It didn't stop him impressing the clockers around the tracks. He was described as not the most imposing physical specimen but very light on his feet, looking as though he was gliding along. He had a sustained burst of raw speed at the end of a race. Riding track work in America, Cliff learned to count the seconds in a furlong, so as to judge what speed he was going. It is not a technique taught in the UK, but it is used by all the top American jockeys, which makes them so good when riding from the front and made Cliff invaluable as a work rider. The English trainer, Mark Johnston, has installed a traffic speed monitor on gallops, so his lads can see how fast they are going! Cliff also kept his stirrups the same length rather than riding 'acey-deucey' as the American jockeys did: because their tracks were all left-handed, the jockeys would ride with their inside (i.e. left) stirrup leather several holes longer than the outside one to compensate for being virtually always on the turn.

The second time Willie Shoemaker came to ride a piece of work on J O, Cliff was to ride a pacemaker for him and jump in at the 5f pole. Pulling up after the work, Cliff turned to see where J O was as he had expected him to pass him. He had decided to go up the shoot Cliff had come down because that was the way back to the stables! Willie didn't ride him in the mornings after that!

Willie 'The Shoe' Shoemaker was tiny even for a jockey! Reportedly weighing only 38 ounces at his birth in 1931, he grew to 4ft 10in and weighed only 91 pounds at maturity; yet his technique enabled him to ride even the largest racehorses successfully, such as the mighty Forego and the great Spectacular Bid. He was one of the most successful American-based jockeys ever, amassing 8,833 victories during his career. At 54, he became the oldest jockey to win the Kentucky Derby aboard Ferdinand, with whom he won the following year's Breeders' Cup Classic. He retired as a jockey in 1990, taking out a training licence for seven years, despite a car crash in 1991 leaving him a quadriplegic. He died in October 2003.

Although Johnny Adams was officially the trainer of J O Tobin, regular reports were sent back to Noel Murless as to his progress and Murless was to receive five per cent of any prize-money he won. Murless suggested Cliff was working the horse too fast, but J O was never off the bridle in his work. As Cliff learned, when two trainers are training one horse it is impossible to keep them both happy!

As a two-year-old in England, J O Tobin had only raced on grass and the conditions were always good or better. His first race in the USA was a 6f exhibition race on fast dirt, starting from the number one stall. He was left three or four lengths at the break but was beaten less than a length by the appropriately named Incredibly Lucky. Adams subsequently reflected they had spent too long at home trying to get him to settle in the gate and blamed himself for the defeat. While he was still at Santa Anita, Bronwell Combs and Nelson Bunker Hunt paid a million and a half dollars for a quarter share in the colt. J O's next test was the Coronado Handicap at Hollywood Park, which he duly won.

That was his prep race for the 102nd Preakness Stakes at Pimlico on 21 May 1977. Following his arrival at Pimlico from Los Angeles, he pleased everybody. His first quick work was over three furlongs, timed by the watchers as being completed in 33 seconds 'as easy as you like'.

Adams decided to forgo a prep race in favour of another piece of work, this time over a mile. He moved beautifully for Cliff, covering the first four furlongs in 52 seconds and completing the mile in 1m 42 seconds, convincing Adams that he would be able to conserve his speed over the extended 9f. Mr Pope invited Murless to come over to watch the race. Seattle Slew, winner of the Kentucky Derby, started odds-on favourite. Sadly, Seattle Slew was the victor and J O Tobin (W. Shoemaker) could only finish fifth. After the race, Cliff took Murless over to the barn to see the horse; Murless was convinced Piggott would have won had he been riding!

When the team transferred to New York to prepare for the Belmont Stakes, Cliff noticed many of the horses were wearing boots over their joints for exercise. J O Tobin exercised without them, despite the dirt track at Belmont was notorious for 'burning' the backs of horses' heels. One morning, J O Tobin jibbed going out on to the track; John Adams was upsides on his pony and told Cliff to give J O a slap under the belly. Cliff did as the trainer told him and J O stepped out on to the track and cantered round. It later became apparent that J O Tobin had bad 'run-downs' on the backs of his heels, which were very sore. Cliff wasn't grooming him, just riding him exercise, so didn't know about the run-downs and the groom hadn't mentioned them. J O Tobin was telling connections he was sore and as a result he ran disappointingly in the Belmont Stakes behind Seattle Slew. As Cliff says, they can't talk but they have ways of telling you.

One morning at Belmont, Johnny Adams asked Cliff to pony J O Tobin with Steven Cauthen on board. Adams had been riding the pony and had much shorter legs than Cliff. However, the stirrup leathers were knotted up to the correct length for Adams and Cliff couldn't undo the knots to let the stirrups down to a length that suited him. Cliff had his knees under his chin and couldn't keep his balance to lead J O Tobin. Cliff had to tell Steve he couldn't manage to pony him: it wasn't something the young American jockey was used to and he was rather dubious. However, Cliff gave him instructions to keep to the middle of the track: that way J O Tobin would hack canter. Once Cauthen reached his start point, he was to move the horse across to the rail and he would automatically switch to work pace. Luckily, all went smoothly, but it was possibly Cauthen's first time riding a racehorse without a pony to lead him.

Revenge for J O Tobin's defeat by Seattle Slew in the Belmont was just around the corner! On 4 July 1977, the two horses met again in the Swaps Stakes. Seattle Slew had completed the American Triple Crown, winning the Belmont Stakes after the Preakness, and taking his winning sequence to nine. J O Tobin broke well and led from start to finish, while Seattle Slew struggled and just didn't fire, finishing fourth and only beating three other horses home. Shoemaker said, 'I thought we would be lying second, following Seattle Slew, but J O broke like a bullet and I wasn't going to try and change anything. I tried to give him a breather down the backside, but he just ran strong. I figured Seattle Slew was back there, but I didn't really know how close he was. I couldn't hear him. Once, I looked round and I couldn't find him: it was no fluke, he just couldn't keep up with us.'

After the Belmont, Cliff returned to the UK. J O Tobin was transferred to Laz Berrera for his four-year-old career. When he arrived, Berrera thought he looked thin and he had bad run-downs in his susceptible heels. He also felt the dirt track at Santa Anita at that time of year was just too fast for him, so decided to give the horse some time off. Berrera also changed J O's tack, swapping his tongue tie and old metal bit for a rubber bit with a figure of eight (Citation) noseband. The break paid dividends and on his first start as a four-year-old, J O Tobin started the season with a five-length victory in the Malibu Stakes at Santa Anita in January, ridden by the 17-year-old Steve Cauthen. Under Barrera's guidance, he went on to victories in six Graded Stakes races, including the Californian Stakes, the Tom Fool Handicap, Los Angeles Handicap, San Bernadino Handicap and Premiere Handicap. Such was his reputation, by the time he was entered for the San Bernadino Handicap, his mere presence reduced the field size from 14 at the entry stage to six at post time. He was voted American Champion Sprinter in 1978 and Barry Irwin in *The Thoroughbred Record* described J O Tobin as 'the most exciting and gifted runner to appear on the local California scene since 1971 Horse of the Year Ack Ack, and before that maybe only Swaps was more gifted.' Despite this success, Pope later admitted to Cliff that leaving J O Tobin in New York was the wrong thing to do. The atmosphere there was too frantic and really didn't suit this nervous colt's temperament. Murless concurred that the American style of hard training wouldn't have suited this highly strung colt but still believed he would have won the Derby at Epsom had he stayed in training in the UK and had Piggott been available to ride him.

A few years later, when Steve Cauthen was riding in the UK, Cliff asked him what he made of J O Tobin. Cauthen's reply was, 'He wasn't a racehorse: he was a machine.'

J O Tobin was retired to stud in 1979 and his first crop of foals was hugely popular in the sales ring: he even beat his old adversary Seattle Slew into second place, taking the Freshman Sire at Keeneland Yearling Sales in 1981. However, despite being by the same sire as the great Mill Reef, J O Tobin was not a great success as a stallion. He died in 1994 in New Mexico.

While Cliff was in Santa Anita with J O Tobin, George Best was also there. George Best was a Northern Irish footballer who played his club matches for Manchester United. His unique skills and goalscoring ability, along with his good looks and playboy lifestyle, saw him become a darling of the tabloids. When Cliff met him in Santa Anita, George was playing football for Los Angeles Aztecs. He and fellow footballer, Bobby McAlinden, also owned and ran a pub on the beach called 'Besties'. The stable lads would sometimes pop in for a drink and Cliff and George became friends. Cliff went to some of the Aztecs matches and was amazed to see that the team were made to run round the pitch after the match, presumably as a warm-down. However, McAlinden and Best were generally tailed off, so they could make a quick exit to the beach bar. When Richard came over for a two-week holiday (which stretched to six weeks), George kindly took them both out for dinner to a seafood restaurant on the sea front. Cliff still has the autographed photograph he took of them both at the time.

Another familiar face he came across while in America was Peter Richards. Cliff initially thought it was Sir Gordon himself before realising his mistake. Peter was the only one of Sir Gordon's offspring who showed an interest in horseracing but was too large to follow in his father's footsteps as a jockey. Peter had worked with Murless for a while before being sent initially to Paddy Prendergast in Ireland and then on to America to learn more about other aspects of racing.

Cliff also rode some of John Adams's other horses while he was in America. It was here he learned how to stop a horse that was running away with him. Like many others, he would shorten the reins to stop, keeping a tight hold of the horse's head and leaning back, sticking his feet forward to try to pull against the horse to stop it. One day, one of the other work riders said, 'Drop your reins and stand up straight.' He did this and it worked. It was no longer a fight between the horse and jockey, both trying to prove they were stronger: the lad is never going to win that one! The method worked for him back in the UK on many occasions. The one thing that still rankles with Cliff concerning his year in America was the prize-money. The groom and work-rider for each horse were each supposed to get one per cent of any prize-money a horse won. Murless and Adams got five percent each; the groom got his percentage, but Cliff received nothing. He didn't even get a photograph of the horse from Mr Pope! Although Shergar was probably the best horse Cliff was associated with, J O Tobin was his favourite.

When Cliff was at Murless's, both John Gosden and William Hastings-Bass (now Lord Huntingdon) were there as assistant trainers, learning the trade. While Cliff was in America with J O Tobin, Pope asked Cliff whether he knew of anybody who might be interested in running the California pre-training ranch, El Pico at Fresnau. Cliff suggested John Gosden who, by then, had moved to Vincent O'Brien to further his experience. Cliff rang the O'Brien office at Coolmore and spoke to Gosden. Having spent a couple of days thinking about it, he accepted the position and Pope sorted out the work permit, plane tickets, etc., for him. A few weeks later, Cliff contacted him again to see how things were going. He replied that every time he spoke to Pope the salary decreased! Eventually he went to America but not to Pope – he took a job as a hot-walker at Santa Anita. The next thing he knew, he was being sent horses to train by Robert Sangster. The following year, Mr Pope saw Cliff again and said Gosden had never turned up at El Pico!

Cliff continued to visit Sir Noel and Lady Murless after their retirement, in their bungalow at Wood Ditton, often taking Lady Murless a plant or a bunch of flowers at Christmas. One year, he turned up after lunch on Christmas Day to discover Lady Murless's sister and husband were visiting. All the leftovers, dirty dishes and cutlery were still on the table when the relatives decided it was time to leave and return to Yorkshire. Fond of Lady Murless as he was, Cliff wasn't prepared to hang around and help clear up either! Sir Noel sadly died in 1987 from the effects of smoking, wasting away to about 7st and spending much of his time during his later years in an oxygen tent. Lady Murless died in 1993.

SIR MICHAEL STOUTE

MICHAEL STOUTE was born in 1945 in Barbados. He was the third son (of four) of the local chief of police. His family had no connections with racing, but their house backed on to the Garrison Savannah, the racecourse in Barbados. As a small boy, Michael would climb over the back wall of his garden and slip into the racecourse. His interest initially lay in the media side and, while helping out at the yard of three-times Barbados Derby winning trainer Freddie Thirkell, he got a job commentating on Radio Barbados. He left Barbados in 1964 to audition for a job with the BBC, but although he got down to the final six he eventually lost out to Julian Wilson. To be fair, he had never seen a hurdle race before! However, there was no animosity and the two became lifelong friends. Instead, Stoute took the opportunity to become assistant to North Yorkshire-based trainer Pat Rohan. After three years, Rohan sent him to Newmarket where he became assistant to Doug Smith, who soon put him in charge of running Lord Rosebery's yard at Park Lodge, from where, in 1969, Lord Rosebery's filly, Sleeping Partner, won the Oaks. Stoute then moved on to assist Harry Thomson Jones at Green Lodge Stables, from where, in 1971, Athens Wood won the St Leger.

That autumn, Stoute branched out on his own, bravely buying a few yearlings and renting Cadland Stables to train them from. Taking out a training licence for the 1972 season, he didn't have to wait long to get the ball rolling, his first win as a trainer coming in April that year when Sandal, a horse owned by his father and ridden by Lester Piggott, won at Newmarket. Within a season, he landed the massive sprint handicap double of the Stewards Cup with Alphadamus (one of

Stoute's bargain-basement yearling purchases, having cost just 1,200 guineas as a yearling) and the Ayr Gold Cup with Blue Cashmere. By the end of 1972, he and his wife Pat were able to secure a mortgage on the vacant Beech Hurst stables on Bury Road, Newmarket, and this was his training yard when Cliff joined the team.

In 1976, the hot, dry summer led to many trainers struggling to find suitable gallops for their horses. Newmarket trainers had an old tan woodchip canter up Long Hill, which led to Jeremy Tree, who was then training at Beckhampton, sending two of his horses, Intermission and Bright Finish, to Newmarket to be cared for with the Stoute string. Once the dry spell ended, he left them with Stoute and, that autumn, Intermission won the Cambridgeshire and Bright Finish won the Jockey Club Cup. These high-calibre successes were to draw the attention of other owners and breeders.

As well as a natural talent for training horses, Michael has an amazing memory: he will air-write something on his hand with his forefinger while whistling tunelessly and that seems to stick a mental post-it note in his head. Dates of races, the horse's bodyweight before and after a race, pedigrees, which jockey had ridden which horse – very little is forgotten using this method.

THE STOUTE YEARS 1978–93

The first head lad for Michael Stoute at Beech Hurst was Andy Andrews. He and Stoute met while they were both working for Harry Thomson Jones. Andy had been attached to the stable as a jump jockey. He was known as Each-Way Andrews (because his initials were EWA, nothing to do with his riding ability!). Andy's wife, Rita, was secretary at Thomson Jones's, but when Stoute set up and Andy took the position as head lad at Beech Hurst, Rita stayed with Thomson Jones. It was Andy who got Cliff the job with Stoute when Murless retired. Cliff can't remember where he and Andy first met, but he had known him a long time and they had one particular interest in common: racing pigeons!

To begin with, Cliff moved into a caravan outside Beech Hurst. Danny, Richard and Adrienne remained in the house at Red Lodge.

The draw of birds (of the feathered kind!) had recently become too strong again for Cliff to ignore: he and his son, Richard, had rescued two young jackdaws which had fallen out of their nest on the heath. They raised them successfully until Cliff went to get the car out of the garage one day. Despite seeing Richard jumping up and down and gesticulating wildly, Cliff reversed out of the garage, running over one of the poor birds which had been seeking some shade by the back wheel. However, it meant Richard could teach the other bird, uninspiringly named Jack, to talk. It took a year and unfortunately it learnt to copy Cliff's voice rather than Richard's: its favourite phrase was 'Richard – come here!' Cliff took it to live with him in the caravan at Beech Hurst. Michael Stoute retained a 'tack man' in each yard. They were old stable lads who were no longer able to ride out, but they supplemented their income by cleaning and mending the tack. One day, the tack man at Beech Hurst, Jack Greensmith, knocked on the caravan door. Cliff opened it: 'Hello, Jack, what do you want?' 'You called me just as I was leaving,' came the reply. After much head scratching, the pair realised it was the jackdaw who had called, 'Jack – come here!'

As well as Jack the jackdaw, Cliff took his Jack Russell terrier, Suzie, to live with him in the caravan. One afternoon, he noticed her trotting off across Bury Hills with Stoute's two terriers. They were Indian-file with Suzie at the back. Unfortunately, the dogs discovered a coop of chickens at Moulton Paddocks, where the main Godolphin training yard now is. Between them, they slaughtered every chicken! Cliff had to reimburse the owners £1 per carcass, although he still maintains it was Stoute's dogs leading Suzie astray!

In 1976, the Swedish owner/breeder, Sven Hanson, sent Stoute four yearlings. Among these was one of the first horses Cliff was to become involved with at Stoute's: Fair Salinia (1975 bay filly by Petingo out of Fair Arabella). She was beaten three-quarters of a length in the 1,000 Guineas ridden by Greville Starkey and Cliff recalls she didn't even get a smack. Afterwards, Cliff asked why Greville didn't give her a harder race and the reply was that they were saving her for the Oaks, which she duly won (by a nose!) at 8-1. Cliff had ridden her work a few times and had backed her for both! She subsequently won both the Irish Oaks and the Yorkshire Oaks. Michael Stoute missed his first Classic victory when Fair Salinia won at Epsom: having grown up in Barbados he had missed all the childhood illnesses that do the rounds in the UK. On Oaks Day 1978, he was ill in bed with mumps, having caught it from his children!

Fair Salinia was looked after by Angus 'Silky' Brown who was known to be a 'lucky lad'. Other good horses he looked after included Vaigly Great and Royal Heroine. Angus worked for Stoute for years and never changed: he was always jolly, never got annoyed; he was just a kind, bubbly person and, Stoute recalls, a shrewd punter. Is there such a thing as a lucky lad or is it just that lads who are recognised as lucky have more empathy with their horses? The empathy between a horse and his lad should not be underestimated. Piggott recognised straight away the relationship between Cliff and J O Tobin. Without Cliff, J O Tobin would never have been the horse he was; likewise, Landau, Queenborough II, Shareef Dancer and Sonic Lady – they were all tricky horses, but Cliff developed a relationship with each one of them. Paula Roberts who looked after Pilsudski was another; she also looked after Red Cotton, Pilsudski's half-sister who achieved very little, but she received the same treatment and as much love as Pudsey, then along came another very good horse for her in Fantastic Light. There are many other examples of horses needing companionship: they are after all herd animals. However, some make do with a goat or a sheep rather than a human!

Not long after Cliff first started at Stoute's, he was called into the kitchen for a chat. Stoute wanted information about Murless's training methods. The first thing Cliff told him was that once a lad and a horse had struck up a relationship they should be left together, didn't matter if the lad wasn't the greatest rider. Stoute used to have a different lad on a different horse every day. That way, how does the lad know what the horse's 'normal' is? He may always have a scratchy action or a lack of 'bounce', but a lad who has never ridden him before isn't to know that and may assume it is the norm. That way, illness and early injury are easily missed until it is too late. Stoute soon changed his ways and lads would consistently ride the same horse unless they didn't get on with them, only being switched off for senior work riders on work mornings. A good lad can make a horse, but a bad lad will definitely break it.

Another lad in the Stoute yard at that time was 'Monty' Mick O'Neill. He was rather too tall to be a work rider, and so was usually employed as a yard man, although he had a good rapport with the horses and was very helpful with breaking in the yearlings and doing stalls practice with any horses that had taken an aversion to them: Mick's nickname, 'Monty', was based on Monty Roberts, an American horse-whisperer who visited Newmarket demonstrating his 'join-up' technique of natural horsemanship. Mick also liked to claim he had been Robert Mitchum's body double! He was the same height as Mitchum and used to pose for him before takes, so the cameras could be set up at the correct angles for filming. The film Mick was involved with was called *Revolution*, but it was a box office flop despite Mick forcing everybody he knew to go and see it because he claimed he had had a fling with Mitchum's Russian female co-star!

That autumn, the first yearlings belonging to HH Aga Khan were to arrive in Britain since the 1960s. They were split between Stoute and Fulke Johnson-Houghton. There were some nice horses in among them, but the best would arrive in autumn the following year – 1979.

One morning in 1979, Cliff was put on a horse, Black Earl, who had only been in the yard a few days. He was to ride it on Railway Land and, coming to the end of the canter, he realised Black Earl wasn't going to stop. He stood up in his stirrups, turned the horse round and went back to the bottom of the canter but it still had no intention of stopping; it was back up to the top again before he was able to pull up. Mrs Stoute walked over to Cliff and invited him to come into the house for a brandy to recover! The horse had run away with the pupil assistant/amateur, Edward Hamner, the day before and with a third jockey on Bury Hills the day after. He didn't stay in the yard for long. Black Earl became a very moderate mile handicapper on the flat, but did eventually win a few National Hunt races; hopefully the obstacles slowed him down!

HARD FOUGHT
1977 chesnut colt by Habitat ex Ambrosia

Hard Fought was owned by Brook Holliday, the son of Cliff's ex-boss Major Holliday. The size of the Holliday string had significantly diminished since the Major's time, with many of the mares, foals and yearlings having been sold, as well as the yards and studs, to pay death duties. Brook Holliday kept a few horses which were scattered among various trainers. Hard Fought was from a family Cliff knew well with his dam, Ambrosia, being a half-sister to Hethersett and Proud Chieftain. Cliff remembers him as a nice, big horse and a fair sort, although he could be edgy before his races and needed strong handling. As a two-year-old, Hard Fought used to hang in behind the horses in front of him and was a far from easy ride. However, there was never any doubt that he had some ability and, as a three-year-old, he won the John of Gaunt Stakes at Haydock and the Jersey Stakes at Royal Ascot before finishing fifth to specialist sprinter Moorestyle in the July Cup at Newmarket. He got no run in the Hungerford Stakes, being held on the fence throughout the race, and was then stepped up to a mile for the Waterford Crystal Mile at Goodwood, where, under a classic Piggott ride, and despite doubts about his ability to stay the trip, he took the lead over a furlong out and stayed on well to finish second, with Known Fact only forcing his neck past him in the dying strides. He then disappointed again when finishing only fourth to Known Fact in the Queen Elizabeth II Stakes at Ascot.

Brook Holliday was offered £100,000 for the horse at the end of his three-year-old career and was ready to sell, but Michael Stoute recommended Hard Fought should remain in training with him as a four-year-old and, according to stable rumour, he would get Holliday £2m for him. Holliday agreed and he promised Cliff a painting of him as a thank you for all the work he had done on him should he get the £2m. Hard Fought had never been an easy ride although Piggott had had a good rapport with him; however, the decision was made and Hard Fought stayed in training with Walter Swinburn as the new stable jockey taking over the reins. Stoute continued to gradually increase the distance Hard Fought would race over as a four-year-old. His campaign started with a comfortable victory in the Earl of Sefton Stakes at Newmarket, which was followed by victory in the 10f Westbury Stakes at Sandown. His next start was the Prince of Wales's Stakes at Royal Ascot in which he put up a good display to win by three-quarters of a length from Vielle and Magesterial. Unfortunately, in the Coral Eclipse he hung badly and got himself boxed in behind Master Willie with Vielle on his outside and Swinburn had nowhere to go. Eventually, Swinburn threw caution to the wind and Hard Fought and Vielle became involved in a barging match, leaving Master Willie to win the race by three-quarters of a length. Hard Fought won the contretemps and finished second but was disqualified and Swinburn banned for ten days. Hard Fought ran again in the Benson and Hedges Gold Cup at York, but disappointed, finishing seventh to Beldale Flutter and again he hung badly.

Hard Fought definitely had a stallion's pedigree and Habitat was proving very popular at stud. Stoute obtained the promised sale price of £2m and the horse was sold to stand at Baroda Stud in Ireland. When Stoute asked for his percentage of the sale, Holliday told him he was getting nothing; they had no written agreement to that effect. Stoute, who believed a gentleman's word should be his bond, told Holliday to remove his other horses from the yard; one went on to win a small race and the other never won. Cliff also never got his painting! They weren't the only people short-changed by Brook Holliday – Lester Piggott never got his additional percentage for the Group race wins as a three-year-old.

Michael Stoute's star continued in its ascendancy: his string was rapidly expanding and in 1980 he bought Freemason Lodge as a second yard. It was conveniently situated just across the Bury Road from his first yard, Beech Hurst. There were two flats above the stables in the front yard and one was to be Cliff's. The other flat was to house the head lad for Beech Hurst, Andy Andrews, and his family, wife Rita, and their two daughters, Nicky and Fiona, as well as Andy's rather large, loud German Shepherd dog Boyboy. Andy and his family had been living on the Exning Road, but it was more convenient to have him on site and it became a Jockey Club licensing requirement to have someone living on the yard.

Once the flats at Freemason Lodge were renovated, Cliff moved across to the yard as head lad. Andy Andrews and his family moved into the other flat and Andy kept his racing pigeons in a loft behind the two flats. However, as the Stoute string expanded, more boxes were built and eventually the pigeon loft had to go. The old boxes in the front yard were wood lined with large, built-in managers across the back of the boxes. One night, Cliff heard a noise in the yard and, thinking a horse was cast, he went to investigate. When he turned the light on and opened the door, the horse was lying down, but there were hundreds of mice running all over him! The horse was unperturbed, but hygiene is one of the essential requirements of healthy horses. The boxes in the front yard were all completely stripped out, the mouse droppings and nesting material rose to about 4ft high behind the wooden boarding! One of the stables was on display at Newmarket Horseracing Museum for many years.

MARWELL
1978 bay filly by Habitat out of Lady Seymour

Marwell was a homebred filly belonging to Sir Edmund Loder who lived at Eyrefield Lodge Stud in Ireland. She was from a speedy and precocious family, her year-older brother Lord Seymour having won the Mill Reef Stakes and her dam Lady Seymour the Phoenix Stakes in Ireland. Cliff recalls her as being a kind-natured filly who was very switched off for a sprinter. She was good as gold and never did anything wrong, giving him a lovely feel on the gallops. Although only medium-sized, she was attractive and a good mover. Most importantly, she had the ability to quicken in a single stride.

Not only did she impress at home but, as soon as she hit the racecourse, everybody could see she was a potential superstar: she was unbeaten in five races as a two-year-old, winning her Newmarket maiden, quickening clear, effortlessly, then following up with a stylish performance in the Group 3 Molecomb Stakes at Goodwood, beating subsequent Phoenix Stakes winner Swan Princess by 2½ lengths. The Queen Mary winner, Lady Tavistock's Pushy, was in third place. Marwell's next intended race, the St Hugh's Stakes at Newbury, was rained off, so instead she lined up for the Prince of Wales's Stakes at York. She started at 9-4 on despite having to concede 7lbs to the likes of Welshwyn, who had been second to Pushy at Ascot. She sat in behind Welshwyn until 3f out when Piggott drew alongside the leader and, without moving a muscle, Marwell shot clear to win by 1½ lengths. Her next appearance was in the Flying Childers at Doncaster. Piggott was suspended so Greville Starkey got the leg up. She again settled well, but with just over a furlong to go, Starkey loosened the reins slightly, asking her to quicken, and she immediately shot clear, eventually winning by three lengths, easing down. For her final start of her two-year-old campaign, Marwell was stepped up to six furlongs for the Cheveley Park Stakes at Newmarket. She only had to stay to win and the opposition should have taken their cue from that, and made it a blistering pace from the start. However, no one was keen to go on, so Piggott was able to sit in behind and quicken past them in the final furlong, winning by a length from Welshwyn with Pushy half a length further back in third. She was obviously the leading two-year-old filly in 1980.

Up until this point, Stoute had been using the best jockey available, with Lester Piggott coming in for many of the top rides, but with so much ammunition going into the 1981 season it was decided to have a retained jockey for the stable. Walter Swinburn, son of Wally, was 19 when he was offered the prestigious job of stable jockey to the rising trainer Michael Stoute. That year one horse was to ensure both their names were in the spotlight: Shergar. Walter had been apprenticed to Frenchie Nicholson and Reg Hollinshead. He had ridden a few winners for Michael Stoute while in his apprenticeship. Stoute recognised him as a very gifted jockey with a great temperament and beautiful hands. He offered Swinburn a modest retainer, bearing in mind his age and with the view that Piggott would still ride for him in the major races when available. However, Swinburn's talents hadn't gone unrecognised among the other flat trainers and Walter was also offered a retainer by Peter Walwyn who trained at Seven Barrows in Lambourn. Stoute had already won the Oaks in 1978 with Fair Salinia but was only 36 himself. He was forced to bite the bullet and told Swinburn to join him. They were to become one of the most successful teams in racing for a very long time.

The big question going into the winter was whether Marwell would stay the mile of the 1,000 Guineas. Timeform didn't think so and they also thought she would struggle against the sprinters, particularly with the Group 1 penalty she would have to carry for a large part of the season as a result of having won the Cheveley Park Stakes. Her full brother, Lord Seymour, was disappointing as a three-year-old and never ran over farther than seven furlongs. As it turned out, Marwell didn't stay the mile, but only two horses were ever to beat her over sprint distances, Sharpo and Runnett, and Marwell gained her revenge with victory over both of them in her last race, the Prix de l'Abbaye at Longchamp.

Marwell started her three-year-old season in the Fred Darling Stakes at Newbury, a recognised Guineas trial over 7f 60y. Notwithstanding the change of jockey, Marwell started as she had left off as a two-year-old, settling beautifully in the race and quickening clear over a furlong out. In the 1,000 Guineas, she was held up to get the trip; however, she was only able to get within a length of the leader Fairy Footsteps and, in the final furlong, she was also passed by Tolmi and Leasing, grimly just holding on to fourth place from Madam Gay. She went straight back to sprinting. A pleasing win in a prep race over 6f at Haydock led her to be market leader at 5-4 favourite for the King's Stand Stakes at Royal Ascot, a race against the colts and older horses which hadn't been won by a filly since 1973. Standaan made the running at a blistering pace on fast ground, but Marwell was able to keep up with that pace and made her challenge approaching the final furlong, going away to beat Standaan by two lengths. Runnett finished third. The July Cup at Newmarket was to be the first meeting between the champion sprinter of the previous year, Moorestyle, and the new kid on the block, Marwell. Standaan again made the running: Moorestyle and Marwell challenged together, but Marwell soon gained the advantage and won impressively by three lengths, ridden out hands and heels, putting Moorestyle in his place. Their next meeting was in the William Hill Sprint Championship at York, where, although Marwell again beat Moorestyle, she herself was inexplicably beaten by Sharpo and could only finish second. In her next start, the Vernon's Sprint Cup at

Haydock, she was beaten into second place by Runnett in the last few strides. Many onlookers thought she just wasn't at the peak she had been in at the start of the season; after all, it had been a long year. However, connections persevered and she appeared at Longchamp for the Prix de l'Abbaye. Sharpo and Runnett, the two colts who had beaten her, were both in the field. Sharpo started even-money favourite but was on his toes; however, Marwell remained her cool, calm self. Again, they set off at a tremendous pace and it took Marwell until two furlongs out to collar Music Streak. She was pressed all the way to the line but hung on grimly to win by a neck, with Rabdan third and Ancient Regime fourth, only six lengths covering all six runners. At the end of her three-year-old career, Timeform commented, 'Sprinting will be fortunate indeed to see her like among the so-called weaker sex inside another few seasons.'

After her racing career, Marwell retired to her owner's stud where she became the head of a racing dynasty: her daughter Marling was beaten a whisker in the 1,000 Guineas but won the Cheveley Park Stakes, Irish 1,000 Guineas, Coronation Stakes and Sussex Stakes and her son Caerwent won the Irish National Stakes and was placed second in the Irish 2,000 Guineas, while Marwell's great-granddaughter Minaun was winner of the Group 3 Marble Hill Stakes. Marwell was retired from breeding in 2002 at the age of 24. She died the following October. Swinburn paid tribute, calling her 'a fabulous filly who did as much to get me established as Shergar. She was a very special friend.'

SHERGAR
1978 bay colt by Great Nephew ex Sharmeen

Shergar may be one of the most famous Derby winners of all time. Although his winning distance of ten lengths is still a record 40 years later, it is indubitably the subsequent events that elevated him to icon level. In a *Racing Post* Derby supplement from 30 May 2021, Lee Mottershead describes him as 'an incredible, unforgettable, tragic Thoroughbred,' which sadly sums up the Shergar story.

Cliff started riding Shergar at the end of his two-year-old year in 1980. Timeform described him as 'a deep-girthed, good sort, with scope and his pedigree is first class'. Great Nephew was proving himself an influential sire and Shergar's dam Sharmeen traced back to Mumtaz Mahal herself, one of the first mares purchased by the Aga Khan's grandfather in 1922 and the winner of five of her six races as a two-year-old, as well as the King George Stakes at Goodwood and the Nunthorpe at York as a three-year-old. Shergar stood halfway along the backside of the front yard at Beech Hurst. Cliff recognised him as a good horse before he ran, along with many of the other staff at Beech Hurst. Although he was known for galloping with his tongue hanging out, Cliff recalls Shergar as being lovely in every way: 'He had no vices and he enjoyed his work. You never had to ask him to do anything, you just sat still on him and he did it.' Lester Piggott rode him first time out at Newbury in the 23-runner Kris Plate, cruising into the lead 1½ furlongs out, then quickening away impressively. His next start was to be the William Hill Futurity at Doncaster, again ridden by Lester Piggott: it looked a tough task on paper, the inexperienced, once-raced winner of a maiden taking on the likes of Robellino and Recitation who had already won the Royal Lodge and the Grand Criterium respectively, but Shergar's fans were undaunted and he vied for favouritism. Eventually starting third favourite at 5-2 behind those two colts, he beat them both but found Beldale Flutter too good for him on the rain-softened ground. However, it meant that Cliff got 33-1 about him for the following year's Derby, which was to be his primary target as a three-year-old. He wasn't even entered for the 2,000 Guineas.

The following spring, while they were still only on trotting exercise, Cliff noticed Shergar was lame behind. Cliff was on the hack, supervising the exercise, and Dickie McCabe, Shergar's lad, was on board Shergar. Cliff reported the lameness to the boss, although the lad said he felt fine. The vet was called and advised three weeks' box rest. That wasn't on the training schedule! Andy Andrews knew a 'back' man, George Armitage, but he was in Newcastle. George was summoned to fly down to Cambridge and was collected from Cambridge airport. He shut himself in the box with Shergar. After a few minutes he emerged and Stoute asked, with trepidation, how many days Shergar would need off. George's reply was, 'None, you can take him out tomorrow.' Whatever was wrong, George had put it right and Shergar was never lame again.

From that moment, George was an integral part of Stoute's team, with regular visits to the yard.

Back on the heath and being prepared for the Sandown Classic Trial, Shergar put in a sparkling gallop on Racecourse Side, finishing about 12 lengths ahead of his co-workers who included Northumberland Plate winner Dawn Johnny. Not surprisingly, this piece of work inevitably caught the eyes of many senior work watchers. Cliff was riding Shergar and recalls, 'It was an unbelievable feeling; I can't put it into words.' Julian Wilson, a BBC commentator, took some of the 33-1 still available and it gave him enough money to buy an emerald, diamond and sapphire engagement ring, which he presented to his then girlfriend at his favourite restaurant, London's Ponte Vecchio, the evening after the Derby. Richard Baerlin, the *Observer* correspondent, took the price and won enough money to buy a house in Sussex, which he subsequently called Shergar. Unsurprisingly, Shergar's Derby odds tumbled! The team knew they had something pretty special before they headed off to Sandown. He won the Classic Trial by ten lengths and followed up with a Chester Vase rout, winning by 12 lengths, yet he was still available at 4-1 for the Derby at this point.

Derby Day dawned. There were 19 declared runners, but only 18 ran with Lydian being withdrawn at the start for refusing to enter the stalls. Shergar, number 18, was drawn 13. The second-favourite was Shotgun, ridden by Piggott, but he had been beaten in the Dante Stakes, as had market third-favourite, Kalaglow. Beldale Flutter, Shergar's Doncaster conqueror as a two-year-old, had won the Dante, but he was forced to miss the Derby having got loose at home. He had crashed into Moorestyle on the heath, then sustained injuries when falling on the road. Glint of Gold, winner of the Italian Derby, was fourth-favourite. Shergar's odds dipped to 10-11 as the race draw closer. Stoute drove to Swinburn's digs to take him to Epsom. Swinburn had ridden work in the morning but was now asleep on the sofa. He slept in the car all the way to the races; there were no question marks over his temperament! He had confidence in the horse. One morning in the spring, Walter had ridden Shergar at exercise and couldn't pull him up: he didn't ride him at home again, so, before the Derby, Stoute made Cliff walk all the way across the course at Epsom to the start and hide in the woods in case Shergar didn't pull up at the stalls: if this happened, Cliff was supposed to run out on to the course and catch him! Luckily, nothing went amiss and all the horses pulled up together. A few horses were sweating but Shergar hadn't turned a hair. Even Lydian's antics at the starting stalls didn't bother him. Wally Swinburn Senior was then based in Ireland. He and his wife Doreen flew over to see their 19-year-old son ride in his first Derby.

What happened next is in all the racing history books: Swinburn followed the two pace-setters up to the top of the hill. As they swept down the hill, Shergar's white face and lolling tongue were easily spotted. What was more difficult was to see what was happening in behind! Shergar was three off the rail and, rounding the turn, Swinburn let him have his head. In just a few strides Shergar had the field strung out like washing. In the commentary Peter Bromley said, 'Two furlongs out and the Derby is a procession.' Approaching the furlong pole, it was: 'There is only one horse in it, you need a telescope to see the rest.' So far clear was Shergar that John Matthias, riding the second Glint of Gold, reportedly thought he had won. Shergar won pulling up, with Swinburn giving him a pat down the neck before the line. After the race, Walter commented, 'I was just a passenger on a very good horse.' HH The Aga Khan took the reins and led in his first Derby winner. Cliff made it back from the start in time to join the victorious team in the winner's enclosure.

With Swinburn suspended following an injudicious ride on Centurius at Royal Ascot, Stoute called on Lester Piggott to ride Shergar again in the Irish Derby. The going was firm and Piggott was instructed not to let him down unless it was necessary. He didn't move a muscle on him, later reporting it as one of the easiest wins of his career.

Not long before the King George VI and Queen Elizabeth Stakes, Cliff was out on the hack on the Limekilns, and Shergar, ridden by one of the other senior lads, was supposed to canter up a gallop by the hedge. At the start of the canter, Shergar whipped round, the lad fell off and Shergar set sail! He raced straight down the Limekilns, between the trees at the bottom, eventually reaching the Boy's Grave.

Here he pulled off the heath and on to the road, just avoiding a passing car, the driver having to slam his brakes on to miss him. When he came to the crossroads by the Boy's Grave, Shergar went straight across, past Lanwades Stud and into Moulton. Here, he turned right and headed back towards Warren Hill. Luckily, the car which just missed him was driven by a fireman, Andrew Sheldrick, who, having had to make an emergency stop himself, realised the potential for a dangerous accident and followed the horse slowly as he trotted off towards Moulton. Luckily, Shergar calmed down and started to graze on the verge, allowing himself to be caught. He had worn his shoes to nothing. Sheldrick took him to the first stables he came across, Warren Place. He passed the horse over to a girl in the yard and headed off back to work. It was only later he realised the significance of the horse which he had caught! Meanwhile, back at the Stoute yard, Cliff had returned to the yard on the hack and saw Mr Stoute, so asked whether Shergar was OK. Stoute had noticed there was a horse missing from his group as they went past him, so knew something wasn't quite right but wasn't sure what had happened. Cliff replied, 'Well, the last time I saw him, he was galloping down to the Boy's Grave!' Michael Stoute and Andy Andrews jumped straight into the car and drove off like bats out of hell! When Stoute and Shergar were reunited at Henry Cecil's yard, the conversation is said to have gone along the lines of, 'Your hack is here, Michael.' 'Henry, that's the best horse you've ever had in your yard!' 'Well, he has obviously come to find the best trainer then!' Shergar wasn't a difficult ride; the only other person he dropped was Lester Piggott on the gallops one morning, but Lester managed to keep hold of the reins!

For the King George VI and Queen Elizabeth Stakes at Ascot, Swinburn was back on board. Shergar was again red-hot favourite to beat his six opponents, despite the Eclipse winner Master Willie, the St Leger winner Light Cavalry (Lester Piggott) and top-class filly Madam Gay being in the field. But jockeyship came into play. Swinburn planned to come with his usual long sweeping run for home for which Shergar was becoming so well known, but Madam Gay's jockey, Greville Starkey, had other ideas! Just as Swinburn was making his move leaving the back stretch, Greville grabbed his arm and wouldn't let go! It was a trick of the trade among jockeys at the time. Swinburn had to quickly change his plans and take the brave man's route to come up Piggott's inside – not a route many jockeys have chosen successfully! Fortunately, Piggott was seemingly aware of what was going on and let Shergar through to secure his final victory. Swinburn maintained it was Shergar's sheer class and quality that got him home that day and rated it as his best performance for, although the Derby might have been more spectacular, his defeat of older horses in difficult circumstances was every bit as good.

Shergar was a horse with instant acceleration that allowed him to put a race to bed in a matter of strides. He was unaffected by the pace of the race and would just relax in behind the leaders. It was announced that he would be let down after the King George VI and Queen Elizabeth Diamond Stakes with a view to being trained for the Prix de l'Arc de Triomphe, taking in one prep race en route. The prep race turned out to be the St Leger and he was installed into the market at 2-5 favourite. It was to be his final race. It had been a long season for him, starting in the Sandown Classic Trial and taking in Chester before the Derby. He was a little edgy before the race down at the start but seemed to be travelling smoothly during it. However, three and a half furlongs from home, Swinburn began to look uneasy and, at the three pole, Shergar faltered and Swinburn went for his whip. It was to no avail and he was eventually beaten 11 and a half lengths by Cut Above, whom he had beaten so comprehensively in the Derby. His retirement was announced soon afterwards. The autumn ground had begun to go against him and, although his victories had appeared effortless, he had expended significant energy winning by such impressive margins. With the additional knowledge acquired from quite a few more years of training under his belt, Michael Stoute now admits that he should not have run Shergar in the St Leger. It is always easy to be wise with the benefit of hindsight, but it takes some moral fibre combined with humility to publicly admit to such an error.

In 1981, Michael Stoute became champion trainer for the first time, largely courtesy of Shergar.

The tragedy of Shergar is what happened to him after he retired. The horse was syndicated and retired to HH The Aga Khan's Ballymany Stud in Ireland. He had a successful first season covering with 36 mares scanned in-foal, but at the start of the following season in 1983, with just one foal from his first crop on the ground, he was kidnapped by the IRA. There was no security at the stud and, on 8 February 1983 at about 8.30pm, three masked men entered the house of the stud groom, Jimmy Fitzgerald. The family were threatened at gun point before being locked into separate rooms. Fitzgerald himself was forced to take the intruders to the stallion barn and show them Shergar. The horse was loaded on to a horsebox and driven off. Fitzgerald was made to lie on the floor of one of the gunmen's vehicles; he was blindfolded and driven around for four hours. When he was released, he was on the Naas dual carriageway, only about seven miles from the stud. The Garda (Irish Police) released a statement that Shergar had been kidnapped and a £2m ransom was wanted for his return. What followed afterwards is still shrouded in mystery, unlikely ever to be resolved, and his final resting place remains unknown.

From his only crop Shergar produced five black-type winners – Authaal, Tisn't, Maysoon, Dolka and Tashtiya – the latter two owned by HH The Aga Khan, and, along with Maysoon, they were trained by Michael Stoute, as was another of Shergar's offspring, Italian Derby third, Shibil.

Possibly the most successful would be regarded as Authaal, being the winner of a Classic race. He had fetched a record-beating 3.1m guineas as a yearling when offered at Goff's Select Sale and joined David O'Brien in Ireland, racing for Sheikh Mohammed but was unraced as a two-year-old. He started his career winning a 12f maiden at Leopardstown in July and followed this up with a victory over 9f at Phoenix Park. He was then sent to York in mid-August for the Great Voltigeur, but he disappointed and was outpaced, eventually finishing last behind Nisnas. Returning to Ireland, he quickly resumed his winning ways with a victory at Naas in September and an enterprising ride by Christy Roche in the Irish St Leger, going 15 lengths clear by halfway, ensured his victory in the Classic. Authaal was disappointing in two starts in the UK as a four-year-old and was sent to race in Australia, where he won the Queen Elizabeth Stakes and the Underwood Stakes. After his retirement from racing, he was sent to stud in Japan but produced little of note. He was retired in 1999.

Cliff's favourite, however, would have to be Maysoon. A bay daughter of Triple First, with whom Stoute had won the Nassau, Musidora and Sun Chariot Stakes, Maysoon's pedigree gave her a lot to live up to. She was a tall, rangy filly with a good walk and she started well, winning a newcomers' race at Ascot. She was then outpaced over 6f in the Lowther Stakes at York when finishing third to Kingscote and her final run as a two-year-old in the May Hill Stakes was disappointing. In 1986, the Stoute yards were awash with female talent and retained jockey Walter Swinburn would have some difficult choices to make! Maysoon and Sonic Lady were aimed at the Guineas, with Maysoon (again), Untold and Colorspin all Oaks possibles. Maysoon started her year winning the Fred Darling Stakes at Newbury impressively. Sonic Lady also won her Guineas Trial, the Nell Gwyn at Newmarket. Swinburn chose to ride Sonic Lady in the 1,000 Guineas, but the winner was not from the Stoute stable: they were both beaten by Ben Hanbury's Midway Lady, Maysoon was three-quarters of a length second, with Sonic Lady a short head behind her. The longer distance of the Oaks only played further to Midway Lady's strength and she beat a triumvirate of Stoute horses with Untold second, Maysoon (now ridden by Swinburn) third and Colorspin fourth. Maysoon didn't win again but finished a valiant second to Park Express in the Nassau Stakes, before being sent to compete in the Arlington Million: a tough ask for a young filly and she finished well beaten. Maysoon stayed in training as a four-year-old, but she was prone to breaking blood vessels and, after fourth places in the Coronation Cup at Epsom and the Prince of Wales Stakes at Royal Ascot, she was retired to stud.

SHAREEF DANCER
1980 bay colt by Northern Dancer ex Sweet Alliance

Shareef Dancer was bought as a yearling at Keeneland Sales for $3.3m, the second-highest priced yearling that year. He was only small. At the end of his two-year-old career a leading bloodstock agent, Peter Wragg, came to see him with a view to purchasing him privately. A glance over the box door was enough and he said to Cliff, 'Don't bother tying that one up, he doesn't look big enough to be a pony stallion.' A year later, Wragg return to the yard to see another horse, but he remembered what he had said about Shareef Dancer! There is nothing like a horse to make you look a fool.

Shareef Dancer wasn't a kind horse and would often chase the lads out of their box. He even cornered Cliff's son, Richard, up by his manger one day and Cliff had to rescue him. One morning, Cliff went in to tack him up with his bridle and headcollar over his arm – Shareef Dancer ran at him, but Cliff was turning back from closing the door and the swinging tack accidentally caught the horse across the side of his mouth. The horse stopped and froze. Cliff went up to him and put the headcollar and bridle on him and tied him up. If Cliff had done what the other lads had done and run out, the horse wouldn't have let him back in again. Although they were never best mates, Shareef Dancer had more respect for Cliff after that incident.

The only time Cliff broke a bone was thanks to Shareef Dancer. He used to ride him on work mornings (normally Wednesday and Saturday), although the colt was based at Beech Hurst. One Monday, he had tacked up his normal first lot at Freemason and was ready to pull out when there was a call from Stoute's Beech Hurst yard: 'Where is Cliff? He is supposed to be riding Shareef Dancer this morning!' He had ridden him work on the Saturday as usual, but no one had changed the names on the Beech Hurst riding out board since then. However, Shareef Dancer had to go out first lot, so Cliff had to remove his tack, rush over to Beech Hurst and tack up Shareef Dancer. This meant he was very late pulling out. The lad who normally saw the horses from Beech Hurst safely across the Bury Road to join up with the Freemason string had already gone with the main group of horses. There were three other horses who were late, so the four of them pulled out together, went down the drive and stood on the edge of the road, waiting to cross over. Shareef Dancer didn't take well to standing and fly-jumped straight into the middle of the road. A white van was coming from town. Shareef Dancer slipped over and Cliff came off and was laying on his back in the middle of the road. The van drove straight past, missing Cliff by inches! The driver didn't stop. Shareef Dancer got up, reared over and landed on Cliff's shoulder, breaking his collarbone and fracturing his scapula. Shareef Dancer then continued riderless into Freemason, while Cliff pulled himself across the road. A passer-by helped Cliff stand up and Cliff walked down the drive to Freemason, from where he was quickly taken to Bury Hospital. He was strapped up and told to take six weeks off.

A few days after the accident, Cliff was returning to his flat with a bag full of shopping on one arm and the other arm in a sling. He climbed the steep stairs to the flats and Andy's dog, Boyboy, was lying across the landing outside Andy's flat. Cliff headed to his own flat but the next thing he knew the dog flew at him, ripping the bag of shopping from his hand. Cliff screamed for Andy who came out. Andy blamed Cliff for startling the dog. However, not long afterwards, Richard, Cliff's son, was heading out to go into town. Boyboy saw him walking across the yard and flew at him: Richard just made it to the other side of the gate in time. Strangely, Boyboy never went for Cliff's Jack Russell terrier Suzie. He might well have come off worse because although she was a sweet-natured dog, she was a great ratter and wouldn't have taken well to any aggressive approach from Boyboy.

As a two-year-old, Shareef Dancer won his Newmarket maiden nicely before finishing fourth in a minor event at Doncaster. Unfortunately for Shareef Dancer's connections, 1983 proved to be an exceptionally wet year, limiting the number of racecourse appearances this fast ground-loving horse would make. He made his three-year-old debut in the Esher Cup at Sandown, for which he was favourite but could only finish second. Back home after the race, he was checked by Stoute's vet and was one of the first horses to undergo an endoscopic examination. This showed him to be suffering from a throat infection. Once that had cleared up, Shareef Dancer headed to Royal Ascot for the King Edward VII Stakes (Group 2) which he won comfortably, setting himself up for a crack at the Irish Derby.

Cliff blew him out in preparation for his Curragh race. The heath man asked what the plan was and Cliff said he was doing a sharp four-furlong blow. The heath man drove to the four-furlong mark, so Cliff would know exactly where it was. Cliff told the rider of the lead horse that Shareef Dancer would need a good blow, so they set off. The heath man came up afterwards. 'Do you always go that fast?' he asked.

The Irish Derby drew a top-class field, including both the winners of the Epsom Derby, Teenoso, and the Prix du Jockey Club, Caerleon, as well as the Epsom runner-up, Carlingford Castle, and the first and third in the Irish 2,000 Guineas, Wassl and Parliament. Shareef Dancer trounced them all. It was a strongly run race and Walter Swinburn confidently slotted Shareef Dancer in behind the leading group on his first ride in the Irish Derby. Two furlongs out, Shareef Dancer saw daylight and he put the matter to bed in a few strides, drawing away to win by a long-looking three lengths from Caerleon, with Teenoso two lengths further back in third. It was three Classic winners from four runners in Ireland for Michael Stoute (Shergar and Fair Salinia being the other two, with only Final Straw failing to make it a clean sweep when finishing third in the Irish 2,000 Guineas before reverting to sprinting).

Having won the Irish Derby, Shareef Dancer worked over 9f on the Limekilns on 10 August 1983. He was ridden by Cliff, with Electric and Karadar as his lead horses. Having disappointed in his work after racing on the July course on the Saturday, this work was described by Newmarket work watcher George Robinson as 'full of his old dash' as he quickened away from his companions, putting himself in line for a shot at the Benson and Hedges Gold Cup at York. Teenoso, winner of the Epsom Derby, was also in action on the Limekilns that day and the two were due to meet in the York race.

When York came around it had rained heavily. Cliff and Michael Stoute walked the course and the decision was made that the ground would not suit Shareef Dancer so he was withdrawn. Teenoso was a proven soft-ground performer, having won the Derby at Epsom on ground officially described as heavy, but, in the event, he was beaten by Caerleon. Shareef Dancer went over the top after that: Cliff rode him a piece of work up Long Hill and he didn't fire, so was retired to stud. He had only run five times, winning three and finishing second once, but he had done enough to be champion UK middle-distance horse, despite many of the press describing his early retirement as unsportsmanlike by connections. He wasn't a kind horse to deal with and Cliff wasn't sorry to see him go.

Shareef Dancer stood at Dalham Hall Stud, Newmarket, with some success, being the sire of Possessive Dancer (winner of both the Italian and Irish Oaks), Dabaweyaa (second in the 1,000 Guineas) and the tough campaigner Rock Hopper (winner of five Group 2s and a couple of Group 3 races) as well as the damsire of the outstanding Dubai Millennium. Shareef Dancer was put down aged 19, having injured a hind leg.

ROYAL HEROINE
1980 dark bay/brown filly by Lypheor out of My Sierra Leone

Royal Heroine was initially trained by Mick Ryan in Newmarket. Having won two of her four starts as a two-year-old, including the Princess Margaret Stakes at Royal Ascot, she had kicked off her three-year-old campaign in the 1,000 Guineas at Newmarket in May, where she finished second but was subsequently disqualified for a failed dope test; a urine sample tested positive for caffeine and theobromine. Royal Heroine then failed to stay the trip in the Oaks. After this, she was bought by Robert Sangster and transferred to the Stoute yard, where Cliff was her regular work rider. She was a tough, consistent filly who maintained her form well throughout the year and Cliff thought she was a pleasure to deal with. While trained by Michael Stoute, she won the Child Stakes at Newmarket, the Sceptre Stakes at Doncaster and the Prix de l'Opera at Longchamp before heading to America for the Yellow Ribbon Stakes. Unfortunately, in the Yellow Ribbon Stakes, Angel Cordero gave her an injudicious ride and she had to be snatched up violently, causing her saddle to slip. She was then transferred to John Gosden who was training in the States at that time and she ran again, ten days later in the Hollywood Derby which she won impressively. She remained in training with Gosden as a four-year-old, although her career was almost ended in a three-horse pileup during the running of the Santa Ana handicap. Royal Heroine's jockey, Fernando Toro, was hospitalised and two horses were killed. She went on to win four races, including the inaugural running of the Breeders' Cup Mile at Hollywood Park in 1984, beating nine male horses and setting a new North American track record for a mile on turf.

* * *

In 1985, for Cliff's 50th birthday, Stoute invited him to Beech Hurst for a drink with the other head lads. His present was a stripagram!

At Freemason, Cliff was in charge of feeding the fillies and his standard menu was one level bowl (three pounds) of feed first thing in the morning; a second level bowl after exercise then, after evening stables, two or three bowls depending on the individual horse. Some of the more delicate fillies at both Murless's and Stoute's had draft Guinness and raw eggs in their food in an attempt to build them up, although they might not have got the whole bottle of Guinness – it's just as well the lads weren't into raw eggs! Clive Brittain claims that one of his older horses was getting 21lbs of feed a day – that must have been one hungry horse!

There are three boxes at Freemason underneath the first flat, opposite the greenhouse and Harlech paddock. They are normally used for the best fillies in the yard and have housed some of the greats, including Sonic Lady and Musical Bliss. One year, they had a very special occupant. Cliff's Jack Russell terrier, Suzie, had her puppies in one of the boxes! Michael Stoute had one of the puppies, as did one of the secretaries. However, Suzie was to outlive all her pups and eventually moved with Cliff when he went to Marsh Stables.

James Fanshawe and John Ferguson were the assistant trainers at this time. James used to regularly ride No Bombs as his hack. No Bombs achieved notoriety as the horse who was disqualified for eating a Mars Bar, which his lad had shared with him in the horsebox on the way to the races! He belonged to Dana Brudenell-Bruce, who was an owner at Stoute's and provided a couple of her ex-racehorses as hacks to the yard, Steeple Bell being another. No Bombs was quite a character. He shared his stable with the Stoute children's retired pony, Dusty, who like many rather rotund, old ponies was prone to laminitis: Dusty therefore wasn't allowed mash on mash nights and his feed was restricted to hay. No Bombs used to scoop a pile of his supper out of his manger with his nose and leave it on the floor for Dusty. Mash night meant that the next morning would be a work morning and No Bombs soon worked out where to find some mash to replace the mouthfuls he had shared with the pony. During first lot, there would be two or three 'shots' of work when the work riders would switch on to different horses while on the heath. James had to jump off No Bombs to leg the jockeys up on to the fresh horses and the horse was supposed to wait by the gallops for James to get back on. However, No Bombs soon discovered that if he came back to the yard on his own, crossing the Bury Road at the traffic lights, he could go to the muck pit and help himself to breakfast on any mash that had been left over from the night before!

SHADEED
1982 bay colt by Nijinsky out of Continual

Shadeed was bought as a yearling for $800,000 at Keeneland Select Sale. His name is Arabic for 'strong'. He was a big, powerful horse and one of those horses who knew he was good: he had 'the look of eagles' about him.

The first time Cliff worked Shadeed was on the Limekilns with three others. Cliff sat last and the other three drew upsides each other but left a gap. Cliff just clicked him and he shot through the gap. The assistant trainers, James Fanshawe and John Ferguson, were in a car parked on the Norwich Road watching work. John Ferguson was standing up through the sunroof and Cliff could hear them screaming with excitement! One morning, Stoute, on the hack, took a group of horses cantering down Railway Land to work over on Waterhall. Cliff took Shadeed to the outside of the group and lobbed down on his own. Stoute told him to join the group. Shadeed went from a gentle lob to full speed! After that, he always worked on his own.

His first run was a typical Stoute introduction and he enjoyed a gentle run at home in the Westley Maiden Stakes at Newmarket, finishing third, beaten 1½ lengths and a short head. The winner, Kala Dancer, went on to win the Group 1 Dewhurst Stakes, while at the same meeting, Shadeed contested the 14-runner Houghton Stakes, smoothly moving through the field and pulling clear to win by 2½ lengths. On the basis of this performance, he was made favourite for the 2,000 Guineas and the Derby.

Shadeed started his three-year-old career in the Craven Stakes, again at Newmarket, where, ridden by Walter Swinburn, he impressed, travelling easily through the race, taking the lead two furlongs out and pulling away to win by six lengths.

However, his temperament could be frail and he would easily boil over. He was stabled at Beech Hurst, but, every day before the Guineas meeting, he would come over to Freemason and be led round the front yard with all the staff standing around, clapping and cheering to make a noise to try and replicate the atmosphere he was likely to encounter on 2,000 Guineas day. This was a typical example of Stoute's attention to detail. On the day of the race, Swinburn was suspended, so Lester Piggott got the call up. Piggott had already been booked to ride Bairn for Luca Cumani, but preferred the chances of Shadeed. However, the two horses were owned by the brothers, Sheikh Maktoum al Maktoum and Sheikh Mohammed, and Sheikh Maktoum, being the elder brother, was able to square the riding arrangements with his younger brother, much to Cumani's annoyance. Willie Carson deputised on Bairn. Despite the practice around Freemason, Shadeed became agitated and didn't partake in the parade, earning the trainer a fine. In the race itself, Piggott took the lead about two furlongs out and looked likely to win easily, but was strongly challenged by Bairn, eventually only winning by a head.

Like many who work in the racing industry, Piggott was not a great fan of the parade. The trainer brings a horse to their peak for the major races and they have to be absolutely spot on for the day. However, the parade puts the more highly strung horses at a great disadvantage to the quieter ones. Their instincts tell them there is a job to be done and they are keen to get on with it. Supposedly, parades are for the punters' benefit, enabling them to get a good look at the horses, but there is usually plenty of opportunity to do that in both the pre-parade and the parade ring and, if the horse boils over due to parading on the course, then the punter is going to lose their money, so will also be disadvantaged.

Shadeed's next start was the Derby where he was 7-2 second favourite. Despite remaining calm in the preliminaries, he ran deplorably. He never figured in the race and only beat one home. The connections were called into the stewards to explain the run. They could offer nothing concrete, Swinburn saying, 'He died in my hands, as if he had been shot.'

Shadeed was evidently wrong and a few days later he was covered in ringworm spots, a not uncommon occurrence when horses have run disappointingly. The fungal spores which cause ringworm can remain dormant for long periods and often stress can cause a flare-up. However, although there are different fungi which cause the condition, once a horse has suffered an outbreak, it will have improved immunity from that particular strain. Shadeed was given a good break to recover and returned for the Group 1 Queen Elizabeth II Stakes at Ascot in September. He took the lead at halfway and drew clear to win, beating the Arlington Million winner, Teleprompter, in a course record time of 1:38.8. His final start was in the Breeders' Cup Mile at Aqueduct, but he found the pomp of the occasion was too much: he ran too freely and failed to handle the tight turns, but his class still saw him through to finish in fourth place, although he was later promoted to third.

Shadeed was retired to Sheikh Maktoum's Gainsborough Farm in Kentucky. He was a reasonably successful sire, with offspring including 1,000 Guineas-winning fillies Shadayid and Sayyedati, as well as the colt Alydeed, who was runner-up in the Preakness. He retired from covering duties in 2004 and died the following year. He is buried at Gainsborough Farm.

* * *

One morning, Cliff rode a two-year-old filly first lot. After work, he turned to the boss and said, 'Guv'nor, I think this is your best horse; she's going to be something special.' Second lot, he rode another two-year-old filly. Afterwards, he said to the boss, 'Guv'nor, I think this is your best horse, the other one is only second best!' Cliff claims he was correct; however, although other members of staff remember him saying this, no one can recall which the two fillies involved were, so we will have to take his word for it!

BELLA COLORA
1982 bay filly by Bellypha out of Reprocolor

When Bella Colora was still only a two-year-old and before she ever set foot on a racecourse, the lad who looked after her, Peter Parkin, came to find Cliff one morning and suggested he should find a way to get himself a ride on her because Peter liked her. Peter asked Michael Stoute to give Cliff a piece of work on her and Cliff rode her up the Limekilns. What a feel she gave him! When they came back in, Cliff told Peter, 'This is good.' Cliff backed her for the Guineas at 22-1 and, at the same time, he got 10-1 about Shadeed for the Guineas double.

Over the winter, the prospects of Cliff landing his gamble looked bright, with Bella Colora having won both her starts at as two-year-old, including the Waterford Candelabra Stakes at Goodwood and, despite just losing out to Oh So Sharp in the Nell Gwyn on her first start at three, connections were hopeful that she would be able to reverse the form in the Guineas itself. Unfortunately, she was beaten by a short head. She was ridden by Lester Piggott and it is about the only race Cliff thinks Lester didn't win when he should have done. The race was won by Oh So Sharp (ridden by Steve Cauthen), who went on to win the Oaks and the St Leger. Al Bahathri was second. Bella Colora cut out the running but drifted off the rail rather than keeping a straight line: Piggott was carrying the whip in his right hand. Had it been in his left hand (not that he readily used his whip on the left), he would have been able to keep her straight and she might have won.

Although she was unimpressive when winning the 1m2f Lupe Stakes at Goodwood on her next start, it gave connections enough encouragement to believe she might stay the 1m4f of the Oaks. However, the ground came up soft and, although she wasn't entirely discredited in finishing fifth, she reverted to shorter trips subsequently. After placing third in the Child Stakes at Newmarket on only three racing plates, she was second in the Sceptre Stakes at Doncaster and finished the season with a brave victory against a strong field in the Prix de l'Opera at Longchamp.

She became yet another great broodmare for the Weinfeld family at Meon Valley Stud with Stagecraft (Prince of Wales Stakes, Brigadier Gerard Stakes), Hyabella (Ben Marshall Stakes, Atalanta Stakes) and Balalaika (Dahlia Stakes) among her offspring. Bella Colora retired from breeding in 2003 and died in 2008.

Meanwhile, Bella Colora's year-younger half-sister, Colorspin, was making a name for herself.

COLORSPIN
1983 bay filly by High Top out of Reprocolor

Like Bella, Colorspin won both her starts as a two-year-old, but her second win was in the Rochford Thompson Newbury Stakes. Coincidentally, the first foal out of Reprocolor, Rappa Tap Tap (by Tap on Wood), had also won both her starts at two. Colorspin was a much taller, lengthier filly than her older sisters and always appeared rather unfurnished throughout her racing career. Neither Rappa Tap Tap nor Bella Colora had stayed 1m4f, but Colorspin's sire, High Top, was a stronger influence for stamina than either Tap on Wood or Bellypha and there was every hope that Colorspin would improve, as they had, between two and three years old and stay further. She started her campaign in the Musidora Stakes at York, a recognised Oaks trial, where she finished third before heading to Epsom, where she finished fourth. On Irish Oaks day, she was at her peak and the soft ground proved very much to her liking. Swinburn had chosen to ride stable companion Untold, who had finished more than four lengths ahead of Colorspin in the Oaks at Epsom so Pat Eddery came in for the ride on Colorspin. Swinburn knew his fate early as Untold struggled in the ground, but Colorspin was loving it! She cruised upsides the leader, Fleur Royale, and Eddery eased her into the lead. She won comfortably by three lengths, with Untold a further 12 lengths away in third and the rest strung out like washing. A few weeks later, the first three home met again in the Yorkshire Oaks, with the Stoute stable's Ivor's Image, winner of the Italian Oaks, added to the mix. Although Colorspin beat Fleur Royale again, the faster ground was much more to Untold's liking and she won from Park Express with Ivor's Image in third and Colorspin in fourth.

Following in the tradition of her family, Colorspin proved to be an outstanding broodmare, achieving the 2003 TBA Broodmare of the Year award with Opera House (King George and Queen Elizabeth Stakes, Coronation Cup, Eclipse), Kayf Tara (dual winner of the Ascot Gold Cup, Irish St Leger) and Zee Zee Top (Prix de l'Opera) among her offspring. She retired from breeding in 2008 and died in 2012 at the great age of 29.

GREEN DESERT
1983 bay colt by Danzig out of Foreign Courier

Green Desert cost $650,000 at Keeneland September Sales as a yearling. He was a typical sprinter, neat and compact, like a small rubber ball full of pent-up energy just waiting to be let loose. He was also sharp and he could whip round without warning: he dropped Walter Swinburn one morning going on to the Limekilns and went 100mph up the gallop. Cliff always knew he was a good horse and he arrived on the racecourse with a big reputation but was beaten first time out by Sure Blade in a Newmarket maiden. Undeterred, his next start was the Anglia Television July Stakes at the same course. He had learned his job and, although headed by Atall Atall after making the running, Green Desert fought back determinedly to win by a head with the third horse well back. He was then second to Nomination in the Richmond Stakes at Goodwood, before returning to winning ways in the Flying Childers at Doncaster where he was ridden by Lester Piggott. He put in a smooth performance, racing prominently and easing past Marouble to win by a neck under considerate handling, with Atall Atall further down the field. In his final start as a two-year-old, he faltered before running on again to finish fourth to Luqman in the Mill Reef Stakes at Newbury.

He started his three-year-old campaign with a pleasing display to win the Free Handicap at Newmarket over 7f, earning himself a shot at the 2,000 Guineas, where only the subsequent Prix de l'Arc de Triomphe winner, Dancing Brave, was too good for him. Unfortunately, the ground at the Curragh for the Irish 2,000 Guineas was bottomless: he didn't handle it and was given a sympathetic ride. Next stop Royal Ascot for the St James Palace Stakes where, unfortunately, he bumped into Sure Blade again, finishing second, having made most of the running. Connections reverted to sprinting and with six furlongs proving his forte, he won two of the season's premier sprints, the July Cup at Newmarket (under a particularly adept Swinburn ride) and the Haydock Sprint Cup.

Described by Timeform as a 'bonny colt, beautifully balanced, a good mover and full of quality', Green Desert was always going to prove popular when retired to stand at Shadwell Stud. The sire of four champion sprinters and 72 individual stakes winners was also a sire of sires with Cape Cross (Ouija Board, Sea The Stars, Golden Horn), Invincible Spirit (Kingman, Eqtidaar) and Oasis Dream (Midday, Muhaara and Aqlaam) perpetuating his line. Green Desert was retired from stud duties in 2011 and euthanised on humane grounds at the grand old age of 32 in 2015.

SONIC LADY
1983 bay filly by Nureyev out of Stumped

Interestingly, Sonic Lady's female line originates from a non-Thoroughbred family. Known as the Verdict family, it was only incorporated into the *General Stud Book* as recently as 1969, following the authorities' acceptance of the family. From 1919, with Verdict and Quashed (winner of the 1935 Oaks and 1936 Ascot Gold Cup) to Sonic Lady's own great granddam, Lucasland, as well as Lucasland's half-brother So Blessed, the family kept beating the recognised blue-bloods! Sonic Lady's dam, Stumped, sealed the approval when finishing third in the Blue Seal Stakes and winning the Child Stakes at Newmarket.

Sonic Lady cost $500,000 at the Fasig-Tipton Kentucky sales in 1984. She was a 'talking horse' before she ever hit the racecourse and had been backed down to 16-1 for the next season's 1,000 Guineas before her debut. The first time she caught Cliff's eye was one morning on Side Hill. She was being ridden by a good lad called Derek Parkin and as they were pulling up after the piece of work, Sonic Lady went past but she wasn't stopping! Cliff soon managed to get himself switched on to her. Her first race was in the Blue Seal Stakes at Ascot, a Listed race for fillies which hadn't run before 8 September. Such was her reputation and despite taking on more experienced rivals, Sonic Lady started at odds-on. With Sonic Lady claiming all the allowances for never having raced, Swinburn was unable to do the weight (8st 2lbs), so Brian Rouse got the ride. Breaking smartly, Sonic Lady was soon in control, making all on the far rails having drifted right across the course. It was her only start as a two-year-old and left everybody wanting more.

The following season, with stable companion Maysoon winning the Fred Darling 1,000 Guineas Trial at Newbury, Sonic Lady was routed to the Nell Gwyn at Newmarket, which she won with authority, lobbing along on the bridle before drawing clear when meeting the rising ground. Swinburn decided to stick with her for the 1,000 Guineas itself, but rode her in an ordinary bridle despite, for some reason, being worried she would bolt to the start. By the time she reached the stalls, she was awash with sweat having been made to trot all the way down the course to the start. Having expended so much energy before the race, she did well to finish third, only beaten three-quarters of a length and a short head, with Maysoon second. Sonic Lady then won five races on the trot.

Her next start was to be the Irish 1,000 Guineas and Cliff was to act as travelling head lad, so he could ride her out on the course in the morning. The normal travelling head lad was packing all the equipment for her and Cliff asked, 'Do I need papers or anything?' Horses racing abroad need an export health certificate issued by DEFRA if they are going to race overseas. However, prior to Brexit, a tripartite agreement existed between the UK, France and Ireland and export health certificates were not required to travel between these three countries. There seems to have been some misunderstanding because Sonic Lady arrived in Ireland without her passport! Luckily, the Irish Turf Club gave special dispensation that, on that one occasion, they would accept a facsimile copy of her passport along with a sworn affidavit. It was a weekend: offices were closed and fax machines were not in common use at that time. Entries and declarations were made using a Telex machine and everything else was pretty much done by telephone. There was no need for a computer because the weekly wage run was done over the road at Geoff Wragg's Abingdon Place yard as he and his secretary, Nigel Welham, were technophiles and did have a computer. Technology at Freemason Lodge hadn't advanced beyond an electric typewriter! There was, however, a photocopier, so the hunt for a fax machine was on! Luckily, it turned out that Stoute's solicitor, Jeremy Richardson, had one in his office and he even knew how to use it! A potential disaster was averted.

The Irish 1,000 Guineas was also the first time Sonic Lady wore a citation bridle with an elasticated noseband, which held the bit in place in her mouth. She made short work of the field, settling well and drawing away to win by two lengths. In a post-race interview with Brough Scott, Walter Swinburn commented that she was more accepting of the bit and jockey with that bridle, a situation that helped them both; however, he didn't think it was the reason why she was beaten in the 1,000 Guineas. Cliff rode her out usually in a plain bridle, but a couple of times he put on a leather drop noseband and she was very accepting of it and easy to hold. He never had a problem with holding her, but she never ran in the drop noseband. When Cliff went on holiday, Tommy Murphy was given the ride on Sonic Lady at home. She dropped him going into the canter on Side Hill one day, but otherwise got on with her well. Her own lass, Helen McLeod-Smith, was a lovely girl but not a regular work rider; however, even Helen managed to hold her when she rode her out on Warren Hill one Sunday morning.

Subsequent impressive victories, in the Coronation Stakes at Royal Ascot and the Child Stakes at Newmarket, set her up for a race against older horses and the colts. Well, the three-year-old fillies just couldn't live with her. So Sonic Lady headed for the Sussex Stakes at Goodwood. Dancing Brave was among the four-day declarations but didn't turn up, so it wasn't the strongest race and Sonic Lady started at odds-on. As usual for a Group 1 race, there was a parade, so Cliff and her lass, Helen, walked either side of the filly, keeping her calm. In the race itself, Swinburn settled her at the back before pulling her out in the straight and she quickly established her superiority, with stable companion, the front-running Scottish Reel, finishing a couple of lengths behind in second.

So on to the Prix de Moulin, Longchamp. For some reason, she didn't settle in behind as she had at Goodwood despite a decent gallop. She pulled her way to the front and swung wide coming down the hill. However, this was Sonic Lady: she was still pulling for her head while others were being ridden behind her! When Swinburn let her go, she went to the front, but eventually had to be hard ridden to hold on from Thrill Show and the pacesetting Lirung.

Yet another race was on the cards for Sonic Lady despite her long season. She had eight weeks to freshen up before the Breeders' Cup Mile at Santa Anita. There she finished out of the frame for the first time in her life, weakening in the final hundred yards into seventh, although only beaten about three and a half lengths.

Sonic Lady remained in training as a four-year-old, with the Breeders' Cup Mile her main target, but she was not quite the force of the previous year. Nor did things go smoothly. She reappeared in the Queen Anne Stakes at Royal Ascot but carried plenty of condition, eventually tiring and finishing third, before retaining her Child Stakes title when making most of the running due to a slow early pace. Bypassing the Sussex Stakes due to the number of runners her owner, Sheikh Mohammed, already had in the race, Sonic Lady headed back to Ascot for the Queen Elizabeth II Stakes. Unfortunately, prior to the race, she had had sore heels, which had become infected and required treatment, causing her to miss some vital work. She wasn't as fit as connections would have liked, but she needed another race before the Breeders' Cup. The lack of fitness showed as her stable companion Milligram won, with the French filly Miesque in second and Sonic Lady third.

Milligram and Sonic Lady set off for California four weeks before the Breeders' Cup meeting in the hope that the additional time there would allow them to acclimatise. Lafitt Pincay Jr was to ride Sonic Lady in the race. As an American-based jockey, he would have superior knowledge of the track. However, he didn't know the filly, so he came to ride her work to get to know her, with Cliff riding Milligram to lead the exercise. Cliff set off at a nice pace, but the next thing he knew, Pincay was hissing at Sonic Lady and came upsides pushing her hard. The same thing happened in the race: his style didn't suit her; they didn't gel and she was too free. Despite his knowledge of the track enabling Pincay to save ground on the home turn, she had done too much by pulling and could only finish third to Miesque. Cliff considered that, although Sonic Lady was most impressive when coming from behind and outsprinting the opposition, she could also make the running; she had done so first time out and in the Child Stakes that year: he should have let her go.

Cliff thought Milligram had gone over the top by the time of the race: the lass who looked after her was supposed to be cantering her every morning but was reportedly doing a good half speed. It was too much. She even complained that Cliff wasn't leading her fast enough on Sonic Lady! Come the race, Pat Eddery was riding Milligram and she didn't want to go through the gap in the fence on to the course. It took nearly five minutes to get her on to the grass track. She was telling connections she had had enough. The girl wouldn't listen to what she was being told and was abusive over the phone. Cliff nearly sent her back on the next plane!

It's disappointing that Wikipedia call Sonic Lady 'temperamental'. It's rather extreme because, although she could be a little keen on the gallops and at the races, she was a sweetheart to do anything with at home or in her box. However, it is an impressive race record in mile races for a filly whom both the trainer and her work rider maintain was better at 7f.

Sonic Lady remained in the States after the Breeders' Cup to be covered by Blushing Groom. Her first foal, Hazaam, inherited his mother's bad joints: both horses had their joints regularly treated with hyaluronic acid and Adequan to aid their soundness, but he still won eight races, including the Supreme Stakes.

Sonic Lady died in a stable accident in 1996, but her line continues: a daughter of Sonic Lady, Soninke, was exported to Japan and is the great granddam of Japanese Champion and international star Deirdre, as well as Logi Universe and Northern River.

Cliff took three horses to Ireland for Classic races, Shergar (Derby), Shareef Dancer (Derby) and Sonic Lady (1,000 Guineas). All three won.

While all these top-class fillies were strutting their stuff, there was also a second Derby winner for HH Aga Khan and Michael Stoute in the yard. Shahrastani (1983 chesnut colt by Nijinsky out of Shahdemah). He had only had one outing as a two-year-old when finishing an unlucky head second at Newbury, having had to be switched late. Cliff only rode him once, on the Waterhall Gallop in his first work as three-year-old, and was told to stay behind on him. Even so, he knew he was on a good horse because of the feel he got from the colt. Shahrastani started his campaign with striking displays in the Sandown Classic Trial and the Mecca Dante Stakes at York, thus arriving at Epsom with only three races under his belt. The 2,000 Guineas winner, Dancing Brave, was favourite but there were doubts about his stamina. Discussions about tactics were vital for this inexperienced colt and a great ride by Swinburn, getting first run on the held-up but fast-finishing Dancing Brave, gave the Stoute stable ample compensation for the defeat of Green Desert at Newmarket. Many considered Dancing Brave was unlucky: he had become unbalanced when Starkey pulled him out to make his challenge, but Shahrastani impressed again when he followed up his Epsom victory with an easy win in the Irish Derby, a race which Dancing Brave by-passed, connections preferring to drop back in trip and wait for the Coral Eclipse. Although both colts showed improved form after the Epsom race, it was to be Dancing Brave who finished the season on top, with victories over Shahrastani in both the King George VI and Queen Elizabeth Stakes at Ascot and the Prix de l'Arc de Triomphe. Shahrastani was syndicated and retired to stud at Three Chimneys Farm, Kentucky. He had limited success, possibly his best progeny being Dariyoun (winner of the Gran Premio di Madrid) and was transferred to Ireland, France and then Japan before standing at Walton Fields Stud in Leicestershire. He is damsire of the Aga Khan's stallion Alamshar (winner of 2003 Irish Derby and King George VI and Queen Elizabeth Diamond Stakes). He was put down in 2011 at the age of 28, due to the infirmities of old age.

In 1987, Cliff, although no stranger to royalty having ridden a winner for the Queen and having looked after so many of her horses in training, met Princess Anne. Michael Stoute had agreed to provide a mount for her in the race for amateur lady riders at Ascot on King George VI and Queen Elizabeth race day. However, Stoute had entered two in the race as a precaution against anything going wrong with one, thereby leaving the princess without a mount; so, she came to Newmarket and rode both of them at exercise. Cliff led both the exercise shots. They cantered up Warren Hill, swapped horses in the trees at the top, went down to the bottom and cantered up again on the fresh horses. As they pulled up on the second horses, Princess Anne turned to Cliff and asked which he thought she should ride. Ever helpful, his reply was: 'You've ridden them both, you choose which one you want!' Luckily, she chose Ten No Trumps, a four-year-old bay colt, and the pair went on to win the Ascot race by four lengths. Ten No Trumps followed up with a win in the Listed City of York Stakes on his next start. Both the Ascot and York ladies' races were regularly contested by the Stoute team, usually with Maxine Juster (now Cowdrey) on board. Probably one of the best renewals of the Ascot race was in 1995 in which they scored with Desert Shot, while the next five horses home were ridden by Amanda Harwood (now Perrett), Lydia Pearce, Maureen Haggas, Sara Cumani and Jane Chapple-Hyam. The race still exists but not in the same format, having been downgraded to a 7f handicap, and it seems to lack some of the lustre of those glory days.

AJDAL
1984 bay colt by Northern Dancer out of Native Partner

The bookies were ringing Freemason Lodge to try and glean information about the unnamed Native Partner colt before he had even done his first canter! There had already been punters wanting to get on for the following year's Derby just on his breeding. His breeder sent him to the Keeneland Yearling Sale, but he was led out of the ring unsold at $7.5m:

the underbidders (representatives of the Maktoum family) discovered they were bidding against a representative of the vendor, a tactic that, strangely, was allowed at the time. A private deal was done outside the ring and the colt became the property of Sheikh Mohammed.

Once broken in and out on the heath, he soon caught the attention of the Newmarket work watchers. A strong, handsome colt with plenty of scope, he was a good mover. Michael Stoute has never been one to rush his horses and Ajdal didn't make his debut until September at Doncaster, over six furlongs, where he created a good impression, winning without coming off the bridle. His next start was the Mornington Stakes at Ascot over seven furlongs: a tougher competition but, again, he didn't need to come off the bridle to win. He started 9-4 on favourite for the most prestigious two-year-old race of the season, the Dewhurst at Doncaster, despite being the only horse in the field who had not previously run in a Pattern race. Despite winning, he was not as convincing as he had been in his previous two starts – he had quickened away impressively, but the field were coming back to him in the final furlong. Maybe it was greenness, after all he had never come off the bridle before. Some people questioned his temperament, but that was never in doubt for those who knew him best.

His three-year-old season started with a win in the Craven, beating Don't Forget Me. Again, Ajdal faltered in the final furlong but he didn't look fully fit and was entitled not to be with the 2,000 Guineas, and then possibly the Derby, being that season's main targets. He was, after all, a colt with huge Classic pretentions and a pedigree to match. Ajdal's first defeat came in the 2,000 Guineas where he finished fourth. He had received a bump from Most Welcome in the final furlong which hadn't helped his cause, but the winner of the race was Don't Forget Me, whom he had beaten in the Craven by three-quarters of a length and was now just over a length ahead. The two met again in the Irish 2,000 Guineas and Don't Forget Me again beat Ajdal, who finished just under a length behind in third, although he was subsequently disqualified for the jockey failing to weigh in. On both occasions, he had travelled well and looked threatening two out, but seemed unable to go through with his effort.

Michael Stoute wanted to drop him back in trip and Ajdal was entered in the Newmarket July Cup. However, the owner's connections insisted on taking up the Derby entry he already had. Cliff rode Ajdal in a piece of work before the Derby and couldn't believe the speed he had. He couldn't see how he would stay 1m4f with that speed. Swinburn deserted Ajdal for his stable companion Ascot Knight, who had finished second to Reference Point in the Dante but would be having only his third start, having made his debut five weeks earlier. The search was on for a replacement jockey for Ajdal for the Derby and some came to ride him work. Bruce Raymond was one and Cliff led the work. Bruce told Cliff he thought Ajdal would win the Derby. Cliff is adamant that you should be able to tell when a horse has too much speed to stay 1m4f. Fleet was never going to stay and, in his opinion, Ajdal was in the same mould. Ray Cochrane eventually got the ride and Ajdal did well, racing prominently for much of the race before fading in the final quarter of a mile to finish ninth behind Reference Point, with Ascot Knight in 11th.

A change of training routine ensued: having been trying to keep Ajdal relaxed to ensure he would stay, he needed to be sharpened up to be competitive at sprint distances. Historically, horses used to race over every distance: in the 19th century, Tristan won the July Cup and the Gold Cup, and Ormonde won the Triple Crown before ending his career with a victory in the six-furlong Imperial Gold Cup. However, nowadays horses tend to specialise, provided connections can find their ideal trip!

In the July Cup, over six furlongs at Newmarket, Ajdal started third-favourite behind Vincent O'Brien's impressive Kings Stand winner, Bluebird. Always prominent, Ajdal took the lead approaching the final furlong and won by a head from Gayane, with Bluebird in third. Dropping back in trip again to five furlongs for the William Hill Sprint Championship at York, Swinburn sent Ajdal into the lead early on and they pulled away in the last two furlongs to win by three lengths. Bluebird was fourth. Ajdal's final start in the UK was the Vernon's Sprint Cup at Haydock. Again, he won decisively. He was disappointing in his final start in the Prix de l'Abbaye at Longchamp, having suffered a very poor draw and racing on firm ground, but it had been a long season for a three-year-old.

He was retired to stud at Dalham Hall Stud, Newmarket, but met with a paddock accident in August 1988 at the age of only four. The following stud season saw 35 live foals sired by him, of which the most successful was Cezanne: a backward colt early on, he was switched between Stoute and Godolphin. However, he was the winner of the Group 1 Irish Champion Stakes as a five-year-old when trained by Michael Stoute. After this victory, Cezanne was returned to the Godolphin fold but had no more racing success. From the Reprocolor family, he was retired to stud but proved infertile and was subsequently gelded and sent National Hunt racing. Fortunately, Ajdal has proved a successful sire of broodmares with the stallions Mark of Esteem and Youmzain among his grandsons. Stoute also trained Dilshaan who was by Darshaan out of the Ajdal mare Avila. Dilshaan was lightly raced but won the *Racing Post* Trophy at Doncaster and the Dante Stakes at York.

MUSICAL BLISS
1986 bay filly by The Minstrel out of Bori

Musical Bliss made her two-year-old debut in July in a six-furlong maiden at Ascot. Her home reputation preceded her and she duly won by four lengths at 8-11. She didn't appear again until the Group 3 Rockfel Stakes at Newmarket where she took the lead inside the final furlong, winning by two lengths.

The following year, Michael Stoute had just bought Harlech House, next door to Freemason. However, he was extremely superstitious about anything green. It was unlucky. For example, when the indoor ride was built at Freemason, the council insisted it should be painted green, so that, if it could be seen from the road, it would blend in with the trees behind. Eventually, once it was pointed out that the trees were deciduous, the Council agreed that it would be satisfactory if it was painted brown! Staff were discouraged from buying green cars. Harlech House had green tiles on the garage roof. Michael really fancied Musical Bliss for the 1,000 Guineas, so a couple of weeks before the Guineas meeting, all the staff had no third lots but instead had to remove and smash all the roof tiles. It wasn't in vain! There were only seven runners and none of the jockeys wanted to make the running. Swinburn decided to grab the race by the scruff of the neck and kicked on. Musical Bliss became Michael Stoute's first 1,000 Guineas winner, beating stable companion Kerrera by a length.

She was stepped up in trip for the Group 1 Oaks where she was ridden by Michael Roberts, Swinburn having elected to ride stable companion Aliysa. Musical Bliss didn't stay the trip and tired in the closing stages, finishing seventh of the nine runners, beaten more than ten lengths by Aliysa.

Her final start was a tough ask against colts and older horses in the Prix Jacques le Marois at Deauville and she was never a factor, the race being won by Polish Precedent.

She was retired to Sheikh Mohammed's Dalham Hall Stud, her best progeny being Muscadel, the winner of a listed race at Longchamp. Musical Bliss died in 2006.

ALIYSA
1986 bay filly by Darshaan out of Alannya

An Aga Khan homebred filly, Aliysa was out of a good mare who, despite being a descendant of the flying filly Mumtaz Mahal, had already produced some decent staying horses in Altiyna and Alipour. Aliysa had obviously gone slightly under the radar at home, making her debut at Wolverhampton at a starting price of 7-1. However, she won easily, going six lengths clear before being eased. She didn't run again as a two-year-old but was impressive when winning the Lingfield Oaks Trial by eight lengths on her reappearance the following season.

Despite stumbling coming out of the stalls, Aliysa finished first in the Oaks at Epsom in 1989: going off as the 11-10 favourite she stamped her superiority on the field, squeezing through a tight gap over a furlong out and galloping clear to finish three lengths ahead of the second. She was disqualified when her routine post-race urine sample was tested at the Horseracing Forensic Laboratory, Newmarket, and was positive for detectable amounts of 3-hydroxy-camphor, a metabolite of camphor which is banned by the Jockey Club as it is believed to be a stimulant of both the central nervous and respiratory systems. It made her the first Classic winner since Relko in 1963 to be disqualified for a positive post-race dope test. The race was awarded to the runner-up, Snow Bride.

The Aga Khan had already won hearings disputing positive test results for both Vayraan (Champion Stakes) and Lashkari (Breeders' Cup) and he was not going to let matters lie in the Aliysa case. The row about her failed dope test brewed for the next 18 months with the reliability of both the testing methods and interpretation of the sample by the Jockey Club's Horseracing Forensic Laboratory (HFL) being called into question after HH The Aga Khan commissioned the University of California at Davis and the University of Quebec at Montreal to investigate. The Aga Khan resigned his honorary membership of the Jockey Club in December because of his opposition to the drug-testing procedures used. When His Highness had a fancied runner in the Classic races, he would send over his own security team a week in advance of the race. They lived in a caravan at the yard and would take turns sitting outside the horse's stable 24 hours a day; they accompanied the horses to the races and did the same at the racecourse stables. Robert Masse, the deputy director of the Canadian Centre for Doping Control at Montreal who were testing the samples for Olympic athletes at that time, argued that the screening assays alone were insufficient to support a positive dope finding and were not as reproducible as they should have been.

Neville Dunnett, the director of HFL at the time, explained that this was due to the need for haste to meet a Jockey Club deadline. Furthermore, the investigations at UCL Davis contended that feeding trials with horses at the university had shown that 3-hydroxycamphor could arise from naturally occurring substances other than camphor, including carrots and wood constituents. Aliysa was bedded on wood shavings, which are widely used in the horseracing industry. Part of the panel's case against the Jockey Club was that there should, at least, be a threshold limit to determine whether the metabolite had arisen unnaturally. Dunnett's defence was that the Jockey Club's rules were 'deliberately black and white' to protect the 'integrity of British racing'. The rules were that a horse with a prohibited substance in its blood should not be racing, even if the material got there through a natural route. He admitted, 'Occasionally, it may be a harsh rule.' Threshold levels for many banned substances have since been introduced, but at the time, the High Court ruled that the Jockey Club was a 'private members club' and could not be sued if the members disagreed with the rules.

The Aga Khan withdrew his horses from training in England, which amounted to roughly 90 horses being trained by Stoute and his Newmarket neighbour, Luca Cumani, and boycotted British racing as a result. The Aga Khan had won three Derbys in the 1980s with Shergar, Shahrastani and Kahyasi and his family had a long-standing history with British racing. Among the horses removed from Stoute's yard was Kartajana (1987 bay filly by Shernazar out of Karamita). Kartajana took after her sire, Shernazar (a Busted half-brother to Shergar), and was never going to be a precocious two-year-old type, so she spent time with Cliff at Marsh Stables being broken in and strengthening up. She started her three-year-old career comfortably, breaking her maiden at Leicester before winning the fillies Oaks trial at Newbury. Unfortunately, she didn't handle the track at Epsom at all and finished last of the eight runners behind Salsabil. She returned to winning ways in the Nassau Stakes at Goodwood before winning the Sun Chariot Stakes at Newmarket, with a second place behind stable companion Hellenic in the Yorkshire Oaks in between. With the Aga Khan's boycott of British racing, she was transferred to Alain de Royer-Dupre in France for her four-year-old career. Here, she won the Group 1 Prix Ganay at Longchamp and the Grosser Mercedes Benz Preis in Munich before being retired to stud.

On 15 December 1994, the Jockey Club announced new dope-testing procedures, which would mean Britain operating the same regime as Ireland and France, where the Aga Khan's horses were being trained. The Aga Khan agreed to return to British racing the following year and have horses trained in England again from 1996. Unfortunately, the cost of training compared to the minimal amount of prize-money available for maiden races and smaller handicaps caused the Aga Khan to again withdraw his British-trained horses in the early 2000s and concentrate on training in France and Ireland where costs were lower and prize-money was keeping pace with the cost of training; there would be infrequent raids to Britain for some of the higher-value prizes.

Meanwhile, Aliysa ran in the Irish Oaks to try and gain recompense for her disqualification at Epsom; however, the ground was too firm and, despite finishing second, she returned home badly jarred up. She was declared to run in the St Leger at Doncaster, but the meeting was postponed, so she ended up going straight on to her final start in the Prix de l'Arc de Triomphe. However, it was a rough race and Aliysa suffered more than most in the scrimmaging. She was retired to stud where she became the dam of Desert Story, winner of the Horris Hill and Craven Stakes. She was also the granddam of Alamshar, winner of the Irish Derby and the King George VI and Queen Elizabeth II Stakes, before retiring to His Highness's stud as a sire. Elsewhere, Snow Bride produced Lammtarra, winner of the Derby on only his second start, ridden by Walter Swinburn.

* * *

One cold January morning, Cliff was sent out on the hack with third lot. Stoute told the string to ride down to the wall by Prescott's yard and trot back up Bury Hills. The lads had had enough and argued with Cliff that going halfway would be enough; the boss would never know. Cliff stuck to his guns. Lucky for everybody riding out that lot that he did because, when they reached Prescott's yard, there was Stoute waiting for them, sat in his car on the horse walk.

In 1989, Cliff bought Marsh Stables in Exning. Although, he continued to ride out at Freemason Lodge, he had to retire as head lad now he had his own yard to run. He reflected that being a head lad was probably his least favourite job in racing. It is not an easy position, taking on the responsibility of being in charge of the horses feeding and welfare, as well as trying to manage the staff and who was riding what on a daily basis. Some members of staff had little respect for the trainer or assistants, so it was particularly hard for a head lad. Once again, there was no training when Cliff was doing the job and very few lads wanted to be head lad or travelling lad.

ZILZAL
1986 chesnut colt by Nureyev out of French Charmer

Although Zilzal had an ex-jockey, Charlie Gaston, as his lad, he was ridden on a daily basis by Tommy Whelan who had a great rapport with him because he wasn't a straightforward horse: he was a free sweater and could get very worked up. On the other hand, he was a lazy walker and his trot could be appalling, so he normally skipped that phase of the warm-up exercise! He didn't run as a two-year-old.

One morning, Cliff was riding Zilzal across to the Limekilns but got so fed up with pushing him to keep him up with the two lead horses he was due to be working with that he decided they would trot once they got across the road. The long walk had warmed Zilzal up properly and he trotted perfectly and was happy and relaxed, so they trotted all the way to the gallop! On another occasion, Cliff was riding Zilzal on the Watered Gallop with a lead horse. Unfortunately, the lead horse went so slowly that Cliff was having his arms pulled out! But Cliff didn't dare shout at the lad on the lead horse as that would have set Zilzal off! So, he had to sit and suffer in behind. He eventually pulled out and smoothly picked off the lead horse before going clear. The lad on the lead horse claimed he could have gone with Zilzal if he had wanted to. Cliff pointed out he couldn't even canter fast enough to lead him – the early part of the work was more like a stroll in the park!

At this time, Stoute had a large string and would sometimes split first lot into two groups. On the walking grounds on Warren Hill one morning, the second group were heading to the bottom of the hill from the yard to take their turn to canter when Zilzal noticed several of his stable companions in the first group already cantering up. He ditched his rider and joined the first group of horses: anything to try and get out of his routine daily exercise – he only liked the fast work!

Zilzal didn't make his racecourse debut until 30 May 1989 but he won easily. He was immediately stepped up in class for the 7f Jersey Stakes at Royal Ascot and he took the rise in his stride, moving up two furlongs out to take the lead in a fast-run race and pulling clear. Connections opted to give him more experience with a run in the Van

Gheest Stakes at Newmarket before moving up to Group 1 level in the Sussex Stakes.

In the Sussex Stakes, Zilzal met his stable companion Shaadi, who had won the St James's Palace Stakes at Ascot, as well as Warning (the favourite, now a four-year-old) and Markofdistinction. Zilzal started second-favourite despite his lack of experience. Before the race, the parade took its toll: he sweated up badly and was reluctant to go down to the start but, in the race itself, he showed his quality again, quickening off a strong pace to win by four and a half lengths. After four quick races, Zilzal was given a break and freshened up for an autumn campaign, aiming for the Queen Elizabeth II Stakes followed by a crack at the Breeders' Cup Mile.

The Queen Elizabeth II Stakes was set to be the racing equivalent of the 'Rumble in the Jungle': the young, unproven Zilzal taking on the might of the French in Fabre's Polish Precedent who was unbeaten in seven races that year. In the paddock, it looked as though the competition would be very one-sided. Zilzal was sweating and on his toes as usual and his light frame was completely over-shadowed by the strength and serenity displayed by the French colt as he strolled calmly around the parade ring as though he owned it. Unusually, Swinburn sent Zilzal straight into the lead. He was still making the running coming into the home turn, but then appeared to be swallowed up by the pack. Critics immediately started slating Swinburn for changing tactics on the colt who had previously always come from behind. But Swinburn's tactics were perfect: he was just giving Zilzal a breather and on entering the straight, he quickened away again and ended Polish Precedent's unbeaten run. After the race, Stoute turned to Tommy Whelan and shook his hand: just a mark of respect for a job well done, but a much rarer occurrence than *Bake Off*'s Hollywood handshake!

Sadly, the Breeders' Cup proved a step too far: the pomp and circumstance of the occasion overwhelmed Zilzal; he had stopped at the gate on to the course and was swooped upon by two stalls handlers, manhandled through the gap and thrust into a starting stall. Being drawn wide and missing the break, he gave himself little chance and he was forced to race wide in a rough race. Although closing on the leaders in the short straight, he never looked like winning and he was then hampered, putting an end to his chances once and for all. He eventually finished sixth. He was Horse of the Year and Champion three-year-old in the UK.

Michael Stoute's pleas for the colt to stay in training as a four-year-old, to try and work on his mental immaturity, fell on deaf ears and he was retired to Gainsborough Stud in Kentucky. However, he had fertility issues with short sperm longevity and he wasn't particularly popular with the American breeders. In 1996, he moved to Lanwades Stud, just outside Newmarket, where his fertility statistics significantly improved with the careful management of his mares. He remained at Lanwades until he was retired in 2005 at the age of 19. Among his best progeny were Among Men (Sussex Stakes, Celebration Mile, Jersey Stakes), Faithful Song (Prince of Wales's Stakes), Always Loyal (Poule d'Essai des Pouliches) and Zilzal Zamaan (Ormonde Stakes, Chester). He was also the damsire of No Excuse Needed (Queen Anne Stakes), Darjina (Poule d'Essai des Pouliches) and Hong Kong Horse of the Year, Good Ba Darina. After his retirement, Zilzal was moved to Aston Upthorpe Stud near Didcot where he lived until he was put down at the age of 29 due to the infirmities of old age.

ROCK HOPPER
1987 bay colt by Shareef Dancer out of Cormorant Wood

Rock Hopper was a homebred colt from Maktoum al Maktoum's Gainsborough Stud. He had his own way of going about things. Cliff rode him a few times and didn't have any problems, but his own lad once took him into the ploughed field at Waterhall and couldn't get him to leave it. It's not easy to shift half a ton of horseflesh once it's decided to plant itself!

On his first start as a two-year-old at Nottingham, ridden by Walter Swinburn, Rock Hopper was only fifth over a mile, starting slowly and looking very green. Next time out, back at the same track, he was stepped up to 1m2f and Paul D'Arcy rode him, just getting up on the line to win. It was unusual for a Stoute two-year-old to be running over 1m2f and Stoute obviously thought he might have a 'slow boat' on his hands, so Rock Hopper was sent down the road to former assistant James Fanshawe who had just taken out his licence to train at Pegasus Stables. D'Arcy pleaded the case for Rock Hopper, persuading Stoute that he could be a decent horse, so the colt returned to Beech Hurst and finished the year winning the 1m2f Listed Zetland Stakes at Newmarket impressively, despite hanging to the left. He was ridden by Greville Starkey who had long been associated with Stoute, and it turned out to be Greville's last winner in Britain. Greville's career as a jockey had lasted over 30 years, during which he rode nearly 2,000 winners on the flat and a few more over hurdles, including a Derby and a Prix de l'Arc de Triomphe, the 2,000 Guineas twice and the Oaks twice. He retired at the end of the season and remained with the Stoute stable as a work rider. Greville was known for his sense of humour: his imitation of a Jack Russell barking had grounded a jet for several minutes while crew searched for the missing dog! Sadly, Greville is probably best remembered for Dancing Brave losing the Derby, but he was associated with horses such as Kalaglow, Rousillon, Shirley Heights and Star Appeal during his career. Greville was never champion jockey, but was fourth in the table four times, each time riding over 100 winners for the season. He was a great judge of a horse and generally a good tactician.

Unfortunately, the following season, having won the Lingfield Derby Trial impressively, making him joint favourite for the Derby, Rock Hopper sustained a hairline fracture of his cannon bone. However, he stayed in training and, as a four-year-old, he began to make up for lost time, initially winning the John Porter Stakes at Newbury and following this up with victory in the Jockey Club Stakes at Newmarket. He wasn't a straightforward ride: he had a great turn of foot but would idle once he hit the front, so his victories never looked easy! However, he struck up a great relationship with Pat Eddery. Unfortunately, Pat wasn't available when Rock Hopper ran in the Coronation Cup at Epsom and Willie Carson took the ride. Rock Hopper hung left with him when asked to challenge, but still managed to finish third, beaten less than a length by In The Groove and Terimon. On to Royal Ascot and reunited with Pat Eddery, Rock Hopper finished a short head second to Topanoora in the Hardwicke Stakes. However, the stewards adjudged that Topanoora had bumped Rock Hopper in the final furlong battle and the places were reversed. His next start was the Grand Prix de St Cloud but he couldn't compete with the speed of Epervier Bleu, finishing second, three lengths adrift of the winner. Back to Newmarket for the Prince of Wales's Stakes where Pat Eddery managed to drop Rock Hopper's head right on the line after a ding-dong battle with Mukddaam, ridden by Willie Carson. In order to assist the jockey, Rock Hopper was equipped with blinkers for the King George VI and Queen Elizabeth Diamond Stakes, but he didn't have the class to cope with the likes of Generous, eventually finishing third. Rock Hopper was then given a break, the plan being to return for the Arc with a prep race beforehand. He did himself well during his two-month break and, despite pricking his foot a few days before the race, he took his place in the Cumberland Lodge Stakes at Ascot and lost nothing in a head defeat to Drum Taps. Unfortunately, he returned home very sore and was forced to miss the Arc. Connections, however, did manage one more race with him that year in the Japan Cup where he was out of the placings for the first time in his career.

Rock Hopper stayed in training as a five-year-old. He hadn't raced beyond a mile and a half up to this point and it was decided to try him over a little further and also to try for the elusive Group 1 victory. He started the season with a lacklustre performance in the Jockey Club Stakes at Newmarket finishing well behind Sapience. However, a fortnight later and reunited with his ally Pat Eddery, Rock Hopper turned the tables on Sapience in no uncertain manner in the aptly named Polo Mints Yorkshire Cup. It was a slowly run affair, with Sapience and Ray Cochrane dictating the pace. It being Rock Hopper's first time over 1m6f, he was held up. As Cochrane slowly increased the pace from the front, Eddery cautiously picked his way through the field and quickened past Sapience in the final furlong, winning by a length, with Snurge a further 2½ lengths back in third. Back to Epsom for a second try at the Coronation Cup to try to gain that elusive Group 1, only to be beaten into second by stable companion Saddlers' Hall. On to Ascot and the Hardwicke Stakes for the decider with Sapience. To avoid a repeat of the Yorkshire Cup farce with no pace, Rock Hopper's stable companion Mellaby ran as a pacemaker. This time, Sapience made Rock Hopper pull out all the stops, but it was as though Rock Hopper knew where the finishing line was and his head was in front at the requisite moment, with the third, Luchiroverte, a further three and a half lengths back. Dropped back in trip again for the Coral Eclipse and meeting soft ground for the first time, Rock Hopper failed to shine. The King George VI and Queen Elizabeth Stakes that year was a competitive event, but Rock Hopper, with Walter Swinburn riding, put up a bold show to finish fifth behind runaway winner St Jovite, with stable companions Saddlers' Hall and Opera House in second and third. Rock Hopper was then third in the Geoffrey Freer Stakes at Newbury before heading for his final start in the Irish St Leger at the Curragh. Unfortunately, the ground came up soft and he could only manage fourth place, never able to get close enough to challenge.

Despite his sometimes wayward tendencies in the final furlong of a race, there is no doubt that Rock Hopper was a tough, consistent and genuine racehorse, with seven Pattern race victories and over £500,000 in prize-money to his name. He was retired to Meddler Stud in Kennett near Newmarket before moving to Beechbrook Stud in Ireland. He sired several high-class, middle-distance runners.

* * *

In 1991, Cliff was riding out from Freemason Lodge with one other lad and they were passing Sir Mark Prescott's yard to take the horses up Warren Hill when they heard a huge explosion. Looking up, Cliff saw a parachute floating down from the sky, towards the top of the Bury Road. It carried an escape pod containing the crew members who had ejected. It was 10.20am and second lot was in full swing when a US AirForce F111 bomber on a training flight suffered a malfunction and spun out of control, causing the crew to eject. Cliff watched as the unmanned plane turned above Prescott's and headed up the Bury Road; it flew low over Cumani's yard at Bedford House Stables. Cliff was thinking it was about to crash on his old flat at Freemason Lodge! The plane burst into flames before crashing behind Clarehaven Lodge, in a gap between Clarehaven Stables, where Alex Stewart was training, and narrowly missing the heath men's cottages. The escape pod landed the other side of the road, very close to the water tank at the top of Long Hill. With typical US Airforce efficiency, the aeroplane remains were removed within a couple of hours.

Cliff remembers his 14 years at Stoute's as being the best years of his life in racing due to the quality of horses he was riding on a daily basis. He says, 'Riding good horses is the best feeling you can get.' Cliff rates Michael Stoute as, indubitably, the nicest person he worked for, although there would be many others who wouldn't have had such a good relationship with him as their boss! He feels he was lucky to have worked for three exceptional trainers in Noel Murless, Major Hern and Michael Stoute (in no particular order!).

Michael Stoute was made Knight Bachelor in 1998 for services to tourism in Barbados and to racing. He has won the Epsom Derby six times, won all the British Classics, been champion trainer ten times, as well as winning numerous prestigious races overseas, including various Breeders' Cup races, the Japan Cup twice, the Dubai World Cup and, although primarily a flat trainer, he won the Champion Hurdle at Cheltenham in 1990 with Kribensis.

JOCKEYS

CLIFF NEVER had any help from the other professional jockeys while he was riding; neither Gordon Richards, nor Lester Piggott, nor George Moore spoke to him after his races to give him any help with tactics or riding style. He would even get a lift to the races with Gordon Richards (and his chauffeur) occasionally, but he was never given any tips about how to ride a particular course or horse. The only time Cliff was spoken to by one of his colleagues was after a race at Newmarket: his backside had brushed the saddle coming out of the dip; Gordon Richards appeared in the weighing room, went over to Cliff and, in front of all the other jockeys, said, 'I saw you bounce the saddle once, never let me see you do it again.' Yet, there are plenty of senior jockeys to be seen 'bouncing' their saddles. Indeed, it proved a very effective technique for the likes of Pat Eddery and his style seemed to particularly suit Rock Hopper. In his autobiography, Lester Piggott (who was nine months younger than Cliff) said, 'All the best riders have a natural talent, but they none the less need a good teacher to point them in the right direction at the outset.' Piggott's own father had been a jockey and taught young Lester. Apprentices nowadays, after training at either the British Racing School or Northern Racing College, are given an ex-jockey as a jockey coach who will go through every one of their races with them, discussing the race in depth to see what they could have done differently and whether there would have been a different outcome. It must be a huge help to the young jockeys and it is amazing that Cliff did so well with absolutely no instruction whatsoever.

During his years in racing, Cliff has worked with most of the top jockeys in one way or another. Some were helpful, others less so. There was often no love lost between the top jockeys of their day. Cliff recalls a television interview with Lester Piggott and Willie Carson. Lester was a quiet, thoughtful jockey whereas Carson was always having a joke; he had an answer for everything and an inimitable cackling laugh. Willie had been trying to taunt Lester during the interview, while Lester was being polite and respectful. As they turned to leave, Piggott turned to Carson and suggested he learned to shut up. He also suggested to Carson it might help if he learned to sit still during a race!

An apprentice Frankie Dettori was another to incur the Piggott wrath by constantly being mouthy and showing off to the older jockeys during a race; Piggott leaned over and grabbed him and made him scream – a pretty impressive feat to be riding a racehorse and lean over to grab someone else in the crotch! Frankie had rather more respect for him after that.

On the other hand, Lester Piggott was known for being a bit tight with his cash. As a boy, his mother had drummed into him the importance of being careful with money. One day, while he was still at Murless's, Clive Brittain mentioned to him that St Paddy was going to be a decent horse: Lester duly won on him. He saw Clive in the yard the next day and told him to pop round to his house as he had a present for him. Clive duly did so but didn't receive any cash – it was an old suit; at least it fitted!

Piggott, Murless and Stoute were of the opinion that a horse should enjoy its first race and not be hit with the whip, but that also applied on the gallops. Piggott used to tell Murless's lads off if he saw them using a whip when out at exercise. 'It's no use you hitting him because if you do that now, he'll laugh at me when I hit him in a race.' Lester Piggott was an exceptional horseman and horses would run for him while they would not do a tap for the lads at home. He was supremely competitive as a jockey and would take any ride he could, often switching from the ride he was booked for if he thought another horse in the race had a better chance. Cliff remembers him jocking a young apprentice off in a seller: the kid already had the owner's colours on and Piggott told him to take them off as he was riding the horse. Just for a riding fee! It finished nowhere. More competitively, before the 1984 St Leger he contacted

Commanche Run's owner, Ivan Allen, to take the ride away from Darryl McCargue, telling Darryl it would leave him more time to play tennis. This time, the action had a better result for Piggott with a conclusive victory. Lester Piggott had a remarkable career and is seen by many as one of the greatest jockeys of all time. With over 4,493 individual winners, nine Derby victories among his 30 Classics, 116 Royal Ascot wins and 11 champion jockey titles during his 47 years as a jockey, he spent nearly his entire career at the top of his trade. In 2021, the British Champion Series Hall of Fame was initiated and Lester Piggott was an inaugural inductee: an honour which was thoroughly deserved.

Michael Stoute once suggested to Cliff that Harry Carr was overrated. Cliff retorted that he couldn't have been too bad: he was retained jockey to Capt. Boyd-Rochfort for years and rode many Classic winners as well as winning the Triple Crown on Meld, despite Piggott objecting in the St Leger. Furthermore, he was a nice guy, unlike some others we could mention.

Cliff has always liked to watch jockeys and assess their ability with a view to giving the young ones, particularly the apprentices, a chance. He knows how difficult it is to make it as a jockey. Mick Fitzgerald didn't ride for Stoute but often claims his only riding instruction to a jockey before a race was 'smoothly'. It is an underestimated instruction: you cannot switch a horse off and on: it needs to be balanced to be able to accelerate. So many jockeys lose races by trying to duck and dive through gaps. Very few horses have instant acceleration, particularly if they are on the wrong leg and Thoroughbreds are not trained to switch leads. Often senior jockeys will have a quick word with the lad leading the horse. Although the orders come from the trainer, Cliff thinks it really helps if the lad can tell the jockey a little about the quirks of an individual horse: for instance, when leading up he told Geoff Lewis about Queenborough II and George Moore about Sun Rock and neither would have won if they hadn't known the horse's particular idiosyncrasies.

Cliff watches racing all the time and assesses the jockeys and how 'smoothly' they challenge. He picked out initially James Doyle to ride Proud Chieftain, before James was approached by Roger Charlton and then retained by Godolphin, and finally Hollie Doyle was chosen for Catapult, while she was still an apprentice.

Robert Tart was apprenticed to William Jarvis initially but wasn't getting any rides. A mutual friend introduced him to Cliff and asked him to help. Robert switched his employment to Cliff and moved into Hethersett House! Once Cliff was happy with his riding ability, Rob was sent to Alan Bailey and took his licence out again. All was going well but unfortunately the life of an apprentice jockey is hard graft and Rob found the early mornings too much and began to regularly skip first lots. He got the sack but was lucky enough to get employment with John Gosden as third jockey. In 2017, Gosden's second jockey, Rab Havlin, was injured and Rob was promoted in his absence, getting some fantastic opportunities, such as the winning ride on The Black Princess in the Lancashire Oaks, and his star was rising again. Once more, however, the early mornings began to pall and he was sacked again. Even after getting a second chance with Gosden, he blotted his copybook once more. Having taken a couple of years away from racing, Rob got a job with Jane Chapple-Hyam in 2021 and, catching the eye with a success on his first ride back, has successfully rejuvenated his riding career. Rob has a natural talent as a jockey but his ups and downs are proof that life in racing is not easy.

Cliff learned early on that honest feedback from jockeys and stable staff is crucial. If a horse isn't eating up, the boss needs to know so they can adjust the feeding or exercise accordingly. It's not helpful to tell them what you think they want to hear. Lads have to do as they are told, particularly if they are working a horse on their own. The trainer will have planned the exercise to bring the horse to a peak at race time. If the lad or lass does a half speed when told to canter, the horse will be over the top by the time it has to race; similarly testing a horse out on the gallops in its work can result in a lacklustre performance at the races. Cliff has a saying which he lives by: 'A liar is worse than a thief.'

BREAKING AND PRE-TRAINING

CLIFF BOUGHT Marsh Stud in 1989 and renamed it Marsh Stables. The area was initially known as 'The Swamp' and was part of a large manor attached to the church. The river through Exning rises at Seven Springs in Newmarket and flows through the Swamp. It frequently used to flood the paddocks on either side. The manor grounds extended from the church, through the Swamp, across where the A14 now runs and right up to Newmarket. Part of the original clunch boundary wall still remains, along with the 17th century, Grade II-listed, square dovecote for the manor (also built in clunch) and the latter is part of Marsh Stables. The Jockey Club bought the manor from the original owner and leased it to Mat Dawson when he cut down his string and moved to Exning from Heath House Stables in Newmarket. Marsh Stables was to become his private stud. Fred Archer had been apprenticed to Mat Dawson from the age of 11, while Dawson was training in Newmarket. In 1927, the Jockey Club sold a part of the substantial Exning portfolio, including Marsh Stud, to a Jockey Club steward for £1,200. Much of this area has now been built over and forms St Martin's Close. However, the Jockey Club have retained the area alongside the A14 and the Exning allotments.

Cliff hadn't intended to buy a yard, but Alan Gibson, a well-known Newmarket estate agent, rang him up out of the blue and told him to buy it! The cottage which was to become Cliff's home had been a barn and was converted just before Cliff bought the yard. The original residence was a bungalow attached to St Martin's Close, but Cliff sold this on separately. He also didn't take the furthest paddock from the yard as the vendor wanted an additional £50,000 for it. It was eventually sold for £20,000 to Sue McGuiness, who lived round the corner on Ducks Lane and had ponies, so it was useful for her to be able to keep them just over the road from her house.

There were already quite a few trainers based in Exning when Cliff moved into Marsh Stables. They included Dave Thom (Harraton Court), Peter Feilden (in what is now Queen Alexandra) and Bill Holden (Exeter Stables). Roger Harris was also training from a small yard, Priory Stables, which was opposite the church in Exning, but to make ends meet he also had a horsebox business, often taking horses across to the continent. He offered to take Cliff's horses if he had any European runners. Luckily, Cliff preferred to keep his horses racing in the UK because Roger Harris was caught importing cannabis resin under the floorboards of his horsebox! He and his business partner, Terence Miles, were estimated to have imported nearly £4m worth of cannabis resin and, in 1998, they were sentenced to seven and five years in prison respectively.

As soon as Cliff told Michael Stoute he had bought the yard, Stoute said he'd like to use it as his pre-training yard with Cliff in charge. Stoute initially supplied the lads to ride out his horses which were at Marsh Stables and the staff would go to Exning for their third lot. Meanwhile, it meant Stoute could keep Cliff's expertise riding out first and second lots at Freemason before the latter returned to Marsh Stables to supervise the third lot with the Stoute horses.

Cliff built the indoor school himself. The supports are old telegraph poles and the men who delivered them kindly set them into the ground, each pole being held up by a cherry-picker while they were bolted together to hold them in place. Jean-Luc Chouvier, who was a stable lad with Michael Stoute at the time but is now an internationally renowned equine dentist, came to the yard to help Cliff put in the fence posts and attach the plywood boards around the sides of the school. One day, when Cliff was loose lunging, as he normally does, one of the panels blew out! Luckily, it fell outwards and not into the school. The horse didn't notice it had gone, so Cliff was able to retrieve the horse and put him safely back in the stable before replacing the panel. Jean-Luc swears it wasn't one of the panels he put in! Cliff put the roof up on his own. He did realise, once he was up there, that it was not one of his brightest ideas because it was quite high! Despite all this, the lunge ring is still there after more than 30 years, so they can't have done too bad a job. Jean-Luc continued to work for Cliff, riding many of the Stoute yearlings, and even looked after the house and yard one winter when Cliff and Sue were in Florida. However, following Cliff's make-do-and-mend philosophy, a lot of the guttering and downpipes around the yard were held up with blue bandage tape!

Cliff's next job was to get the garden dug. There was always a rumour around Newmarket that Cliff kept a stash of spare cash from his betting in a tin in the garden. Cliff was known to be a shrewd punter and he certainly saved plenty of money from his successful bets, hence he could afford to buy Marsh Stables. He let the lads discover that he had buried the tin, with cash in it, in the garden at the back of the yard. A few days later and the garden had been nicely dug over but no tin had been found. There never was one!

To keep the number of mice down, Cliff found himself a kitten. She became very attached to Cliff and when he came home from riding out at Stoute's, she would rush out from behind a chair and throw herself at him, attaching herself around his leg with her claws and refusing to let go. Luckily, he still had his top boots on and he learned not to take them off until this ritual had been performed each day! He brought his terrier, Suzie, with him from Freemason but also acquired Skunk. She was a sweet dog who needed rehoming and he was persuaded to take her by his head lad at the time. Since she was a possible German Shepherd/Collie cross, Cliff took her on as a potential guard dog. However, she was far too friendly for this role and used to go walkabout around the village looking for new people to meet and greet!

Cliff initially took in horses from a selection of Newmarket trainers. One of the first horses he was sent had a reputation for bolting across the heath whenever it went out. Cliff wasn't going to risk one of his staff on a runaway, so he made up a Guy Fawkes-style dummy which he tied on to the saddle while the horse was still in its stable. He put the lunge rein on, planning to take the horse into the school. The minute it walked out of the stable, the horse bolted across the yard and galloped like the clappers into the first paddock. Cliff had to let go! He waited until it came to a halt and stood still for a few minutes; the dummy had slid round and down one side. The horse was standing frozen in a corner of the paddock, allowing Cliff to quietly remove the dummy. He didn't use it again, but the horse certainly got smaller feeds after that and gradually started to calm down. The trainer took him back, but even with the best lads on board he still went his own way – usually straight across the gallops at 90 degrees to everyone else and up over the Devils Dyke! He did get to the races eventually where he was ridden in a hackamore with no bit. The jockey got to the start safely and eventually finished about fifth or sixth, but the horse was evidently nothing out of the ordinary and was too dangerous to persevere with.

KRIBENSIS
1984 grey gelding by Henbit out of Aquaria

Kribensis was bought by Sheikh Mohammed's racing manager, Anthony Stroud, for 125,000 guineas as a foal for a Flat-racing campaign. He was never over big, even for a flat horse; however, as a two-year-old he was very colty and always had to lead the string. Unfortunately for him, one morning at the top of Warren Hill, he went too far and pulled a lad, who had gone in front of him, off his horse. His next trip, later that same day, was to the vet's to be castrated. Luckily, this seemed to settle him down. He showed some class on the Flat, breaking the 8f track record for two-year-olds at Ayr on his second start despite being hampered. Unfortunately, he returned home with a hairline fracture of his cannon, strangely enough a similar injury to the one his sire, Henbit, had suffered when winning the Derby. However, Kribensis raced on while Henbit was retired to stud. As a three-year-old, he won his first two starts at Salisbury and Sandown before running creditably to finish third in the King George V Handicap at Royal Ascot. Despite these achievements, his forte was to be over hurdles. Despite having a combined licence, Stoute didn't really train any National Hunt horses, but he had spent time with Harry Thomson Jones and Stoute's assistant at the time, James Fanshawe, had come from David Nicholson, 'The Duke's', academy, so they decided to pop Kribensis over some straw bales in the paddock. He took to it like a duck to water. Steve Smith-Eccles was called upon to school him up at the Links over the baby hurdles, using the hack No Bombs as a lead horse. Kribensis was a natural and the decision was made to aim for Cheltenham! It bought a buzz to the yard that was normally missing during the long, dark days of winter. There was a distinct Flat racing season then, between March and November, with no all-weather racing.

Smith-Eccles rode Kribensis in his first hurdle race at Doncaster and he won, although not impressively. However, for the next race at Huntingdon, Smith-Eccles was unavailable and was replaced by The Duke's retained jockey, Richard Dunwoody. What a partnership they became! Winning at Huntingdon, they were on course for the 1988 Triumph Hurdle. After just two hurdle races and only six weeks after his hurdling debut, Kribensis was sent off a 6-1 chance, but he hurdled well and surged up the hill to victory. KB briefly returned to a flat campaign for the summer, but the Champion Hurdle would be his main aim. However, he needed more experience. Two wins at Newbury, one in the Gerry Feilden, and victory in the Christmas Hurdle at Kempton put him on course for Cheltenham. However, despite leading into the last, he tired up the hill in the rain-softened ground. It was a big ask after all for a horse straight out of his novice campaign: not many manage, with See You Then (1985), Katchit (2008) and Espoir d'Allen (2019) being the only recent notable exceptions. In autumn 1989, after a short break with Cliff at Marsh Stables to freshen up after his flat campaign, Kribensis set off on his preparation for Cheltenham once more, winning the Fighting Fifth (Newcastle), the Christmas Hurdle and the Kingwell at Wincanton before finally heading to Cheltenham once again. This time, all went to plan. Challenging between the final two hurdles, Kribensis and Dunwoody forged into the lead, and despite a rather awkward, cat-like jump over the last victory in the Champion Hurdle was theirs. The second horse home was Nomadic Way, trained for Robert Sangster by Barry Hills; two primarily Flat-based owner/ trainer combinations leading the field home at Cheltenham was an unusual sight! Sadly, we were not to see the best of Kribensis again after that. Shortly before trying to defend his crown, he bled badly at home.

He was turned out for a year and on his next visit to Cheltenham he badly skinned a hind leg, catching it on a hurdle.

Once it was decided to retire Kribensis from racing, a new home was found for him as a lady's hunter in Rutland. He returned to Marsh Stables to be let down and prepare for the hunting season. Kribensis didn't take to hunting and let everybody around him know about it! His will to win would come to the fore as he would try to kick any horse that wanted to pass him out on the hunting field. He returned to Freemason Lodge where he took up residence as the head lad's hack. He was very spoiled for the rest of his life: he developed such a liking for Yarmouth rock that any lads going racing at Yarmouth had to bring some back for KB as he was known, and fans would send some through the post. Sadly, having reached the grand age of 23, he died of cancer in 2007.

* * *

Old friends and their families featured strongly among Cliff's head lads over the years. John McGarr was one of the first, having returned to the UK from Australia and John Snaith, son of the jockey Willie Snaith, was another.

In 1993, Cliff was to meet his second wife, Sue Cawthorn, thanks to some subtle matchmaking by his sister-in-law Rene, the wife of older brother Dave. Sue was working for Tanner's Frozen Foods and had a meeting with the manager of De Niro's night club in town. She had arrived early, so was browsing the shops and went into the RSPCA Charity Shop where Rene was working. The two of them got chatting and somehow the conversation turned to ponies: Sue's daughter, Zoe, had a rescue pony with bad feet and Rene recommended that Sue should consult Cliff and that she would get Cliff to call. A week later, Sue's phone rang. Cliff didn't bother to introduce himself but launched straight into the recommended treatment of Stockholm tar and cowpats. Eventually, Sue realised what he was talking about! Sue had recently helped a friend with the catering at a charity cricket match and had the friend's knives and baking tins in the boot of her car. The friend had asked her to return them to her at Newmarket races. Sue had never been racing, so Rene again recommended Cliff would be the person to ask. Sue plucked up the courage to call Cliff and he grudgingly agreed to take her. Sue turned up at Marsh Stables where Cliff was waiting for her. His first words to her were: 'Here's your badge: if anyone asks, you are Mrs Lines.' Sue thought that was a bit quick, but then discovered it was the badge meant for the trainer's wife! However, despite this dodgy start, the relationship blossomed and many years later he did actually propose.

While they were still courting, Sue invited Cliff and a friend to a fancy-dress barbecue. They decided to go as Arab sheikhs; however, Cliff's friend, John Gowing, was rather a large man and his sheet was rather short, whereas Cliff's reached the ground. They needed to stop for petrol on the way to the party in Bassingbourn, near Cambridge, and got some very strange looks from other customers in the petrol station! Cliff used his outfit for future fancy dress parties, but John quickly disposed of his!

It wasn't long before Sue and her younger daughter, Zoe, moved into Marsh Stables. On the day they moved in, Cliff walked in for breakfast after first lot to see Zoe standing in the kitchen, a saw in one hand, skirting board in the other! Sue had wanted to fit her own fridge under the countertop, but it stuck out. Zoe had ambitions to be a structural engineer and, luckily, removing a piece of skirting board to fit a fridge was well within her capabilities. Zoe and failed guard dog Skunk quickly became firm friends. Zoe would take Skunk for a walk to an abandoned airstrip in the village, strap on her roller-skates and grab hold of Skunk's lead. Skunk would set off at full pelt down the runway! Zoe was also a keen amateur polo player and spent some time in Argentina on a polo ranch. Here, she learned the polo technique of bandaging tendons: a vital skill in polo, and it was very different to the way it was done in racing. The end of the bandage is run down the tendon and then wrapped anti-clockwise around the leg with the crossovers of the bandage on the bone at the front of the leg, rather than around the tendon. To Cliff, this makes a lot of sense as the tender tendon is protected. So many people put bandages on the wrong way round and, if they are done up too tightly, the crossovers can cut and damage the tendon.

Zoe's bedroom was above the stables. She remembers one horse which seemed to get cast every night: she regularly had to go and help it right itself. One night, it had got particularly well stuck, with all four feet against the wall. She couldn't manage on her own, so Sue came to help. They still weren't strong enough to move the horse, so went and woke Cliff. He just said, 'Pull it round by its tail,' and went straight back to sleep! Eventually, he had to get up and help because it was stuck at such an angle it wasn't possible to roll it, push it or pull it!

Cliff and Sue regularly held yard barbecues for staff and friends at Marsh Stables. Everyone would sit around the yard on hay bales and Cliff would take the children for rides on a small tractor and trailer he used around the paddocks. They had a full tour of the heath from Exning, across a little wooden bridge over the river, through the tunnel under the A14, to the Racecourse Side gallops, but they thoroughly enjoyed it! One year, Zoe brought a friend along who was registered blind. Cliff had done a couple of tours and fancied a burger, so tossed the keys over to her: 'You take them now' and off they went again! Despite Cliff's pyromania tendencies as a child, he was initially allowed to be in charge of the barbecue; however, his fascination with flames meant that all the food was charred outside and raw inside! Luckily, Johnny McGarr's years in Australia were not wasted and he took charge, teaching everybody that bringing sausages to the boil in a pan of water before putting them on the barbecue stops the skins splitting: a handy tip for those who listened! Cliff's cookery skills have never quite made cordon bleu level: after all, he is the person who tried to make Yorkshire puddings with 20oz of flour, having misread 2oz! More recently, he heated a pot of hummus in the microwave and ate it with a fork, thinking it was curry.

Cliff's attempts at repairs around the yard didn't always go well. Zoe recalls that in the late-90s, she was helping John McGarr clean up in the yard, while Cliff was playing around with a small tractor he had. Suddenly, she heard a bang like a car backfiring. John went to see what had happened and Cliff was stood with his hands over his face. The battery had exploded and Cliff thought he had got acid in his face. John dragged him into the yard and washed his face and hands over and over again before taking him to the doctor's. It turned out to be water rather than acid, but the doctor had to give him eye drops: there were silvery flecks in his eyes for days afterwards – presumably tiny pieces of plastic, but it made him look like a character from *Dr Who*!

One morning, Cliff was riding out and left Sue with instructions to give one of the colts the contents of a bowl, which he would leave outside the horse's box, half an hour before the vet was due. Sue was dressed to go to work in her suit and heels but went down to the yard. The bowl was outside the horse's box but was completely empty! Cliff returned and asked Sue whether she had done as he had requested, but she told him there had been nothing in the bowl. Cliff was baffled until he noticed the dogs. Skunk was fine, running around as normal, but Sue's Lhasa Apso, Honey, was very wobbly walking back towards the house. As she got close to Sue, she just collapsed in a heap on her belly, a leg stuck out from each corner! The bowl had had two ACP tablets (tranquilisers) in it. Sue picked her up and carried her up to the house. Honey was completely out of it! Sue rang the vet who said just to put her in the recovery position and let her sleep. Twelve hours later, Honey woke up!

FUJIYAMA CREST
1992 bay gelding by Roi Danzig out of Snoozy Time

Fujiyama Crest was bought by John Ferguson for one of his Japanese clients, a Mr Seisuke Hata, who wanted to have a racehorse in England. He was a tall horse and was sent to Cliff to be broken in before being transferred to Michael Stoute for his racing career.

When Fuji arrived, Sean Posner was helping Cliff at Marsh Stables. Sean Posner's father, Merv, had been a leading jockey in Australia and Sean was following suit with only a few months more of his apprenticeship to run until, in January 1987, Sean had a bad fall while riding at his home racecourse, Ascot in Perth. His mount stumbled badly, throwing Sean head first into the ground, giving the riders behind no chance to avoid the stricken jockey. Sean was airlifted to hospital where doctors found he had a depressed fracture of the skull, which resulted in a degree of paralysis to his left arm, so he was unable to continue to ride professionally. The horse merely suffered a lost racing plate.

* * *

Sean met Cliff's son, Richard, through a mutual friend while Richard was visiting Perth. When asked what he planned to do, Sean said he fancied travelling, so Richard gave him Cliff's address and soon afterwards Sean arrived at Marsh Stables for a short visit. The boys had forgotten to mention these plans to Cliff, but Sean eventually stayed for five months! In view of Sean's injury, Cliff was rather dubious about allowing him to ride out, but Sean was desperate. Eventually, Cliff allowed him to ride out on Conkers, the hack, who was probably the worst ride in the yard. Sean used to place the reins in his left hand in the correct position, then, using his right hand, he would squeeze the fingers of the left hand together until the reins were firmly in his grip. Conkers was a solid pony cob with his own ideas about how he should be ridden, but Cliff legged Sean up and, with Cliff on Ball Gown, they headed on to the heath. Conkers bolted! Ball Gown had to become the hack and gallop after the pony and pull him up! Sean subsequently fell off a two-year-old filly and needed to be legged back up by Bob Champion, so it was agreed that a two-year-old Fujiyama Crest might be the safest conveyance for him and Sean became his regular pilot until Fuji moved to the Michael Stoute yard.

When Cliff went abroad to visit Richard that spring, he left Sean in charge of the house. Sean managed to get himself an invitation to the local Hunt Ball and found Cliff's evening suit hanging in the wardrobe. Luckily it fitted, so off he went. When Cliff returned and went to get his evening suit, it was hung back in the wardrobe but covered in white dog hairs! However, Cliff wasn't all innocence as Sean clearly remembers a punting trip in Cambridge where Cliff tied the punt to a 'No Mooring' sign when they stopped for a picnic!

Another of Sean's abiding memories of his trip to England was spending time in the company of Cliff and Greville Starkey. Neither of them can remember where they were or what they were celebrating but only that they were drinking Guinness, which probably explains the memory failures! It may have been as a precursor to Sean's trip to Ireland with ex-jockey Johnny Roe, who introduced him to such legends as John Oxx and Dermot Weld.

As a two-year-old, Fuji had three runs without showing much promise and as a result he was gelded over the winter. However, at three, his strength was beginning to catch up with his size and he won his first start that season at Folkestone, despite jinking in the final furlong. He followed this victory up with a win at Windsor before a couple of below-par efforts, including one at Ascot where he was nearly put through the rails. However, he finished his three-year-old season in style with consecutive victories in staying handicaps at Chester, Sandown and finally the Gordon Carter Handicap at Ascot. He appeared to have lost his confidence when among other horses following the incident at Ascot, so for the last three races he was allowed to make his own running, which helped him regain his self-belief. However, he was still only rated as a decent staying handicapper: his glory moment was to come the following year.

It took Fuji time to come to himself as a four-year-old, but he certainly chose the right day to show he was back to his best. He had been carrying top weight of 10st around in some minor handicaps but had finished third with that weight at Kempton, before running respectably in front of his owner at Royal Ascot to finish ninth in the 2m4f Ascot Handicap, but then was tailed off in the Northumberland Plate at Newcastle. He was given a break and freshened up with the hope that he would put on a better show when attempting to retain his Gordon Carter Handicap victory. Stoute's Ascot runners at that time would travel the day before. However, one of his runners on 28 September 1996 was Soviet Line, a six-year-old gelding who was a very good miler but could be quirky and didn't like being away from home. Pandering to his requirements, Stoute's runners that day were sent off to Ascot early in the morning on race day. When the betting shops opened later that morning, Fujiyama Crest was available at 16-1. Despite his patchy form, the jockey Frankie Dettori, who had won on him the previous year when he was carrying 8st 8lbs, stayed loyal. This year Fuji had 9st 10lbs to carry. Fuji's lad, Derek Heeney, had faith that his mate was back to his best, despite his not having won for a year, and asked his wife to put a bet on for him on her way home. However, the bookmaker's shop was busy when Floss finished work, so she went to do her weekly shop, planning to return to the bookie's to place the bet on her way back to do evening stables. While Floss was shopping,

Frankie was doing something unheard off. He won the first race on Wall Street, not an unexpected victory. However, the second race played into the hooves of Diffident, being slowly run and this 12-1 shot duly provided Dettori's second winner of the day. The third race was billed as a duel between Cumani's good miler, Mark of Esteem, and Cecil's filly, Bosra Sham. Mark of Esteem proved the better on the day and Frankie was three from three. Race number four was a handicap, never easy to win, particularly when you are carrying top weight, which Decorated Hero was. However, at 7-1, he was obviously not a forlorn hope and he kept the ball rolling. Four from four. How long could Dettori keep this up? Race five was Fatefully's turn: she was better fancied at 7-4. Ray Cochrane got Abeyr's head up to Fatefully's girth but couldn't get past. Five from five. Next up was Lochangel, a daughter of the speedy Lochsong with whom Frankie had had so much success. Lochangel didn't let the side down. It was all up to Fuji: his price had been slashed into 2-1, but he couldn't possibly win, could he? Floss returned to the bookies and decided the price wasn't worth taking. Fuji wasn't really likely to win despite Derek's faith in him. He did: history was made and the story of Frankie Dettori's Magnificent Seven was written. The stunned bookmakers had lost over £30 million. For once, racing made the headlines and pictures of Fuji, Derek and Frankie were on the front pages of all the newspapers the following day.

Fujiyama Crest was eventually sold to Nicky Henderson to go jumping, but he never really took to it, despite winning a 2m6f hurdle at Stratford the following year. He then changed hands a couple of times but, in 2000, was entered in the Ascot Sales. Derek saw the entry and contacted Frankie, who had an offer accepted on the old horse. Fuji joined Decorated Hero at Frankie's own yard and lived his life out there as a pampered pet.

Some years later, in 2006/7, Sean spent a couple of weeks at St Pete Beach in Florida with Cliff and Sue over the winter. Cliff has a terrible habit of poking your arm while he is telling you a story to ensure you are paying attention. Unfortunately for poor Sean, Cliff was sat on his wrong side and was poking his bad arm. Sean slowly, surreptitiously, removed the cushion from behind his back and slipped it over his arm for protection. Cliff carried on with the story and didn't even notice!

* * *

Embracing was a filly, by Reference Point out of Hug Me, who was sent to Cliff to be broken. She developed a very large haematoma on her quarters, which needed fomenting twice daily before the vets could lance it. She went on to win four races consecutively as a staying handicapper before retiring to stud.

PILSUDSKI
1992 bay colt by Polish Precedent out of Cocotte

A homebred from the Weinstock's Ballymacoll Stud, Pilsudski was sent to Cliff to be broken in before joining the Stoute yard. A backward colt, Pilsudski found life as a two-year-old was hard work. Although he liked to help sweep the yard, exercise was exhausting and he would often spend most of the day lying down, fast asleep in his box! He was exactly the late-developing type that Michael Stoute excelled with. He had two unremarkable, educational runs at the backend of the season as a two-year-old. He was always going to develop and improve, but he met with interference when challenging on his first run as a three-year-old and was beaten into second place. Nothing went right for him in the King George V Handicap at Ascot next time, so it wasn't until his fifth start that Pilsudski eventually got his head in front, winning a competitive Newmarket handicap under Kevin Darley, but he quickly followed that up with an impressive victory in the Tote Gold Trophy at Goodwood. He then had a couple of months off and, showing the benefit of the break, he looked rather burly for his final start as a three-year-old, taking on older horses for the first time. He was not disgraced in finishing third, having been given plenty to do, behind the more experienced Taufan's Melody at Ascot.

Pilsudski strengthened again from three to four years old and he was thrown in at the deep end first time out, taking on more experienced stable companion Singspiel in the Gordon Richard's Stakes at Sandown. Pudsey showed the expected improvement in form, with only Singspiel too good for him on that day and, with Singspiel not in opposition,

Pilsudski won the Brigadier Gerard at the same course on his next start. Unfortunately, the firm ground in combination with racing too freely at Royal Ascot scuppered his chances in the Prince of Wales's Stakes. He was given a short break and returned to winning ways in the Royal Whip at the Curragh. Back on track, he headed to Baden-Baden to compete for some of the good prize-money available there in the Grosser Preis von Baden. His travelling companion, Luso, from Clive Brittain's yard, sustained an injury on the plane and was withdrawn from the race, leaving Pilsudski to show the Germans that his starting price of 11-1 was just plain rude and he beat the previous year's winner, the appropriately named Germany, into second place! This victory over 1m4f meant Pilsudski would challenge for the Prix de l'Arc de Triomphe. The French also showed little respect and Pilsudski went off at 22-1 for the Arc; however, he did find the French-trained Helissio had too much speed for him, but it was a cracking effort to finish second in that high-class race. The dismal record of Arc winners and runners-up in the Breeders' Cup did not deter connections from taking that route. Pilsudski broke the trend, beating stable companion Singspiel into second place, the pair drawing clear of the third-placed Swain. He was Stoute's first Breeders' Cup winner, with the trainer having achieved no success with such excellent horses as Shadeed, Sonic Lady and Zilzal. It would be fair to say that Stoute has now pretty well cracked the Breeders' Cup nut however! On this occasion, it was a tearful event with Pilsudski's part-owner, Simon Weinstock, having died earlier in the year from cancer and the emotion of a difficult year for Walter Swinburn coming to the fore. It was Walter's crowning achievement that year, having suffered a horrific fall in Hong Kong early in the year. He had spent a long time on the side lines recuperating from the multiple skull fractures and associated head injuries that were ultimately to lead to his premature death.

Pilsudski stayed in training as a five-year-old. He had developed into a big, strong, good-looking colt and he didn't let anybody down, continuing to show improved form throughout the year. Pilsudski started the season in the Prix Ganay at Longchamp. However, he had done himself well during his winter break and he was again beaten by Helissio. Giving away weight all round in the Hardwicke Stakes at

Royal Ascot, Pilsudski found Saeed bin Suroor's Predappio half a length too good for him. Back to Sandown for the Coral Eclipse, Pilsudski was at last stripping fit and beat Derby winner Benny The Dip and Bosra Sham, who started at odds on, having won impressively at Ascot. It was back to Ascot for the King George VI and Queen Elizabeth Diamond Stakes, but a torrential rainstorm on the morning of the race turned the ground soft and Swain found the demand on stamina more to his liking than the rest of the field. Pilsudski was unable to find his usual turn of foot but stayed on in the final furlong to take second with Helissio in third and Singspiel in fourth. Predappio, his Hardwicke conqueror, only beat one home. Victory in the Irish Champion Stakes at Leopardstown over the Irish Derby winner, Desert King, put Pilsudski on track for another attempt at the Prix de l'Arc de Triomphe. Unfortunately for Pilsudski, the French three-year-old ace, Peintre Celebre, was heading the same way. Helissio made the running, but Peintre Celebre was five lengths clear of the field at the line. Pilsudski again finished second in the great all-age European championship race, with Helissio and Swain in a photograph for the minor placings.

There was little between Saeed bin Suroor and Stoute at the top of the trainers' championship at that late stage of the season, so Pilsudski, having shown his wellbeing at home, was called out 13 days later for the Champion Stakes at Newmarket to try and clinch the title for his trainer. Of course he obliged, romping home two lengths clear of a small but classy field in what was described in some newspapers as a 'demolition job'. Michael Stoute won his fifth trainer's championship, largely down to the efforts of the five-year-olds Pilsudski and Singspiel, although Entrepreneur had also contributed with victory in the 2,000 Guineas before breaking down when odds-on in the Derby. The championship is assessed purely on earnings in Great Britain; however, the two older colts had also earned more than £2.6 million overseas! Unsurprisingly, Pilsudski was nominated as European Champion Older Horse and polled 21 of the 23 votes available in the British Racehorse of the Year award.

Pilsduski wasn't finished yet and he travelled on. While the form of his final race, the Japan Cup, may not be his best, it certainly showed his grittiness and determination to win, sticking his neck out with his ears flat back to repel the challenge of Japanese-trained filly Air Groove. Pilsudski returned home to Freemason Lodge to complete the quarantine requirements for permanent export to Japan, having been sold to stand there at stud. It was a sad farewell from the yard to such a kind yet tough horse, but the Japanese had promised plenty of his preferred extra-strong mints! After six seasons in Japan, Pilsudski returned to Ireland to stand at the Irish National Stud before moving to Anngrove Stud as a dual-purpose sire.

KAYF TARA
1994 bay colt by Sadlers Wells out of Colorspin

Another horse who benefitted from the individual care and attention the residents of Marsh Stables received was Kayf Tara. He was a very backward horse and not the easiest ride as he had a particularly bad habit of rearing when going out on to the heath. Cliff would often make Sue, in her high heels and ready to leave for work, chase him down the horse walk with a broom! This attention obviously paid dividends because, although he didn't see a racecourse until July of his three-year-old career, he quickly impressed, winning comfortably on his second start in an Ascot maiden. He was then put away to continue maturing, but at the end of that season, Kayf Tara was transferred to Saeed bin Suroor under the Godolphin banner. He went on to win the Ascot Gold Cup twice, the Irish St Leger twice and the Yorkshire Cup, and was Champion European Stayer in 1998, 1999 and 2000. Injury eventually brought his career to an end and he was retired to Overbury Stud with National Hunt horses such as 2016 King George-winner Thistlecrack and champion chaser Special Cargo being among his most successful offspring. After 20 seasons at stud, declining fertility led to his retirement at the age of 26. He has remained at Overbury Stud since his retirement.

* * *

Michael Stoute used to come and check on his horses at Marsh Stables every week, so he knew exactly how Cliff was doing with them. He normally took them back over to the main yards at Beech Hurst and Freemason Lodge once Cliff felt they were ready to start work. One year, however, his yards were full, so he asked Cliff to kick on with a couple of them and three were selected to start faster work at Marsh Stables. One was showing some ability and was taken back to Freemason to prepare for a race. She was Karasta.

KARASTA
1998 bay filly by Lake Coniston out of Karliyka

Having done a little work with Cliff at Marsh Stables, Karasta was ready for the racecourse soon after returning to Freemason Lodge. However, she was an extremely tall filly at nearly 17 hands as a two-year-old. There was some disdain among the crowd around the parade ring when she made her debut at Newmarket, dwarfing her competitors and with connections being asked by the crowd whether she was their next Cheltenham horse! Her faster paces, however, were something to behold: she was extremely well balanced and a long raking stride came naturally to her, soon putting the doubters in their place. Karasta won her Newmarket maiden under Richard Quinn with ease, starting odds-on favourite, she drew into the lead a furlong out and quickened clear of a classy field. The reward for Marsh Stables was a tin of biscuits to share between all the staff.

Stepped up in class for the Group 3 May Hill Stakes at Doncaster, and ridden by Johnny Murtagh, she again impressed. Making smooth headway and quickening clear of the field, she had enough in reserve to jink at a photographer standing near the finishing line! She again started favourite for the Prix Marcel Boussac at Longchamp on Arc day. Unfortunately, she appeared to lose her hind legs early on and didn't seem to relish the track, but was still able to finish second to Pascal Bary's Amonita. Sadly, and somewhat surprisingly, Karasta didn't train on as a three-year-old, only beating two home in the 1,000 Guineas at Newmarket when favourite. A better effort at the Curragh saw her finish five and three-quarter lengths sixth behind Imagine before a final below-par effort in the Jersey Stakes at Royal Ascot saw her retired to stud. Not surprisingly with her size, she has produced a couple of decent National Hunt horses in Solstice Sun and Karasenir, rather than excelling as a Flat-racing mare.

TRAINING

CLIFF PUT into practice what he had learned from his years with Murless and Stoute. The horses were always treated as individuals and with kindness and respect, which paid dividends. Although at first he didn't hold a licence, Cliff trained a couple of horses at Marsh Stables and put them into a nearby trainer's yard about a fortnight before their races. However, Cliff was responsible for all the planning and preparation involved in the horses' racing careers. Cliff first held a trainer's licence in 1993 when Michael Stoute had no horses for him to pre-train. However, at the end of that year, Stoute wanted to use Marsh Stables again, so Cliff handed his licence back in. Despite having horses in training in the meantime, it wasn't until 2011 that he resumed training under his own name.

One of the first horses Cliff had in training was Aquarian Prince, whom he bought from Peter Savill for Richard Lines to ride. Cliff left him in training with Richard Casey in Dullingham, who had already finished second with him three times as a two-year-old. Casey had worked for Michael Stoute, and his wife, Diane, was Stoute's secretary for many years. Cliff would help Casey by riding work from time to time. Aquarian Prince was entered to run at Brighton on 20 June 1988, but he was ridden by John Reid – Richard Lines had taken a ride elsewhere! The horse looked beaten coming up the hill, but Reid pulled his whip through and the horse suddenly took off and won! Aquarian Prince had a reputation for being a bit of a non-trier and Brighton often seems to suit those horses for some reason. Gill Richardson (a leading bloodstock agent at the time) then bought the horse from Cliff for £6,000. Among the Casey horses, Cliff also rode out Hogmanay, a successful jumper, but he could be a strong puller so would work on his own. One morning, Cliff was working him 'across the flat' on Racecourse Side but as he stood up in his irons to pull up, Hogmanay showed no sign of slowing down. Cliff managed to turn him, so he ran across the cricket pitch, rather than across the main road, then hooked him back and he managed to stop him. But the cricket pitch was a little rough for a few seasons! Cliff also often rode Petrullo (1985 bay colt by Electric out of My Therape). The Caseys and Petrullo's owners, the Websters, kindly invited Cliff along to the 1989 Irish Champion Stakes at Phoenix Park in their plane. Petrullo ran a fantastic race to finish third behind Michael Jarvis' Carroll House, who went on to win the Prix de l'Arc de Triomphe.

TIGER SHOOT
1987 bay gelding by Indian King out of Grand Occasion

Tiger Shoot was originally owned by John Greetham, a Norfolk farmer who was a long-standing owner with Michael Stoute and William Jarvis. He only had a few broodmares, but they produced some nice horses such as Whitewater Affair (winner of the Prix de Pomone at Deauville; she also finished second in the Yorkshire Oaks and third in the Hardwick Stakes at Royal Ascot and the Irish St Leger). Tiger was sent to Cliff to be broken, but he sustained a bone chip in one knee. Arthroscopic surgery on horses was pretty much unknown at that time (although it is very common now) and Mr Greetham was advised to have him put down, but Cliff wasn't prepared for this to happen, so Mr Greetham let him have the horse.

Unsurprisingly, Tiger Shoot was unraced as a two-year-old. Initially in training under Richard Shaw's licence, when he moved to Dubai, Cliff switched Tiger to Peter Feilden, who trained in Exning. Cliff was up with the lark and would ride out Tiger Shoot before making his way into town to ride out first lot with the Stoute string. Tiger won his fourth start at Lingfield in a ten-runner maiden in the December. Walking in front of the stands after saddling up, Peter asked Cliff whether he fancied the horse. Cliff had worked Tiger with one of Peter's good horses the week before and Tiger had gone ten lengths clear!

Cliff couldn't understand why Peter was asking whether he would win; however, he gave him the nod and Peter disappeared to the Tote. Tiger bolted up!

Tiger Shoot didn't reappear until June the following year and Cliff is particularly proud of the coup he pulled off on 3 June 1991 at Leicester in the Paul Bentham Westminster Agent Handicap. Cliff was beating even Clive Brittain, a renowned early bird, on to the gallops to exercise Tiger at 4am in the morning, before driving to Stoute's to ride out for him. Walter Swinburn was booked to ride. The early morning odds had Tiger Shoot at 20-1. By the time they reached the course, his odds had tumbled to 10-1 and by the start of the race he had been backed in to 7-2! Swinburn had a relatively straightforward task, making all and quickening clear from two out to beat Officer Cadet by three lengths. It made those early mornings worthwhile! Tiger Shoot then ran in the Ladies Diamond Stakes at Ascot and was ridden by Debbie Camp-Simpson who was a trainer of Arabians, based at Machell Place in Newmarket. She had bought two young horses, a filly and a colt, from the sales very cheaply, the filly having initially been returned for failing a vetting. Cliff used to ride the filly, Duma, while Debbie rode the colt. Duma went on to win 15 races from five furlongs to two miles. Debbie sold the first two foals for a million pounds each to the Maktoum family! Sadly, Duma died shortly afterwards. Tiger performed well in the Ladies Diamond Stakes despite getting into trouble turning into the straight and he finished seventh of the 15 runners.

Later on in his career, Cliff had started schooling Tiger, thinking he might run him over hurdles. However, his plans went awry when the girl who was supposed to be riding him to the Links didn't show up. Julia often rode out first lot for Cliff before work: this is her story!

I overslept when I was supposed to be taking Tiger Shoot over to the Links for one of the top jockeys to school. I leapt out of bed, pulled on my clothes (no bra/no knickers) and drove as fast as I could to the yard – but they'd boxed him up and driven him there.

I drove to the Links and hacked him home. He jig-jogged the whole
way – not very comfortable and a bit of chafing!

A few weeks later Cliff had a winner, Ball Gown, at
Newmarket. I was working at the racecourse then, so went into
the winner's enclosure to congratulate him. Cliff was standing
next to Nick Lees – clerk of the course at the time (and my boss)
– and Cliff asked if I was wearing any underwear. It took a bit
of explaining!

One morning, Cliff was on Tiger Shoot, leading the string up to
the heath, when he noticed a car parked on the horse walk. The
windows were steamed up and it was quite a squeeze to get past,
but Cliff could just about make out two people sat on one another
on the passenger seat and, despite Tiger trying to peer through
the window and one of the lads knocking on the car roof with his
stick, neither would show their face! It pays to know where you are
parking around Newmarket and the local villages if you don't want
to be disturbed!

One problem Tiger did have was he would quite often be a little
stiff. A physio called Isobel Prestwich would come and treat his withers
and across his quarters. On one of these occasions, Cliff also asked her
to check the yard cat who was lame! His diary notes that the cat had
its shoulders and a hip massaged!

Sadly, when Tiger was in training with Dave Thom and ran on the
all-weather at Southwell in 1996 with Lee Newton on board, he was
pulled in for being a non-trier, having started as favourite. He had been
running slightly freely over hurdles during the winter, so Lee steadied
him coming out of the stalls and he stayed on strongly to finish sixth.
Cliff had to attend a hearing at the Jockey Club and, despite producing
a veterinary certificate explaining that the horse had returned home
lame after the race, he was fined £1,000, the jockey was suspended
and Tiger was banned from racing for 30 days. Cliff noticed a similar
incident a few days later, but different, higher-profile, connections
were involved and the connections of that horse received a much lesser
penalty. Tiger was then off for 277 days while he recuperated from the

injury. Perhaps that should have been enough to indicate to the stewards that he had sustained an injury and to allow them to reconsider their verdict! He showed little form in three starts after that, so Cliff retired him. He had won six races and over £28,000 in prize-money. He stayed with Cliff until he sadly died from a twisted gut and he is buried at Hethersett House.

BALL GOWN
1990 bay filly by Jalmood out of Relatively Smart

Ball Gown was also bred by Mr Greetham and, similarly, came to Cliff at Marsh Stables to be broken in before going into training with Michael Stoute. When Ball Gown arrived at Marsh Stables, she was tiny – barely 14 hands – so Cliff left her alone for a while to see whether she would grow. She grew a little, but Stoute was still not impressed and suggested to Cliff that she would be no good. Cliff had seen something he liked but quickly agreed with the Guv'nor as he had plans to train himself! John Snaith was riding her once she was broken in. She used to canter on Choke Jade in the mornings and both Cliff and John loved her action; she would float over the grass. John Greetham asked Cliff if he would like to train her himself if Stoute didn't want her. Cliff was happy to take her on, but things didn't go her way and she kept getting beaten. Eventually, Mr Greetham had had enough and offered her to Cliff. Cliff was convinced she would win and persuaded Mr Greetham to keep her for one more race.

John Lowe rode her, not for the first time, and managed to get her beaten again. She shot clear about 6f out and was understandably treading water in the last furlong but bravely held on for third place. Mr Greetham told Cliff that he definitely no longer wanted her and, if Cliff didn't take her, she would be given to someone else. Cliff agreed to have her and waived the training fees that were outstanding at that point, which were between £200 and £300. Cliff ran her the following week in a seller at Yarmouth, but took John Lowe off and replaced him with Lee Newton, who was still a five-pound claimer in those days. He told Lee to drop her out last until after the two-furlong marker and then let her make her run. She came through the field in a canter! Luckily, she looked like a greyhound in the auction ring after the race and there were no bids for her. The first person to come and congratulate Cliff was Mr Greetham.

At the end of 1993, Cliff handed his licence back in and Ball Gown then ran under Dave Thom's name. Although David Trenchard Thom (born 1925 in Glasgow) is best remembered as a Flat trainer, he had ridden under National Hunt rules, initially as an amateur, then as a professional jockey. When Cliff moved to Exning, Dave was training at Harraton Court Stables in the village. He had significant success with his handicappers, including Prince Hansel who won five times in 1965, the highlights being the Bessborough Handicap at Royal Ascot and the Doncaster Cup, as well as the speedsters Absent Chimes, winner of the Molecomb in 1984, and Touch of Grey, winner of the Wokingham Handicap at Royal Ascot in 1986.

There was obviously a little friction having two people trying to train one horse. Ball Gown, despite her size, could be a bit of a monkey, but Dave insisted his wife Alison, who had an amateur licence, should have a sit on her. The morning dawned; it was thick fog. Cliff was on the lead horse and the plan was to work across the flat. Cliff's instructions to Alison were to sit in behind him and not pull Ball Gown out until they were running up the hill. After only two furlongs, Ball Gown shot past Cliff and disappeared into the distance! Dave didn't ask Cliff again whether Alison could ride her.

Dave Thom had ideas of being Mark Prescott (the king of exploiting a good handicap mark!) and would enter Ball Gown in races a couple of days apart without telling Cliff. On 22 August 1994, she won a mile handicap comfortably at Nottingham; Thom came clean about her having another entry a few days later and persuaded Cliff to run her again. She followed up the Nottingham victory with a win over 1m2f at Chepstow. Thom then admitted to another entry he hadn't told Cliff about and Ball Gown was sent to Salisbury on 1 September. Another victory meant she had won three races in just over a week. Cliff then insisted she should have a short break, but that did her no harm and she won her first start back as well, winning the apprentice series final at Newmarket on 27 September!

In 1995, Ball Gown won a fillies' handicap at Doncaster on her second start. She was then unlucky to be disqualified and placed last at Newmarket when ridden by David McCabe in a 1m2f handicap, being adjudged to have caused interference when squeezing through a tight gap – the race was awarded to the John Dunlop-trained horse Special Dawn, despite the latter clearly being beaten on merit. Following consistent runs in further handicaps, always placed but never quite managing to get her head in front, Cliff decided to be brave and enter her in the Cambridgeshire. There is always a big field for this race and it is often something of a cavalry charge down the Newmarket Rowley Mile course over 1m1f. Numbers are restricted now, but in Ball Gown's year there were 39 runners. Ridden by Tony Whelan and carrying four pounds overweight at 7st 10lbs, Ball Gown settled in mid-division, while Cap Juluca (Roger Charlton/Richard Hughes) made the running. At the bushes, Cliff turned away thinking there was too much traffic; she would never get through and her chance was gone. But Ball Gown weaved her way through the pack, and came racing down the rails with an amazing burst of speed. However, she was just unable to catch Cap Juluca who was racing on the other side of the course. The brave little filly only went down by a head. It was a career-best effort.

Ball Gown might have been small, but she was tough and genuine. However, she certainly had a mind of her own! Tommy Murphy was Ball Gown's regular pilot at home. However, he wasn't a great cleaner of his own tack and one day the rein broke: the stitching had rotted. Tommy bailed out and Ball Gown went 100mph up to the Cambridge Road, slithering to a stop on the concrete. Towards the end of her racing career, Ball Gown became a little reluctant to go out on the heath every morning. She would canter three strides, then stick her toes in and whip round to the left. Tommy Murphy was riding her as usual and she dropped him twice. Cliff made him drop his leathers to stop him coming off, but she continued to baulk occasionally, so Cliff took over riding her. He tried several different methods to encourage her. Initially, he carried a tin of stones which he shook when she stopped and this worked briefly; however, the most successful appliance was a 'Tweety Duck' fly swat, which Sue had bought from the dollar store in

America! Cliff carried it instead of a whip and a quick flash of it in her eye line when approaching the gallops kept her moving! He then tried changing her bridle and put a hackamore on; she was good the first day, but the next day they went down the Sand Canter and she pulled Cliff's arms out! Luckily, she did pull up when Cliff wanted her to.

One day Cliff was riding Ball Gown out and was with John Snaith. He saw a figure in the distance and thought to himself, 'If I didn't know better, I'd say that was Tony Trevor' – his old school friend, whose mother had got Cliff his apprenticeship with Noel Murless. As they got closer, he realised it was Tony! He had been working in New York and decided that was close enough to London, so got on a plane, made his way to Exning and surprised Cliff! Although they had kept in touch, they hadn't seen each other for nearly 40 years.

In 1996, Ball Gown won two further races, both at Newmarket, and the following year she was stepped up into Group class to try and earn some black type, finishing third in the Middleton Stakes at York. Ball Gown eventually won nine races and, thanks to her second in the Cambridgeshire, she amassed over £80,000 in prize-money.

At the end of her career, a decision was made to send Ball Gown to Tattersalls December Sales rather than to enter the risky world of breeding her himself. However, fate decreed otherwise: there wasn't a bid for her, so Ball Gown returned home to Marsh Stables. With the help of John Ferguson, Sheikh Mohammed's bloodstock advisor and ex-assistant trainer to Michael Stoute, Cliff obtained a nomination to Lion Cavern.

MOONSHIFT
1994 bay gelding by Cadeaux Genereux ex Thewaari
Moonshift came to Cliff through a more authentic route than Ball Gown and Tiger Shoot! He had been at Marsh Stables to be broken in when owned by Maktoum al Maktoum before going into training with Michael Stoute. Cliff liked the horse and he had a lovely temperament, but he was very lazy! He didn't run until he was a three-year-old and, when he was racing for Stoute, the jockeys would get tired before halfway in the race! He had two starts and was tailed off on both

occasions. The second race was at Lingfield; Darryll Holland rode him and managed to get him smartly out of the stalls, but by the top of the hill the jockey was exhausted from the effort of trying to keep Moonshift going, so he eventually allowed him to come home in his own time! Unsurprisingly, he was sent to the sales and Cliff was able to buy him. However, he wasn't prepared to pay for a horsebox to take him from Park Paddocks to Exning, so he made Zoe ride him home. He didn't even pay her!

On his first start for Cliff at Nottingham, Jason Weaver rode him and he and Kieren Fallon joked that neither of them had any chance, so they had a £1 bet between them on which would finish in front of the other. Moonshift (at 66-1) was always behind but managed to finish fifth of the eight runners (albeit beaten 24½ lengths!), while Fallon (on Beau Tudor at 100-1) was a further eight lengths behind in sixth. Shifty's reward was to be gelded!

A typical Cadeaux Genereux, Shifty was heavy shouldered and Cliff had to be careful what ground he ran on, so he was only lightly raced the following year, but he even had a run out in a claiming hurdle at Huntingdon in an attempt to get him to the races. By May 1999, his official handicap rating had dropped to 25 and it was nigh on impossible to find a race that he could get into. However, an apprentice handicap at Yarmouth cut up when the ground officially turned firm. Cliff walked the course and decided it wasn't as bad as described. Moonshift's moment of glory had come and, from a pound out of the handicap and with only 7st 10lbs on his back, he hit the front just under a furlong out and, never one to over-exert himself, he held on to win by a head! On Michael Stoute's next visit to the yard, Shifty was rewarded with a carrot by his former trainer. A few more races produced no further victories and Shifty was retired and given to John Gowing's son to be used as a riding horse.

* * *

One of Cliff's best hacks was the ex-chaser Admirals Cup, who had been John Francome's last winning ride as a jockey. At the end of Admiral's racing career, he had been sent to the British Racing School. After a few years there and having reached the age of 18, the manager of the school decided that Admiral was no longer up to the work required and he was put on 'death row' to await the next visit of the vet. Cliff's neighbour and fellow Exning trainer Julia Feilden, realising she had left her riding gloves there after giving a lecture, returned to the school to collect them. She walked past the row of boxes and asked why Admiral was there. She was told the situation and quickly offered to take him. They said she could have him if she could collect him before the vet arrived. She rushed back to her yard to collect the horsebox, headed back to the racing school and loaded him up. Just as she was leaving, the vet arrived. Admiral had escaped being put down by a whisker! The Feildens had Ball Gown in training at the time and Sue was in their yard looking for Cliff. A striped face whickered at her over the box door. Julia offered the horse to Sue as a hack on the spot! Admiral quickly accepted a few polos and pulled some soppy faces. Sue returned to Marsh Stables to collect her tack, so she could try him out, only to be told by Cliff that there was no way she was having a horse of her own! Luckily, Cliff fell asleep in the armchair after lunch, so Sue snuck down to the Feildens' yard and had a ride on Admiral. She agreed with Julia to keep him, but he would have to stay where he was. After a few days, Cliff grudgingly agreed that Admiral had better move to Marsh Stables because Sue was never there; she was always down at the Feildens' with her horse! The next morning, Sue was about to ride out before she went to work but Cliff decided he needed to use Admiral to lead a two-year-old.

That was the end of Sue having her own horse to ride! He did make an exceptional hack, however. Cliff could get off him in the middle of the gallops and he would stand still wherever he was left until Cliff reappeared, unlike No Bombs! Sue and Zoe were allowed to enter him in some local horse shows and he often competed in the trainer's hack class. One day, the judge was an ex-starter and he told Zoe to gallop round the ring. Zoe explained that, at 20 years old, Admiral didn't really do much galloping, so the judge got on the horse and made him gallop. He then asked the competitors to show what made the horses good trainer's hacks. The others hadn't been expecting this and were unprepared! Admiral, however, showed himself to be the perfect hack: Zoe threw a stable bandage on the ground and dismounted. She hooked

J O Tobin wins the
Swaps Stakes

J O Tobin, Cliff, Johnny
Adams, Del Mar

Shergar, Epsom Derby

Relaxing in the paddock with Shergar after exercise

Shareef Dancer, Irish Derby

Princess Anne, Ten No Trumps (Getty)

Sonic Lady, cover girl first
edition Racing Post

Riding Sonic Lady exercise at Santa Anita

Marsh Stables, Exning

*Ball Gown and
Conkers the hack*

Tiger Shoot

Singlet wins at Newmarket

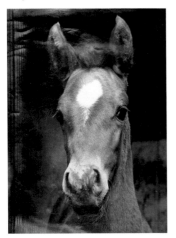

Prima Markova as a foal

Pilsudski sweeps the yard

Leoballero in the dovecot

Fujiyama Crest entering the winner's enclosure with his lad (Getty)

Pilsudski wins the Breeders' Cup (Getty)

60 years: Cliff and Lester Piggott

60 years: Cliff and Michael Stoute

60 years: Group photo

Cornelious wins at Lingfield

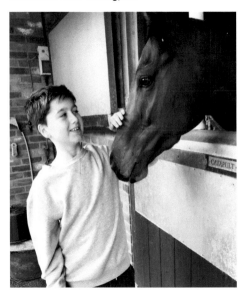

Catapult with Sue's grandson, Jed

Proud Chieftain wins at Doncaster

*Aaranyow in his
new home*

Cliff's final runner, Catapult

The Memento Cabinet

Relaxing in Florida with vet Mathilde Texier

Relaxing in St Marks Square, Venice

the reins around Admiral's saddle and left him standing in the middle of the ring. The judge told the others to gallop around the ring, shouting to try and upset Admiral. He stood stock still while Zoe collected the bandage and remounted him. He still only got third place!

SHERZABAD
1997 bay/brown gelding by Doyoun out of Sheriya

Sherzabad was a homebred of the Aga Khan's with a lovely nature but not a huge talent! On discovering the limited talent, Stoute sent Sherzabad to Tattersalls Newmarket Sales. Cliff had a soft spot for the horse, having had him at Marsh Stables for a while. And, after all, he was Cliff's 'lucky' dark bay colour! Sue offered to buy him if he went for £1,500 or less. She didn't tell Cliff that she was actually prepared to go to £5,000 if necessary. There were a lot of withdrawals that day, but luckily Cliff and Sue arrived at Tattersalls in plenty of time as Sherzabad went through the ring almost an hour before his advertised time. They got him for the agreed £1,500 and were immediately offered £3,000 for him. Unlike Cliff as it was to turn down an immediate profit, Sherzabad joined the team at Marsh Stables.

He won two races for Cliff, showing a distinct liking for the 1m3½ furlongs of Lingfield! The first race was a handicap where, on 10 August 2001, he was ridden by Paul Quinn, claiming three pounds and taking the lead over two furlongs out, he just needed to be shaken up to win a shade cosily from Michael Bell's Activist.

In the summer of 2003, Jimmy Quinn was riding work for Hugh Collingridge, under whose licence Sherzabad was running. Sherzabad, ridden by Alison Hutchinson, was in the group of workers and they were headed towards the Cambridge Road all-weather track. Quinn asked who Sherzabad was and decided he was no good, so he would give Sherzabad a six-length start. He regretted that move: he couldn't get near the first two! Strangely enough, when Sherzabad was next entered, on 8 August 2003, Jimmy Quinn rang and asked to ride him. Going down to the start, the jockey pulled up near the bookies and gave them the nod. Sherzabad's odds tumbled from 14-1 into 8-1 despite his having been beaten in a seller on his previous start. Once again, he was settled in the rear with a strong pace up front. Despite meeting trouble in running, he battled through, taking the lead in the final furlong and, by the line, he had pulled five lengths clear of the second!

Soon after this, Sherzabad was sold for £10,000 to Iona Craig, who had taken out a licence to train National Hunt horses in Wales.

THE HOME BREDS

DESPITE HH The Aga Khan considering that breeding good racehorses is 'akin to playing chess with nature', Cliff managed to breed a couple of winners from his one mare, Ball Gown.

LEOBALLERO
2000 chestnut gelding by Lujain out of Ball Gown

As Cliff didn't hold a licence at the time, Leoballero initially went into training with Hugh Collingridge, who trained at Harraton Court Stables in Exning. Hugh was one of the long-term Newmarket trainers, having landed the Royal Hunt Cup and the Queen Elizabeth II Stakes with Buzzard's Bay in 1982 as well as winning the Lincoln with Cuvee Charlie in 1988.

Leo made his debut at Newmarket in the Wood Ditton Stakes, which is for unraced three-year-olds. He made a pleasing start to his career, finishing third, despite showing his inexperience by pulling early on. Following a couple of near misses (seconds at Leicester and Nottingham and a third, also at Nottingham), he broke his maiden at Lingfield, winning a 16-runner race under Michael Tebbutt.

The following season Cliff switched his horses to Declan Daly. Declan had been head lad at Michael Stoute's for eight years before returning to his native Ireland to further his knowledge under Aiden O'Brien's tutelage. He returned to Newmarket in 2004 to train in his own right, alongside pre-training for Sir Michael Stoute at Machell Place Stables, and asked Cliff to be his assistant. After only a few years, despite being tipped for the top by many onlookers, poor prize-money levels meant the books wouldn't balance: the financial constraints were too much and despite success at the top level, Declan was unable to continue training. Declan then joined Godolphin, heading up their pre-training yard.

Sadly, despite many more placings, including a second at Newmarket ridden by John Egan when seven pounds out of the handicap, Leo was unable to win again. Leo was a miler, which is a particularly competitive division for Flat handicappers to find themselves in. On one occasion, when ridden by John Egan at Kempton, Leo finished fourth. Connections had fancied him and Cliff's instructions to the jockey were to have him in behind the leaders and pull him out – he should win. Leo broke well in fourth. Egan took him back until he was last, waiting until the last couple of furlongs, he cruised up through the field and, ignoring the gap between the first two, swerved in behind them, finishing fourth with just a slap down the shoulder. He never said anything to Cliff but told the stewards he was hanging badly, obviously expecting to be pulled in as a non-trier. A little while later, Egan asked Cliff why he wasn't getting any rides. Cliff told him politely that he didn't use stopping jockeys.

Leo was quite a tall horse and, when at Marsh Stables, he lived in bottom of the old dovecot which was the highest stable Cliff had. He was such a kind-natured horse that when he had his head over the box door watching the yard goings-on he would allow the swallows to swoop in and out through the box doorway, flying between his ears and ruffling his foretop, to reach the nests they had built in the dove nest boxes.

SINGLET
2001 chesnut gelding by Singspiel out of Ball Gown

Singlet was Ball Gown's second foal. He had an educational outing at Newmarket as a two-year-old and two summer-time runs at three before being gelded. It wasn't until he was a four-year-old that he got his head in front. Before this run, however, Cliff decided Singlet could do with a break from the training routine and put him in the small paddock by the yard. There was an electric fence around the top of the paddock railings, which, of course, Singlet decided to investigate.

Although the electric-wire voltage was set quite low, the shock when he stuck his nose on it was enough to make him jump in the air and gallop back across the paddock. This wasn't enough for Singlet, so he walked back to the fence, turned around and backed slowly towards the electric wire, and touched it with his backside; this resulted in him fly-jumping back across the paddock! The shock seemed to do him good because a few days later he won his next start at Newmarket at 33-1, ridden by Micky Fenton. The stewards enquired into his improved form and Cliff was unable to give them an explanation. He didn't think they would be impressed that Singlet had given himself an electric shock!

His form was certainly more consistent after that with a dead-heat for second at Salisbury, followed by a head third at Nottingham. On his final start, Singlet looked as though he was coming through to win his race, but Cliff noticed him change his legs and his stride pattern was wrong. He had broken down a furlong out and yet he still stayed on to finish second.

* * *

Tragically, Ball Gown's third foal, a filly by Lujain, died when being weaned. She was separated from her mother at dusk and left alone in a field for the night. The next morning, she was found collapsed and exhausted: she had been galloping round the field all night looking for her mother. Sadly, the vets were unable to save her.

PRIMA MARKOVA
2003 bay filly by Mark of Esteem out of Ball Gown

Prima was Ball Gown's fourth foal. When Cliff and Sue took Ball Gown up to Dalham Hall Stud to be covered by Mark of Esteem, she had the Lujain foal at foot. Cliff and Sue were watching the action from a viewing gallery around the covering box when they heard footsteps on the stairs. John Ferguson appeared, accompanied by Sheikh Mohammed and Sheikh Maktoum. John Ferguson went to make the introductions, but Sheikh Mohammed remembered Cliff from his work with Sonic Lady and needed no introduction. Meanwhile, Sue was trying to find somewhere to hide as she was dressed in her mucking-out clothes with dirty hands! But there was no escape, Sheikh Mohammed insisted on shaking her by the hand as well. Like her parents, Prima was on the small side, but she never grew as her mother had done. She made little impact on the racecourse, so Zoe retrained her as a polo pony which proved to be her forte. She even had a trial for Guards polo before retiring and becoming a successful polo pony broodmare.

BRAIN TUMOUR

IN 2007, Cliff went into hospital to have a cataract removed. He had been diagnosed with cataracts in both eyes and was booked in to have them removed one at a time. Once the first (left) one had been removed, he went back for a check-up but complained that his vision was worse rather than better! Luckily his optician took him seriously and he was eventually sent for further tests. A brain scan at Addenbrookes Hospital in Cambridge showed a large tumour at the front of his brain. The surgeon wasn't sure he would be able to restore Cliff's vision in his left eye because the scan appeared to show involvement of the optic nerve within the tumour, but he was admitted on Sunday night and taken down for surgery at 6am the following morning, undergoing nine hours in the operating theatre. The tumour was removed in its entirety and later testing thankfully proved it to be slow-growing and benign. When Cliff came round from the surgery, he noticed a clock on the other side of the ward. He closed his left eye, then his right, then looked again with both eyes open. He could see out of both eyes! The clock said 6.20pm. Cliff had had no symptoms and had he not had the cataract operation, the tumour would never have been diagnosed. The surgeon said he would have been dead within 18 months had he not had the tumour removed when he did. Unfortunately, when Cliff came home, he found he had a constantly running nose. It turned out there was a leak of cerebral fluid from the surgery where the skull hadn't completely closed. He was rushed back in to have a patch placed over the gap, but that was only a three-hour operation – so easy!

By 2009, Cliff had spent 60 years in racing. A party was arranged at Newmarket's Rowley Mile Racecourse for friends and family. Among those in attendance were Lester Piggott, John Ferguson, Willie Snaith and his son, John, and fellow Exning trainer Hugh Collingridge. Cliff was presented with an engraved fruit bowl by Sir Michael Stoute, who had kindly delayed his departure to the Breeders' Cup to supervise Conduit's successful defence of his Breeders' Cup Turf title. Later that afternoon, Cliff presented Frankie Dettori with the jockey's trophy for his win on Quick Wit in the Cliff Lines 60 Years in Racing Maiden Stakes.

HETHERSETT HOUSE

AFTER HIS brain tumour, Cliff decided to cut down significantly on his racing commitments. He split the land at Marsh Stables and obtained permission to build a house with a four-stable block in the back paddock. Marsh Stables was sold and Cliff and Sue had Hethersett House built and moved in in 2010.

Shortly after the move, the new owner of Marsh Stables, Jo Fenton, rang asking for help because someone was walking round the yard. Sue gallantly jumped over the fence to find Jo hidden behind a stable door and Jo's mother behind a bush in the yard. Sue had a quick look round, then went down to the stables. Seeing nothing immediately amiss, she went to the feed house and called, 'Come out, come out whoever you are!' and seconds later a small, grey pony emerged: he had obviously been bored, so had gone for a little wander and was enjoying a midnight feast!

PROUD CHIEFTAIN
2008 bay gelding by Sleeping Indian out of Skimra
Proud Chieftain was bought as a two-year-old out of a field in Soham from a small breeder Cliff knew called Rob Robinson, through their mutual connection John James. Chief's dam, Skimra, was getting on in years, but she herself had been bred at the famous Lanwades Stud by Kirsten Rausing. Chief was named after a half-brother to Hethersett whom Cliff had ridden at Holliday's. This new version was a backward individual and only had a couple of quiet, educational runs while racing under Hugh Collingridge's name as a two-year-old. In 2011, Cliff took his licence out again and took over Proud Chieftain's management.

As a three-year-old, Proud Chieftain grew and strengthened. Cliff was looking for a jockey for him. Alison Hutchinson was working for Cliff and had had her own horse, Strike Force, at Marsh Stables. Ali used to ride as an amateur and suggested Cliff try James Doyle. Cliff didn't know him, but Ali insisted he was a good horseman. James rode Proud Chieftain for the first time at the Newmarket July course on 24 June, finishing third, running on strongly over a mile. James commented that he could be a nice horse, so he kept the ride! Proud Chieftain showed a liking for the July course and he and James won their next two starts there in July and August, both over 1m2f, despite a six-pound weight rise for the first success. Chief followed up with a third consecutive win at Kempton in November, but James wasn't available and Jim Crowley got the ride. Proud Chieftain was still maturing, so Cliff was careful to give him plenty of time between races.

On one occasion, Cliff quite fancied Proud Chieftain's chances. However, he was watching what was happening down at the start and saw the assistant starter go across to tighten Chief's girths. The horse kicked out. Cliff knew then that his girths had been over-tightened and he wouldn't run a good race because he wasn't the sort of horse to kick unless he was uncomfortable. True enough, he ran disappointingly and trailed in. Running with over-tight girths will stop a horse: it can't breathe. The assistant starter then had the audacity to tell Cliff afterwards that Chief tried to kick him and he had marked him down as a kicker for future handlers. It's hard enough to get a horse to the races with a chance without a pompous official ruining it all!

The following year, Proud Chieftain took a little time to come to himself but hit his stride once his favoured Newmarket July Course was in use, winning there in July. His official handicap rating was already in the 90s and this pushed it up to 95, making it hard to place him in handicaps as he was giving weight away all round, so Cliff routed him to a Conditions race at Doncaster on 12 September: the Kat Communications Conditions Stakes (Class 2) over 1m2½f. It was a competitive affair and Proud Chieftain was 16-1 in the market. He had been working well once on the gallops and Cliff advised connections he was worth a bet, although some were dubious as it appeared the conditions wouldn't be in his favour. It was pouring with rain and he was giving weight to higher-rated horses. When they met the jockey, Darryll Holland, in the paddock, he asked whether he could make the running. Darryll had ridden him in his previous race at Haydock and, despite finishing second, he had never been able to get a clear run. Cliff reluctantly agreed. Darryll rode an outstanding race from the front. His rivals allowed him to make all, so set his own pace and kept enough up his sleeve to repel raiders when challenged two furlongs out. Cliff hates to watch a race live when there's a fancied runner, so was hiding round a corner and Sue was standing downstairs in the trainers' area. A friend, Tahl Holzman, had accompanied them to the races and claims he could hear Sue screaming Chief home from the owners' and trainers' bar two floors above!

Barry Foley was Cliff's main lead-up man on racing days. There were a couple of occasions when Cliff had two runners, such as when Cornelious and Tyrsal both ran at Yarmouth. Barry would lead up both horses which kept him on his toes: he certainly had to keep his fingers crossed that the races weren't going to be run consecutively and certainly got lucky when Catapult (2pm) and Tyrsal (3.05) both ran at Yarmouth on 26 July 2018 – that was all a bit rushed! When Chief won at Doncaster, Barry hadn't taken his waterproofs and was absolutely soaked, but the smiles afterwards proved this omission didn't matter at all! Barry had started in racing as an apprentice with Harry Blackshaw in Spofforth near Wetherby before moving to Middleham and joining Neville Crump, then Billy Haigh. Barry had about 50 rides and rode a winner before deciding to follow the masses and move to Newmarket where he joined the Captain Boyd-Rochfort stable at Freemason Lodge.

There was a regular racing team from Hethersett House: David Jenkins, who lived over the road at Exeter Stables, was the box driver and he, Cliff and Cliff's brother-in-law, Malcolm, would sit in the front of the cab with the heating on, while Sue and Barry sat in the back with no heating, so had to wrap themselves in blankets to keep warm! Sue provided a picnic to eat on the way back and there was always a packet of wine gums secreted at the bottom. Barry ate the black and red ones;

Sue ate the yellow and green ones, then the leftovers were passed to those in the front of the cab!

Proud Chieftain went into plenty of notebooks on 12 September 2013 when ridden by a young William Buick, finishing fifth in a Class 2 1m2f handicap at Doncaster, a track for which he had already shown his liking. He was travelling well but had to wait for a run and then got shuffled back. He was better than he showed and came out of the race kicking and bouncing, without a blow on him. Proud Chieftain was proving difficult to place with his high handicap rating and he struggled to get his head in front. However, he did finish the year very respectably when, reunited with James Doyle, he finished second in the Listed James Seymour Stakes at Newmarket, only beaten a neck by an odds-on Gosden-trained horse, Nabucco.

Cliff was normally a very reasonable employer. One morning, a young apprentice, Nathan Alison, was riding Proud Chieftain at exercise, but the horse refused to go past the bushes on to the gallops. Cliff was on his hack and getting rather irate, effing and blinding at both the jockey and the horse. Nathan eventually said, 'If you swear at me again, I'm getting off the horse and walking back home!' The next thing Cliff knew was Chief was standing jockey-less in the middle of the horse walk! Luckily, Cliff managed to flag down a passing couple, who were out for a walk, to leg Nathan back up and they returned home uneventfully. When Cliff checked the horse over at home, he realised that Chief hadn't wanted to go on the gallops because he had a sore joint. Cliff always maintains that the horses will tell you if something is not right, but you need to be prepared to listen to them.

In 2014, Steve Williams joined the team at Hethersett House. At breakfast time, they would sit around the kitchen table and Steve would pore over the racing calendar, looking for races for the horses. Cliff was always keen to have a runner in the Shergar Cup competition. The Shergar Cup is a unique event: it is a team competition held annually at Ascot racecourse and named in honour of Shergar. Internationally renowned jockeys are invited to join the teams and they wear team colours with distinguishing caps rather than the owners' racing colours.

Teams can be split on countries of origin or gender and jockeys are allotted to horses by the organisers, using a complicated formula to try to ensure it is as equal a competition as possible. Points are awarded for finishing position in the races and there is a silver saddle trophy for the leading rider. It is a popular event with the crowds, but the drawbacks for connections could be seen as being unable to choose your own jockey and not seeing your own colours. Steve managed to convince Cliff that Chief would stay 1m4f if ridden correctly, so an entry was made for him.

Preparing for this race, Chief was again being a little awkward about going on to the canters. Steve Williams was riding him out and Tahl Holtzman rode the hack, Robbie. One morning, just as Chief started to baulk at the canter, Tahl leaned over and grabbed the cheek piece of his bridle. Chief jumped backwards, the cheek piece snapped and the bridle fell apart! Steve jumped off and Chief headed back home! Luckily, he misremembered the route and, thinking he was heading for the gap in the fence, he ended up getting himself cornered and the heath man, Mick, caught up with him. Mick luckily had a spare bridle in the back of his van and Steve and Chief were reunited.

So it was that on 9 August 2014, Proud Chieftain and the team all set off for the races. Steve had the honour of leading up: Barry Foley was given the day off and went as Cliff's guest. Arriving at the racecourse in good time, Chief was settled in his stable and Cliff and company made their way to the owners' and trainers' dining room where videos of Cliff riding work on Shergar were being shown on a loop. The hospitality was fantastic. As race time approached, they went to saddle up and meet the jockey they had been allotted, a German rider on the girls team named Stefanie Hofer. Steffi is tiny at only 4ft 11in; in fact, she is so petite that she rode a promotional 'human horse' formed by ten acrobats before the competition. When Cliff saddled up, Chief's saddle nearly weighed as much as Steffi and when Cliff went to leg her up, he nearly threw her straight over the top of Proud Chieftain! It was Steffi's Shergar Cup debut, but she had had plenty of experience under her belt having ridden more than 300 winners. Steffi rode a cracking race to pinch second of the ten runners on the line, despite starting at 20-1! Steffi was nearly as thrilled as Cliff and Sue! In the overall competition, the girls' team were beaten by one point by the Frankie Dettori-led European Team, with the girls' captain, Canadian Emma-Jayne Wilson, also coming second in the Silver Saddle competition to Olivier Peslier.

Chief won five races and £78,394 in prize-money, having cost £3,000 as a yearling. A horse like him doesn't come along often in the lifetime of a small trainer.

* * *

The horses trained by Cliff ran under the Prima Racing Partnership banner. It was an all-inclusive package with 'hands on' access to the horses and exceptional hospitality, although mucking out and poo picking the paddock were not compulsory! Debs Keppey, who, together with her partner Gary, joined the syndicate at Hethersett House, reflects on her experience as an owner with Cliff and Sue:

> To be part of the Prima Racing Partnership was nothing but a privilege and an honour. It was a once in a lifetime opportunity for us to experience racehorse ownership and we wouldn't have wanted to have done that with anyone else. To watch Cliff train and care for his racehorses was a joy. The passion, dedication, attention to detail and the understanding of the horse, both physically and mentally, were testament to the consummate horseman he is. Nothing was missed, even the beautiful, pristine little yard – never a thing out of place. Also, every horse ran on its merits – Cliff's integrity and respect towards the sport he has made his life was always paramount. Every horse was also found a loving, forever home after their racing career was over. The horse truly came first. On a more personal note, the welcome and hospitality we received from Sue and Cliff was second to none. We were welcomed into their home with open arms and made to feel part of the Prima family. Overnight stays, trips to the races with the horses in the box, many wonderful social occasions, held in thrall by Cliff's stories of his life in horseracing and the legendary horses and trainers he was involved with,

not to mention the treasured gift of a set of Prima Racing silks hanging on the wall at home. Unforgettable memories and two very dear friends made.

AARANYOW
2008 Chesnut Gelding by Compton Place out of Cutpurse Moll

In 2013, Cliff was looking for another horse, so he would have the requisite three for his licence. He had already been to see a horse with a well-known retired trainer who was based in one of the nearby villages, Kirtling, at the time. On being shown the horse, Cliff pointed out that it was lame. The trainer pointed out that it had a shoe missing but also claimed that it always moved like that anyway! Having been told the owner wanted £12,000 for it, Cliff decided to look elsewhere. He heard that Taffy might have something suitable, so went to the yard on the Hamilton Road where Taffy was just coming back from the heath on Aaranyow and he confirmed that Aaray was for sale. Cliff asked how much he wanted for the colt and Taffy replied that he owed the blacksmith £50. The blacksmith was in the yard, so Cliff gave him £50 and took the horse! Aaranyow had been being campaigned by various trainers over every distance between 6f and 1m4f, without ever troubling the judge and normally finishing nearer last than first. Cliff had one look at the horse and realised he was a typical sprinter: short backed, strong. On his first run for Cliff, he finished fourth over 6f ridden by Jimmy Quinn. The new connections were delighted with their latest purchase.

At this time, Cliff had Rob Tart living at Hethersett House and riding out every morning, so he became Aaray's regular pilot, sharing the rides with fellow apprentice, Nathan Alison, and they followed up this promising first run with places at Kempton (second), Yarmouth (third) and Nottingham (second). However, the handicapper kept increasing Aaranyow's official mark accordingly and Aaray struggled, and combined with getting a throat infection early in the summer, he wasn't able to trouble the judge again until late August, when he finished a good second over five furlongs at Lingfield. Unfortunately, during that race, he sustained a tendon injury and the vets advised

Cliff to finish his racing career and rehome him for hacking. Cliff had a think about it: the horse wasn't lame, but his tendon was thickened. Cliff decided to proceed with caution. He walked him around the lunge ring every day for a week. Twice a day, Cliff would massage the tendon for ten minutes with DMSO. After a couple of weeks of walking, Aaray decided he wanted to trot round the ring, so Cliff let him and he went two or three times round the lunge ring every day. Slowly and cautiously, Cliff increased his trotting until he decided he was ready to resume exercise on the heath. He bandaged the injured tendon, took Aaray over to the round canter and did a slow hack canter, barely out of a trot. He then built this exercise up until Aaray was going round the round canter four times a morning, a daily distance of three miles hack cantering.

Aaray was away from the racecourse for nearly a year on Cliff's rehabilitation programme. During this time, Rob Tart moved out of Hethersett House. After a few warm-up races, Aaray was entered at Wolverhampton. Rob Tart didn't answer the phone for the ride, so Cliff eventually booked Toby Atkinson. Aaray started at 50-1 for the 5f race, but connections were confident he was ready! Aaray won his first race, a maiden, at the age of six. He and Toby won their second race, again over the minimum distance, at Kempton a month later, making all the running. Cliff decided he had proved his point and Aary was rehomed. He is now thriving as a show jumper in Norfolk – his approach to the jumps is rather speedier than many would like, but he is a careful, accurate jumper and has quite a few red rosettes to his name! Sadly, Toby Atkinson was not getting enough rides in the UK, so left for Australia.

TYRSAL
2011 bay gelding by Jeremy out of Blanchelande
Tyrsal was initially trained by Robert Eddery, who won with him as both a two- and three-year old. Unfortunately, the owners could no longer commit to his training fees when he turned four, so Robert gave him to Cliff to train.

Tyrsal hit peak form in summer, winning a 1m2f apprentice handicap at Yarmouth, ridden by Daniel Cremin, and following this up with a victory in another 1m2f apprentice handicap at Leicester, ridden by Paddy Pilley. Paddy got on well with him and won on him again at Kempton in a 1m2f handicap on the all-weather in October.

The following year, the ground went against Tyrsal in the summer and he was twice withdrawn on fast ground, but he got his head in front again in another Yarmouth apprentice handicap, this time ridden by Cameron Noble. It was Truck Fest day! Cliff decided they were celebrating Tyrsal's victory when there was a lot of vehicle horn honking between the horsebox and the lorries; you'd have to have felt sorry for the locals!

As a six-year-old in 2017, Tyrsal's results became more consistent, but were, at the same time, frustrating with four second places. However, ridden once again by Paddy Pilley, he strode clear in the 1m4f Kube Exhibition Centre handicap at Leicester in July. In 2018, Tyrsal was again placed four times but was unable to achieve another elusive win.

CORNELIOUS
2012 bay colt by Cape Cross out of Fantastic Spring

In 2016, Cliff once again needed a third horse to be able to hold a licence, so Richard Lines kindly bought him Cornelious for £8,000. Cornelious was another horse who had previously been trained by Robert Eddery. He hadn't made his debut until he was a three-year-old, but made up for lost time when he won at Windsor in April, but then blotted his copybook at Leicester in June by refusing to settle when he was odds-on. The result was that he was gelded soon afterwards. This, the cruellest cut as many seem to think, did the trick and Cornelious was second at Salisbury, before winning again at Chelmsford in October.

After being transferred to Hethersett House, it was July before Cornelious showed his true form, when, ridden by Darryll Holland, he was second at Kempton, making the running until just being headed near the finish. Darryll was back on him when he won a 1m4f handicap at Leicester, when a change of tactics did the trick and he was held up before taking the lead inside the final furlong.

Cornelious and Tyrsal were both due to run in the last race at Yarmouth, but their race was abandoned due to the racecourse doctor having travelled on the ambulance with an apprentice who had fallen off in an earlier race. The apprentice can't have been badly injured because he rode the next day. However, the only way connections of the runners found out that the race had been abandoned was because Ryan Moore had the courtesy to come out and tell the connections of Michael Stoute's runner. Sadly, the racecourse and the BHA refused to pay any costs for those whose horses hadn't been able to run. The jockeys had weighed out, so their riding fees had to be paid, which, along with the cost of the horsebox and grooms' wages, came to over £1,200 – a significant amount of money to find for a small owner/trainer only to later discover they have no chance of getting anything in return.

CATAPULT
2015 bay gelding by Equiano out of Electrona

Catapult was another to be transferred to Cliff from Robert Eddery. He hadn't shown much form for Robert in five starts as a two-year-old but, once switched to Hethersett House, he finished second on his first start in a seven-furlong handicap at Yarmouth, ridden by Hollie Doyle. He was beaten by Mutafarrid, trained by ex-Stoute assistant Owen Burrows and ridden by Jim Crowley, who had come up the centre of the course while Catapult was in a small group on the stands rail.

Encouraged by that run, Cliff then stepped him in class for a seven-furlong novice stakes at Newmarket. Unfortunately, Catapult became very upset in the horsebox. Cliff took him into the yard to wash him down and Catapult started to purge badly. A racecourse vet was standing in the yard watching but didn't say anything, so Cliff decided to let Catapult take his chance. It was the wrong decision. Rob Tart rode and said the horse was completely flat and unresponsive. That wasn't Catapult – he was normally a bubbly little thing.

Not surprisingly, it took Catapult a while to get over whatever had been ailing him and it wasn't until winter 2018 that he began to show some consistently decent form again.

HEART ATTACK

Towards the end of 2018, Cliff hadn't been sleeping well, so was using a bed in the office downstairs in order not to disturb Sue. He got up to use the bathroom but when he went back into his room, he sat on the side of the bed and realised he couldn't breathe. He went to the bottom of the stairs and tried to call for Sue. Sue came downstairs at 6am as normal and found him collapsed in a chair, weakly waving an arm. An ambulance was called; the lodger, David Letts, was woken to run up the drive in his nightwear (and Sue's Crocs, which were four sizes too small!) to open the gates and let the ambulance in. The paramedics quickly diagnosed a heart attack. They sat him in an armchair, put an oxygen mask over his face and gave him intravenous drugs in both arms: Cliff's blood pressure was spiralling and his heart racing. Once he was stable enough, the paramedics tried to get the gurney in but couldn't get it through the door, so Cliff was carried out to the ambulance on a Victorian chaise longue! On arrival at West Suffolk Hospital, Bury St Edmunds, he was rushed into the emergency room and hooked up to saline drips, which sent his blood pressure soaring again. It took five days to stabilise both his heart rate and his blood pressure before he was allowed home. Cliff claims the specialist said the heart attack was caused by stress, probably from a nagging wife!

However, there was to be one final runner. With such a small string, Cliff had gone 559 days without a winner, but he knew Catapult was in good shape and had him aimed at a seven-furlong maiden handicap race at Lingfield on 30 January 2018. Hollie Doyle was booked to ride. It was the 3.20 race, The @SunRacing Maiden Handicap. It fell just 16 days before Cliff's 84th birthday and two days before Cliff would have had to renew his training licence! As ever in racing, there were last-minute dramas with a National Hunt meeting, due to be run at Lingfield a few days before, being called off due to the course being frozen. But when the curtain finally fell on Clifford Victor Lines' lifetime in horseracing, it was to be a fairy tale ending: the four-year-old gelding shot out of the stalls to make the running. Despite Exning neighbour, Gay Kelleway's Global Goddess coming out of the pack to chase them down, Hollie and Catapult held on to reward all Cliff's fans who, probably largely for emotional reasons, had backed the gelding in from 9-1 to 4-1 joint-favourite at the off. It was Hollie's first winner for Cliff despite his support for her the previous year. She had a soft spot for Catapult, about whom she said after the race, 'always tried his best but could just curl up in the dying strides'. Luckily, he chose this day to run to the line: perhaps he had picked up on the atmosphere. Once Cliff saw the way he jumped from the stalls 'like a greyhound', he was always confident. He even found himself trending on Twitter after the emotional farewell victory from Catapult!

In the post-race interview Cliff said, '... 70 years in racing: it couldn't have been a better life – I wouldn't have changed it for the world.'

A week later, on Thursday, 7 February 2019, the British Horse Racing Authority cancelled all British racing due to an outbreak of equine flu detected in vaccinated horses in a training yard in Cheshire, which was continuing to have runners. Cliff had got his last runner in just in time!

Shaun Keightley, who was based in Exning at Harraton Court at the time, leased the boxes at Hethersett House for a few of his overflow horses. His backer, Simon Lockyer, bought Tyrsal and Catapult. Tyrsal won once more for seven-pound claimer Gavin Aston. When Keightley and Lockyer split, Tyrsal moved to Phil McEntee with the rest of Lockyer's horses but retired soon afterwards and is now living in the lap of luxury in Norfolk with one of Carrie Massingham's clients. Keightley kept Catapult and he has been earning his living as a great lead horse and also as an apprentice ride, notching up another three wins. He has now run 58 times under rules and accrued more than £27,000 in prize-money. He will return to Cliff and Sue as soon as he retires.

POST-SCRIPT

IN RECOGNITION of his 70 years in racing, Cliff and Sue were invited to Royal Ascot in 2019 as the Queen's guests. They found themselves on a table with Black Caviar's representatives, possibly because of the Australia connection. Black Caviar, known as Nelly, was the leading Australian racehorse between 2010 and 2013. She was undefeated in 25 races, including 15 Group Ones. In June 2012, her connections took the brave decision to take on the Brits in their own backyard and she came over for Royal Ascot. When travelling, she wore a specially designed 'compression suit', which was supposed to help blood circulation and supply more oxygen to the muscles. The suit was recommended by Australia's Olympic 100m hurdle hope Sally Pearson. It was made of a revolutionary moisture-management fabric and fitted with zips. It was certainly very different from what Landau was wearing on the boat to Australia, or J O Tobin's stable rug in which he flew to the USA! It was a wet year at Ascot and Black Caviar wasn't used to the rain-softened ground she encountered in the 6f Diamond Jubilee Stakes. Her jockey Nolen was also unused to the style of racing here. He sent her into the lead inside the last quarter mile and, having established a lead, he began to ease up on her, not realising the European sprinters would come back at him. He managed to galvanise the mare to win by a head in the final strides from the French filly Moonlight Cloud. At the time, he blamed himself for over-confidence, although later connections claimed she had torn a muscle in the race. The trainer, Peter Moody, also felt she had not coped as well with the 11,000-mile journey from Australia as he had expected and she appeared flat and tired. She returned to Australia after the race, again wearing the 'compression suit' for the flight. During the pre-export quarantine she was required to complete before returning to Australia, she was stung by a bee. Such was the importance of Nelly that vets from all three Newmarket practices were called on to attend to her! She was fine. Despite all this, she was the first non-European horse to be named Champion European Sprinter at that year's Cartier awards. She continued racing and in February 2013 was inducted into the Australian Racing Hall of Fame, only the second horse to be so honoured while still competing. She retired to stud at the end of that season in April.

Cliff continues to 'bodge and mend' anything which offers itself. He has made blue tit nest boxes for many friends from old pallets. On holiday in Marie-Galante, Guadeloupe with good friends Jean-Luc and Robin Chouvier, Cliff was put in charge of the chickens who lived in a run under the holiday cottage. Every morning he would collect the eggs for breakfast until, one day, he saw a mongoose running off with an egg in its mouth. He swore revenge! He spent hours combing the beach for a pebble which resembled a chicken egg. Once found, he put it just inside the hole in the wire the mongoose was using to get into the run and kept watch. The mongoose duly appeared, collected the pebble egg and ran off with it. Cliff thought he had won the battle, but the mongoose reappeared the next day!

Cliff has been a long-term fixture of the Newmarket racing community and, although he no longer has horses himself, his years of wisdom and experience have not been lost. He rents out his four stables to Carrie Massingham who is primarily a BAEDT-approved equine dentist but is also involved with helping to find new homes for some of her clients' horses when their racing careers come to an end. Cliff is chief advisor on exercise, feeding and treatment of any injuries.

CLIFF'S VIEW OF THE FUTURE

AFTER HIS retirement, Cliff reflected that in many ways very little had changed in racing in the UK during his time, although the world had opened up and there are many more opportunities to race overseas, which bring with them significant prize-money.

At the beginning of 2022, the BHA Press Office issued a statement confirming the following information: 'British Racing generates an annual expenditure of £4.1 billion, a tax contribution of £300 million and directly employs over 20,000 people, principally in rural areas.' It is indubitably a large industry but for how much longer?

When Cliff became involved in horseracing in the 1950s, the majority of the owners were owner/breeders such as Sir Victor Sassoon, Major Holliday, the Queen, HH The Aga Khan and indeed the Murless's themselves. However, by the late 1970s, many of these names were lost to racing, with their estates being split between families and often sold off to pay for death duties, as in the case of Major Holliday. Luckily their place was to be taken by the Arabs, who became involved in British Racing in the early 1980s. At the time, their investment was very welcome but what happens next? In 2021, leading owner/breeders HH Sheikh Hamdan al Maktoum and Prince Khalid Abdullah died. Although it has been announced that both bloodstock empires will continue, it will be at significantly reduced sizes. Sheikh Hamdan's daughter, Sheikh Hassa, will manage his Shadwell Stud interests, but has already sold some of the property in America and many horses globally. There is no direct family involvement in Khalid Abdullah's stud interests. Sheikh Mohammed is not getting any younger and there is little sign of any family members taking over his huge British-based racing and breeding empire. Racing authorities in Dubai, Saudi Arabia and Qatar have received huge investments over the last few years, making prize-money in those countries much more worthwhile and encouraging international runners from around the globe to compete there. HH The Aga Khan is the fourth generation of his family who have run successful Irish- and French-based studs, reaching their 100-year anniversary in 2022. The different generations all used to have horses trained and raced in England but no longer: the current Aga Khan withdrew his horses initially due to issues with dope testing in this country but, although that issue was eventually addressed, he no longer has horses based here because it is just not economically viable. The level of prize-money in the day-to-day races goes nowhere near paying the costs. The royal colours go back even further, having first been registered in 1875 by Edward VII, although the royal family had been involved in racing for many years previously. The Queen funded her racing interests from her private purse and she was forced to sell her mare Height of Fashion to Sheikh Hamdan so she could buy the stables at West Ilsley, meaning the resident trainer would pay her rent to cover her training fees. There are still a few family-owned studs around, such as Hascombe and Valiant Studs and Cheveley Park Stud but for how long? Without the support of the overseas owners, how long can British Flat racing survive, particularly while it is blatantly failing to attract new generations?

As already indicated, the prize-money available in the UK, particularly for day-to-day racing, remains pretty static and has become a serious issue. It was an issue raised by Murless towards the end of his career and has continued to be raised regularly since. In the mid-1950s, Cliff was looking after a horse for the Queen, which won about £500 in prize-money for a Thirsk win. Now it would be nearer the £3,000 gross mark if you are lucky; while this is an increase, it is nothing compared to the significant increases in costs such as feed, training fees, transport costs and staff wages. Some English-based trainers are setting up satellite yards in France to take advantage of the better prize-money available there: it is possible to win £10,000 for a claiming race and if your horse happens to be French-bred, there will be an additional £8,000 breeders' premium. In just three months in 2022, Newmarket trainer, Amy Murphy, earned over £180,000 in prize-money from a handful of horses based in a satellite yard in France. This surpassed her prize-money total for the whole of 2021 for horses racing on the Flat in the UK. Meanwhile, a Saturday afternoon race at a televised meeting at Newbury, a Group 1 track, attracted no runners having only offered £3,500 to the winner. The level of prize-money in British racing has long been an issue. It was a problem as long ago as in 1968 and even for the major races: Vaguely Noble was transferred to France to be trained because the maximum prize-money he could win in a race in England, having not been entered for the Derby, was the £25,000 available to the winner of the King George VI and Queen Elizabeth Stakes; in France the equivalent race, the Grand Prix de Saint Cloud, was worth twice as much and the Arc was worth £100,000 to the winner. Not quite so long ago in 2000, in a speech at the Cartier Awards, the Aga Khan himself called for a revision in the distribution of prize-money at the lower levels of racing to prevent smaller enterprises from going out of business during the fallow periods. He noted, 'The current trend appears to be a global competition as to which country can disburse the highest amounts of money to the winners of its premium Classics. Is this really good for everyone in the industry? Or is it only good for those bloodstock operations which have the highest probability of winning the most numerous Group races?' He went on to say that he would rather see a much wider distribution of prize-money to increase significantly the probability that more horses in more yards would bring back at least some income every year to offset the costs. The prize-money for a maiden win needs to be able to cover at least the cost of getting the horse to the course, if not a reasonable proportion of the horse's training fees for the year. Australian connections say they get more prize-money for a 'bush track' win than is available at the majority of UK courses. It is interesting to compare how house prices have changed: when Muriel and Malc moved to Newmarket 60 years ago, they paid £3,000 for their house, much the same then as the prize-money for winning a maiden race. The house is now worth about £360,000. The two Guineas races at Newmarket this year were worth around £250,000 each and a maiden on the same card paid about £8,000 to the winner:

that is for a premier day's racing on a course that charges £100 a head for a fish-and-chip dinner! Prize-money really isn't keeping up with the constantly increasing cost of living or keeping a horse in training.

Another seemingly insurmountable problem currently is the lack of staff. Instead of the two or, occasionally, three horses each lad did when Cliff first came into racing, lads are now having to ride out three, four or sometimes even five lots and to do as many as ten horses at evening stables, and these numbers continue to rise. There are currently over 130 stable staff jobs being advertised on the *Careers in Racing* website, mostly comprising riding out 3–4 lots per day. One even proudly states that wages 'are above the national living wage' and most include working either one weekend in two or sometimes one weekend in three.

Training techniques are little changed since Cliff came into racing. Michael Stoute was intrigued by different training methods in athletics and was more prepared than most to explore new options. So much so that he went to Newcastle to meet Olympic medal-winning, middle-distance athlete and coach Peter Elliott, who was competing at the same time as the other great British athletes, Sebastian Coe, Steve Ovett and Steve Cram, during a golden age for British athletics. Stoute wanted to discuss various schedules, techniques and methods the athletes used to improve their performance. On his return to Newmarket, he tried interval training with some of the two-year-olds, but it wasn't a success – Walter Swinburn reported it as being like the Charge of the Light Brigade – so he reverted to more traditional methods.

Although the safety of riding is under constant scrutiny and the introduction and constant review of both crash helmets and back protectors is to be welcomed, there are still safety issues in racing that need addressing. The first of these is the starting stalls, which are unchanged since their inception in 1965. Cliff believes there is an accident waiting to happen. On numerous occasions, a stalls handler is seen to lead a horse into stalls, then the handler ducks out under the front and the horse tries to follow, as was demonstrated in the horrific incident in the 2012 1,000 Guineas at Newmarket when Gray Pearl tried to follow her handler under the front gate of the stalls but got wedged under the gate. Although she was eventually extricated by the vets on duty, she had suffered a spinal injury and had to be put down. There was also the incident in 1981 when Lester Piggott's horse, Winsor Boy, ducked under the stalls at Epsom: Piggott's ear was badly torn and he needed surgery. For the handlers, if you are not quick enough to duck under, the horse could trample you while you are still in the stall with it. In America, there is a running board along the inside of the stall and the handler climbs up on this, rather than ducking under the front gate, meaning the horse won't try to follow. The handler can then either climb out over the back gate or remain in the stall until the off: the latter position would also enable the handler to remove any extraneous equipment not needed during the race, such as the blindfold often used for stalls entry. It also means stalls handlers can be of a larger build as they don't need to duck under the front of the stalls, enabling the front of the stalls to be made lower, stopping the horse from trying to duck out underneath. A horse ducking under the front of the stalls can shift the saddle back on to its flanks, which will cause it to bolt believing it has a predator on its quarters. If all horses wore a breast girth, this eventuality could easily be prevented. It is becoming a more and more common occurrence to see horses leave the stalls with the blindfold only partially removed, if at all, meaning the horse is running blind and could cause a serious accident during the race. If the stalls handler was standing on the running board in the stalls, then they could remove the blind as the gates opened, leaving the jockey free to ride. Finally, Cliff feels the stalls should be made high enough in front that horses can't get their foreleg over the top in front. The reason given for the British stalls being so much smaller than the American ones is that they have to be transported from one course to another. Surely, in this day and age, every course should have its own starting stalls? All the courses in Australia and the USA all have their own stalls. The design of starting stalls in this country hasn't changed since they were first introduced in 1965. How much have telephones advanced during this time? Mobile phones hadn't even been invented when starting stalls came in: they've been bricks, now they are mini-computers!

There would also be advantages to having outriders on ponies to catch loose horses. In the Winsor Boy/Piggott incident at Epsom, the horse crashed to death in the crowd. Another near miss occurred when a Hugh Collingridge-trained horse, Eaubinite, nearly drowned at Huntingdon: the jockey went to turn left when going down, but Eaubinite jinked and the jockey came off, while the horse kept going right and ended up swimming in the lake. Luckily, Eaubinite swam back to the edge of the lake and then galloped down to the start. One further example is the incident involving Cliff himself with Chiperone at Lewes.

Despite rehoming of racehorses having become a hot topic recently, is there enough being done? Some owners take their responsibilities seriously; Godolphin have a rehoming programme where horses no longer suitable for racing are retrained and have been successful in various new disciplines: one of the most unusual must be the one-eyed Caymans who has successfully become an integral part of the Dartmoor Hawking team, one of only two organised mounted falconry teams in the UK. The Queen also rehomed some of her string: initially, they are sent to the Royal Mews for assessment and retraining, before moving to their new homes. Once rehomed, they are still checked from time to time by the Queen's head stud groom to ensure they are being properly cared for. Some, such as First Love, join the Royal Mews and take part in Trooping the Colour; while Quadrille, who finished second at Royal Ascot when in training, is strutting his stuff very successfully in the dressage arena with Louise Robson. There is also the Rehoming of Racehorses Charity and many private individuals, such as Carrie Massingham, who do their bit. However, there are many more horses who are just sent to the sales and never heard of again, often being exported to countries such as Kuwait who have little use for these horses if they are not up to racing. What might have happened to Fujiyama Crest had Frankie not saved him when he was entered at the Ascot Sales?

Tony McCoy makes a good point that extending the Cheltenham Festival from three days to four, and now possibly to five, days not only results in a dilution of the quality of the fields but also results in smaller fields. The same would appear to have happened at Newmarket with the Guineas Festival reverting to three days; despite perfect ground some of the Group races only had three or four runners. Genuine seven-furlong horses are already poorly catered for in the Racing Calendar and moving the Charles II Stakes back to the Guineas meeting prevents a trainer who runs a horse in the Guineas and discovers they don't quite get the trip, then having the Charles II Stakes as a springboard to assess whether to head for the Jersey Stakes at Ascot or whether to step further down in trip and revert to sprinting. When there are more opportunities, it does make winning a race at a festival meeting feel a little less elite.

Why are races such as the Grand National and Derby so special? Surely it is because there is only one opportunity a year to win that race and for the Flat horses it is one opportunity in a lifetime to win the Derby? A view has to be taken about the quality of racing in this country. There seems to be a continual increase in poor-quality racing, which leaves everybody in the industry out of pocket, with only bookmakers and punters making money. When Cliff started, racing was six days a week, with set seasons for National Hunt and Flat racing and no racing on religious festivals such as Good Friday, Easter Day and Christmas. When Sunday racing came in, the following Monday was supposed to be blank to allow staff to spend time with their families but that never happened. With the advent of all-weather racing, both codes are now continuous, with the National Hunt Season finishing one day and starting again the next day. Flat racing is now all-year-round, although, weirdly, the Flat jockeys' turf championship does not start until Guineas weekend, over a month after the actual start of the turf season! It is well established that there is a lack of stable staff and with seven-days-a-week racing throughout the year, anti-social hours, never a break and little financial reward unless you happen to do a Classic winner, is it a surprise that it is difficult to recruit people? Why do lads have to start at 6am? Is there any good reason that their normal day can't start at 9am like any other industry? The horses have to race in the afternoon, so it can't be the weather conditions. It seems to just be habit. The typical cry in racing is 'That is how it has always been done,' and no one has the inclination to try something else. The BHA recently suggested axing 300 races from the calendar but that was met with a hostile reception. Those in the industry are really not helping themselves. The fields are seldom full. Trainers are struggling to find staff to take horses to the races, as well as have staff at home riding out and doing evening stables. If a concertina effect by cutting races leads to increased prize-money and encourages more people into racing, surely that is one way forward?

The racing industry in the UK is a cruel and fickle mistress: it is a difficult industry to survive in, with even the greats such as Henry Cecil having long, fallow spells. The opportunities appear to be few and far between, forcing many young talents to move overseas – for instance, Annabel Neasham and David Eustace are making a living training in Australia, while Sophie Doyle and Adam Beschizza are plying their trade as jockeys in the USA, despite Adam recently becoming one of the few jockeys to complete the autumn double, winning both the Cambridgeshire and the Cesarewitch in 2015. While the bloodstock market remains strong, it is hugely dependent on sales to overseas investors. Even winning the Derby at Epsom is no longer a guarantee of a stud career, Coolmore having subsequently gelded their 2020 winner, Serpentine. Stud land is being sold for housing developments and compulsory purchase orders are in the offing to build huge solar farms on stud land in the Newmarket area. There has even been a proposal for a wind farm on the Newmarket gallops on racecourse side!

Finally, the lack of appreciation for retirees from the industry is sad. Cliff had dedicated his whole life to the sport, but, because he wasn't a licenced trainer for 15 years, he can't get a badge to go racing without paying for one. NARS (the National Association of Racing Staff, the lads' Trade Union) have given him a card for entry to the silver ring, but he'd like to be able to go maybe to one or two of the smaller days, particularly at Newmarket, but access to the members would be nice and would allow him to mix with fellow trainers but it costs £40 to £50 per person each time.

As Cliff says, 'You fall in love with horses and that's it,' so let's hope the situation is sorted out soon. Otherwise, in another 70 years, will anybody have been in the racing business for as long as Cliff and still be able to say, 'I wouldn't have changed it for the world'?

BIBLIOGRAPHY

Clive Brittain, *The Smiling Pioneer: Robin Oakley* (Racing
Post Books 2012)

Her Majesty's Pleasure: Julian Muscat (Racing Post Books 2012)

Lester, The Autobiography of Lester Piggott: Lester Piggott
(Partridge Press 1995)

Men and Horses I Have Known: The Hon George Lambton (J A Allen
& Company Ltd 1963)

My Story: Sir Gordon Richards (Hodder and Stoughton 1955)

Nature, Vol 348, 13th December 1990

Racing Post Derby Supplement, 30th May 2021

Ruff's Guide to the Turf ... year by year series from 1953 onwards

The Guv'nor, A Biography of Sir Noel Murless: Tim Fitzgeorge Parker
(Collins 1980)

The Magnificent Seven. Graham Sharpe (Aurum Press 2001)

Timeform's Racehorses of ... year by year series from 1967 onwards
(Portway Press)

Newmarket Pony Academy (NPA)

The Newmarket Pony Academy, at the British Racing School, is a community project designed to use horses and ponies to positively affect mental health and wellbeing for the children in Newmarket. Newmarket, despite being the headquarters of racing, does not offer affordable access for children to learn about, ride or look after these animals. These children see horses around Newmarket town and surrounding areas every day and the Newmarket Pony Academy is going to give them that chance.

The Newmarket Pony Academy has been designed to give young people the opportunity learn new skills such as team work, confidence and resilience. They will have the chance to learn about these animals and the hard work and dedication it takes to look after them. They will benefit enormously from developing life skills from this unique experience by participating in a five-day primary school program, designed to mix equine care with core subjects and team building activities embedded into this diverse learning experience. The courses build on the curriculum and work on key skills, such as confidence, resilience and overall engagement in learning, through delivering practical and theory lessons to the students.

Further to this, afterschool and holiday clubs will be delivered for local young people who have been referred to the project by teachers and social workers. It is hoped that ongoing engagement with the NPA will give these young people a positive constant. We really believe in the social and mental health benefits from this type of learning and are incredibly excited to empower these young people.